Grow Your Own Teachers

Grassroots Change for Teacher Education

EDITED BY

ELIZABETH A. SKINNER
MARIA TERESA GARRETÓN
BRIAN D. SCHULTZ

FOREWORD BY
CHARLES PAYNE

Teachers College
Columbia University
New York and London

Published by Teachers College Press, 1234 Amsterdam Avenue, New York, NY 10027

Library of Congress Cataloging-in-Publication Data

Grow your own teachers : grassroots change for teacher education / edited by Elizabeth A. Skinner, Maria Teresa Garretón, Brian D. Schultz ; foreword by Charles Payne.
     p. cm. — (The teaching for social justice series)
  Includes bibliographical references and index.
  ISBN 978-0-8077-5193-0 (pbk. : alk. paper) — ISBN 978-0-8077-5194-7 (hardcover : alk. paper) 1. Teachers—Training of—United States. 2. Critical pedagogy—United States. 3. Community and school—United States. 4. Educational change—United States. I. Skinner, Elizabeth A. II. Garretón, Maria Teresa. III. Schultz, Brian D.
  LB1715.G76 2011
  370.71'173—dc22

                           2010054358

ISBN 978-0-8077-5193-0 (paperback)
ISBN 978-0-8077-5194-7 (hardcover)

Printed on acid-free paper
Manufactured in the United States of America

18 17 16 15 14 13 12 11   8 7 6 5 4 3 2 1

The Teaching for Social Justice Series

William Ayers—Series Editor
Therese Quinn—Associate Series Editor

Contents

Series Foreword

Schools serve society; society is reflected in its schools. Schools are in fact microcosms of the societies in which they're embedded, and every school is both mirror of and window into a specific social order. If one understands the schools, one can see the whole of society; if one fully grasps the intricacies of society, one will know something about how its schools are organized.

In a totalitarian society schools are built for obedience and conformity; in a kingdom, schools teach fealty and loyalty to the crown; under apartheid, schools inculcate that privilege and oppressions are distributed along the color line. These schools might be "excellent" by some measures, but whatever else is taught—math or music, literature or science—the insistent curriculum under all else is the big lessons of how to function here and now: German schools in the middle of the 20th century produced excellent scientists and athletes and artists and intellectuals, and they also produced obedience and conformity, moral blindness and easy agreement, obtuse patriotism, and a willingness to give orders that led to furnaces.

In an authentic democracy, schools would aim for something entirely different: a commitment to free inquiry, questioning, and participation; a push for access and equity and simple fairness; a curriculum that encouraged independent thought and judgment; a standard of full recognition of the humanity of each individual. In other words, schools in a vibrant democracy would put the highest priority on the creation of free people geared toward enlightenment and liberation.

When the aim of education is the absorption of facts, learning becomes exclusively and exhaustively selfish, and there is no obvious social motive for learning. The measure of success is always a competitive one—it's about comparing results and sorting people into winners and losers. People are turned against one another, and every difference becomes a potential deficit. Getting ahead of others is the primary goal in such places, and mutual assistance, which can be so natural, is severely restricted or banned. On the other hand, where active work is the order of the day, helping others is not a form of charity, something that impoverishes both recipient and benefactor. Rather, a spirit of open communication, interchange, and analysis becomes commonplace, and there's a recognition that the people you're trying to help know better. Of course, in these places, there is a certain natural disorder, a certain amount of anarchy and chaos as there is in any busy workshop. But there is a deeper discipline at work, the discipline of getting things done and learning through life, and there is an appreciation of knowledge as an inherently public good—something that can be reproduced at little or no cost, and unlike commodities, when it is given away, no one has any less of it. In a flourishing democracy, knowledge would be shared without any reservation or restrictions whatsoever.

The education we're accustomed to is simply a caricature—it's neither authentically nor primarily about full human development. Why, for example, is education thought of as only kindergarten through 12th grade, or kindergarten through university? Why does education occur only early in life? Why is there a point in our lives when we no longer think we need education? Why, again, is there a hierarchy of teacher over students? Why are there grades and grade levels? Why does attendance matter? Why is punctuality valuable? Why, indeed, do we think of a productive and a service sector in our society, with education designated as a service activity? Why is education separate from production?

The development of free people in a free society—this is the central goal of teaching for social justice. This means teaching toward freedom and democracy, and it's based on a common faith in the incalculable value of every human being; it assumes that the fullest development of all is the condition for the full development of each, and, conversely, that the fullest development of each is the condition for the full development of all. One traditional way of expressing this ideal is this: Whatever the wisest and most privileged parents in a democracy want for their kids becomes the standard for what we as a community want for all of our children.

The democratic ideal has policy implications, of course, but is deeply implicated as well in questions of teaching and curriculum. We expect schools in a democratic society to be defined by a spirit of cooperation, inclusion, and full participation, places that honor diversity while building unity. Schools in a democracy resist the overspecialization of human activity, the separation of the intellectual from the manual, the head from the hand and the heart from the brain, the creative, and the functional. The standard is fluidity of function, the variation of work and capacity, the mobilization of intelligence and creativity and initiative and work in all directions.

While many of us long for teaching as something transcendent and powerful and free, we find ourselves too often locked in situations that reduce teaching to a kind of glorified clerking, passing along a curriculum of received wisdom and predigested bits of information. A fundamental choice and challenge for teachers, then, is this: to acquiesce to the machinery of control, or to take a stand with our students in a search for meaning and a journey of transformation. To teach obedience and conformity, or to teach its polar opposite: initiative and imagination, curiosity and questioning, the capacity to name the world, to identify the obstacles to your full humanity, and the courage to act upon whatever the known demands. On the side of a liberating and humanizing education is a pedagogy of questioning, an approach that opens rather than closes the prosy process of thinking, comparing, reasoning, perspective-taking, and dialogue. It demands something upending and revolutionary from students and teachers alike: Repudiate your place in the pecking order, it urges, remove that distorted, congenial mask of compliance. *You must change.*

A generous approach to teaching grounds itself in cherishing happiness, respecting reason, and—fundamentally—in honoring each human life as sacred and not duplicable. Clarity about classrooms is not based on being able to answer every dilemma or challenge or conundrum that presents itself, but flows rather from seeing classroom life as a work-in-progress— contingent, dynamic, in-the-making, unfinished, always reaching for something more. The ethical core of teaching is about creating hope in students. Because the future is unknown, optimism is simply dreaming, pessimism merely a dreary turn of mind. Hopefulness, on the other hand, is a political and moral choice based on the fact that history is still in-the-making, each of us necessarily a work-in-progress, and the future entirely unknown and unknowable. Teaching for social justice provides images of possibility—*It can all change!*—and in that way rekindles hope.

A robust, humanistic education for today can draw on the diverse threads spun by our freedom-seeking foremothers and forefathers. We begin by embracing the importance of dialogue with one another, and dialogue, as well, with a rich and varied past and a dynamic, unfolding future. Dialogue is both the most hopeful and the most dangerous pedagogical practice, for in dialogue our own dogmas and certainties must be held in abeyance, must be subject to scrutiny, and there will be, to be sure, inevitable mistakes and misunderstandings. But the promise remains that if we unlock the wisdom in the room, if we face one another without masks and as the best we can be, we each might contribute a bit, and we each might learn something powerful and new.

The core lessons of a liberating education—an education for participation, engagement, and democracy—are these: Each human being is unique and of incalculable value, and we each have a mind of our own; we are all works-in-progress swimming through a dynamic history in-the-making toward an uncertain and indeterminate shore; we can choose to join with others and act on our own judgments and in our own freedom; human enlightenment and liberation are always the result of thoughtful action.

There are a series of contradictions in these propositions that must somehow be embraced, and not fled from: a focus on changing oneself, and a focus on engagement and change within a community; a concern with the individual, and a concern with the group; the demands of self-activity and self-education, and the location of that self within the social surround. An emphasis on the needs and interests of each individual must become co-primary with faith in a kind of robust public that can and must be created. To be exclusively child centered, to the extent that the needs of the community are ignored or erased, is to develop a kind of fatalistic narcissism, or, too often, a performance of whiteness; to honor the group while ignoring the needs of the individual is to destroy any authentic possibility of freedom. The challenge is to somehow hold on to the spirit of the old saying, "I am because we are, and we are because I am."

Education is an arena of struggle as well as hope—struggle because it stirs in us the need to look at the world anew, to question what we have created, to wonder what is worthwhile for human beings to know and experience—and hope because we gesture toward the future, toward the impending, toward the coming of the new. Education is where we ask how we might engage, enlarge, and change our lives, and it is, then, where we confront our dreams and fight our notions of the good life, where we try to comprehend, apprehend, or possibly even transform the world. Education is contested space, a natural site of conflict—sometimes restrained, other times in full eruption—over questions of justice.

William C. Ayers
Therese Quinn

Foreword

The recent and long-overdue national appreciation for the importance of improving teaching in urban schools comes, ironically, at a moment of growing national disregard, even contempt, for people who teach. Just fifteen years ago, scholars were still publishing books wondering whether anything schools did, let alone taught, was going to make a difference for the outcomes of poor children. There was a feeling that urban children were so damaged by the conditions of their lives that there was little schools could do about it. That debate is over and we have entered a period in which all the complex, twisted, long-developing problems of urban schools are reduced to bad teachers defended by protectionist unions. One oversimplification is replaced by another. (And if it is true unions have been *part* of the problem, it is also true they are showing signs of changing.) In a bizarre way, this represents progress; it is a step better than blaming children and their parents, which is what much of the national discourse in the decades following the Coleman Report amounted to.

If good teaching has become more valued in the abstract, then, it has not necessarily become better understood. In too many policymaking discussions, good teaching comes to mean just improving test scores. Ron Ferguson has compiled a body of data that suggests that certain teacher characteristics—how relentless about student learning, how engaging, how thought-provoking the teacher is—can affect how much work students do, whether they seek help from the teacher, whether they misbehave, whether they even show up for class. Importantly, these effects are generally greater for Black and Latino students than for others. These teacher characteristics are precisely what one would hope to find in Grow Your Own (GYO) teachers—although they may not show up in teachers' test scores or grades. Adults who have themselves gone through an arduous process of re-invention of the self, who have discovered unsuspected powers and talents in themselves, should be more likely to understand that the same potentials exist in the young people they teach, even though those young people may be doing everything they can to hide their own potential. As Lisa Delpit says, majority group children learn for their future; minority students learn for the teacher.

Good teaching holds students accountable to their best selves, refuses to let them yield to the temptations that can derail their lives, and envisions for them futures that cannot be seen from the vantage point of ghettoes and barrios and reservations, and keeps them moving toward those futures. Let us say it again, test scores are important, they matter. But to act as if that is the end-all of teaching shows little understanding of children or poverty. Grow Your Own understands both. I don't know exactly the steps by which their vision grew into a program of national importance. I'm sure it was the kind of process one sees so often in organizing. You do one thing and that puts you in position to do another thing that you couldn't see until that first thing was done. Even without knowing the details, we can be sure that this program was predicated on confidence in the ability of ordinary people to do some extraordinary things. This represents the community organizing tradition at its finest; it represents the American tradition at its finest. It represents a new hope for the young people we give up on so quickly.

Charles Payne

Acknowledgments

This book, much like the Grow Your Own (GYO) teacher project, is a truly collaborative effort that could not have happened without the support of many individuals and groups. First, we want to express our gratitude to the GYO students who openly shared their stories that are at the heart of this book. Our sincere appreciation goes to those who have worked within our colleges of education, community-based organizations, and public schools to make GYO a reality. Many thanks as well to our university and community colleagues for your insight and expertise. And to those of you who helped during the writing process—you know who you are—we are grateful. Our chapter contributors as well as others on the ground have turned this idea into a movement that will continue to evolve and impact schools and communities in powerful ways. Finally, we are so fortunate to have worked with Carole Saltz, Emily Renwick, and the rest of the incredible folks at Teachers College Press.

Grow Your Own Teachers

1

Rethinking Teacher Preparation

ELIZABETH A. SKINNER & BRIAN D. SCHULTZ

This is my dream: I want to work, I want to go back, believe it or not, to the neighborhood where I grew up. I want to go to Little Village or Pilsen and when I graduate I want to be there helping the children. I know that I could make a difference with one child, and maybe in the future he or she could be someone to help an entire family.

The above quote encompasses the fundamental rationale and goals of the Grow Your Own teacher initiative (GYO) that began in one Chicago neighborhood and evolved into a statewide movement. Although these sentiments come from a single GYO graduate, they represent the hopes and dreams of all involved in the undertaking. This grassroots political work is a catalyst for change in historically marginalized urban schools and communities. By developing partnerships between colleges of education, community-based organizations, and public schools, GYO has created a pipeline of teachers of color in Illinois. These culturally competent and committed individuals are from the communities in which they will one day teach. GYO is not only a unique approach to teacher preparation; it is also a vehicle for school reform that provides hopeful opportunities for the often-marginalized students in urban public schools.

In order to understand GYO as an organizing campaign for robust education reform and consider its potential on a national scale, it is necessary to examine the local partnership and program that inspired the movement. Following Chicago's path-breaking 1988 School Reform law, the Logan Square Neighborhood Association, a 44-year-old, multi-issue community organization on Chicago's Northwest side, began working with public school parents and their neighborhood elementary schools. *Mark Warren* discusses the historical trajectory of school-community organizing, illustrating the potential for ongoing partnerships. One of the most successful organizing efforts in the Logan Square schools is the Parent Mentor Program, which began in 1995. This Parent Mentor Program is articulated in *Joanna Brown*'s description of Logan Square Neighborhood Association's educational organizing work and subsequently elaborated upon in *Soo Hong*'s ethnography of parent mentors. The guiding philosophy of the Parent Mentor Program is the desire to create schools that are centers of community and representative of the organization's strong belief in the funds of knowledge that parents bring with them into the school (Moll, Amanti, Neff, & Gonzalez, 1992). The education organizing and the Parent Mentor Program laid the groundwork for the partnership with the Bilingual Education Program at Chicago State University.

The original goal of the federally funded (Title VII) partnership between the Logan Square Neighborhood Association and the Bilingual Education Program at Chicago State University, called Project Nueva Generación, was to prepare community members to become bilingual teachers for the neighborhood schools. Although the two are very different institutions, the personnel at both believed in the potential of preparing non-traditional students to become teachers—issues of community, culture, and language were all priorities in program design and implementation. *Maria Teresa Garretón* highlights the critical negotiations, institutional barriers, and collaborative processes that ensued when these organizations began working together. The first students enrolled in the fall of 2000, and during the first 2 years of the program, they all took their classes at the community center located within one of the neighborhood elementary schools. The classes were held in the evenings or on Saturdays. In addition, the federal grant provided monies to cover tuition, onsite child care during class time, and books. The idea was to create opportunity and access to higher education for non-traditional students from historically marginalized communities. In order to do so, funds were used to eliminate or lessen known barriers to higher education, including the financial limitations and familial obligations of the community members. *Christina Madda and Morgan Halstead* provide the story of two current GYO teacher candidates as they journey through the program and adapt to life as college students.

Following the example of the original partnership, the statewide GYO movement, the evolution of which is detailed by *Anne Hallett*, is designed to recruit and retain highly qualified teachers for hard-to-staff schools and hard-to-fill positions. However, the foundational community-based, collaborative nature of the program indicates that there is more at stake than simply filling teacher vacancies. At the heart of this justice-oriented campaign is the inherent value of challenging the existing social order of schools and colleges of education while preparing community members to serve as educational leaders, dynamic teachers, and change agents once in these schools (Schultz, Gillette, & Hill, 2008). A social reconstructionist view is a common belief that underlies the collective efforts between the community-based organizations and the colleges of education. This construct and further theoretical underpinnings of GYO are presented by *Brian Schultz, Maureen Gillette, and Djanna Hill*. The authors contend that urban schools can and should be locations where inequality and oppression are challenged. Illustrating this point, *Gregory Michie* describes practicing teachers of color working for change in urban schools who exemplify the GYO teacher. In order to prepare teachers who will understand and accept the transformative nature of their work, a focus on critical pedagogy, hopefulness, and leadership must be present throughout the teacher preparation curriculum, practicum, and student teaching assignments, as well as organizing activities outside the coursework. *Kathleen McInerney*'s analysis of teaching and learning in GYO presents insights about successful GYO professors who demonstrate how GYO is not interested in producing candidates who will enter the school system and accommodate to the existing system. Rather, GYO aims to educate community teachers who will challenge, question, and improve schooling practices to include much stronger connections to their own culture and that of the students (Murrell, 2001). *Elizabeth Skinner* portrays the transformation of one GYO graduate as she evolved from college student to public school teacher.

Such a framework makes it imperative that colleges of education rethink the nature of their community-based teacher education programs and initiatives. Describing the pitfalls and potential of such programs, *Maureen Gillette* shows how scaling up such reform efforts can be problematic while elucidating promises of what has worked in ongoing partnering efforts. In order to create a pipeline of teachers of color from the community who will change the current climate and resist the pathology commonly associated with urban schools, colleges of education must first question their own practices and adapt as necessary in order to ensure the success of the GYO candidates. This does not mean lowering entrance requirements, designing routes of alternative certification, or accepting substandard academic performance. Instead, it means looking for ways to tap the enormous assets that the GYO teacher candidates bring into the program and to support them when and where they need it. This approach views the urban communities (and their residents) as assets, not just locations for diverse field experiences for traditional teacher candidates (Skinner, 2010). The GYO teacher initiative acknowledges that the university and the community partner share responsibility and accountability for the program and its impact on neighborhood schools.

By including the perspectives and experiences of community organizers, students, and teacher educators in this collection, we challenge readers to think about ways in which teacher preparation programs may be improved by developing meaningful partnerships among universities, community-based organizations, and public schools. And although there is a danger in the broad replication of any successful program (Payne, 2008), the central goal of this volume is to show how community-centered teacher preparation programs can instill agency and empower their future educators, while situating this particular effort within the broader national reform movement. *Linda Darling-Hammond* points to how GYO fits within the landscape of other educational reform efforts.

Those of us involved in the work of the GYO movement for the past 10 years learned as we went along. The community organizers, teacher educators, and students all brought different expertise and perspectives to the project, and this book represents our collective efforts. The chapters tell the Grow Your Own story both conceptually and practically, from a unique example of education reform in one Chicago community, focused on educating bilingual teachers, to the subsequent growth of the statewide initiative and its potential as a national example of educational reform. By sharing our acquired knowledge, we offer more than a policy recommendation. Instead, we show how we put into practice a social justice–oriented approach to teacher preparation—what Jean Anyon (2005) calls a new social movement.

REFERENCES

Anyon, J. (2005). *Radical possibilities*. New York: Routledge.

Moll, L., Amanti, C., Neff, D., & Gonzalaz, N. (1992). Funds of knowledge for teaching. *Theory Into Practice, 31*, 132–141.

Murrell, P. (2001). *The community teacher*. New York: Teachers College Press.

Payne, C. (2008). *So much reform, so little change*. Cambridge, MA: Harvard Education Press.

Schultz, B., Gillette, M., & Hill, D. (2008). A theoretical framework for understanding Grow Your Own teachers. *The Sophist's Bane, 4*(1/2), 69–80.

Skinner, E. (2010). Project Nueva Generación and Grow Your Own Teachers. *Teacher Education Quarterly, 37*(3), 155–167.

2

Teaching as Political

Theoretical Perspectives for Understanding the Grow Your Own Movement

BRIAN D. SCHULTZ,
MAUREEN D. GILLETTE, & DJANNA A. HILL

The notion of teaching as political is exemplified by the theoretical underpinnings of a Grow Your Own teachers (GYO) project, a community-centered program of teacher education whose mission is to improve teaching and learning in high-needs schools by recruiting and preparing community-based teachers and returning them to their local schools. Although this chapter details perspectives of the program at Northeastern Illinois University (NEIU) in Chicago, it is reflective of statewide efforts of Grow Your Own Teachers Illinois and is situated in the broader national school reform movement. Beyond the Chicago context, this unique collaborative effort builds upon the strengths of all its entities, which include coalitions of community-based organizations, institutions of higher education, and school districts, and seeks to offer a hopeful alternative to the pathology and despair that often characterize large urban school districts nationwide.

At a time when much of the school reform debate focuses on looking to ill or underprepared and uncommitted outsiders as a remedy to solve dire teaching shortages in many U.S. inner cities (i.e., Teach for America), the GYO model offers a distinct alternative. The partnerships that have evolved through GYO—partnerships that embrace people from historically marginalized communities as assets to help solve the grave issues within their own communities—offer promising possibilities for educational change through university-community collaboration that can prompt not only reflection, but also the potential to transform teacher education.

REFRAMING URBAN TEACHER SHORTAGES

Finding, hiring, and keeping teachers in urban classrooms are paramount issues in current educational policy. Many reports caution policymakers of massive teacher shortage trends. This may be accurate for specific demographics or content-specific areas, but the reality is that for many affluent school districts, teaching positions receive an excess of applicants. Scarcity of qualified applicants exists in poor, urban areas where teachers are often placed in classrooms for which they underprepared, and have little to no experience working with the population of students. Further, teacher retention and teacher experience are extreme challenges in most urban schools. Research conducted by Christenson and Levine (1998) for the National Center for Educational Statistics (NCES) found that in schools where a majority of the students are of color, 14% of teachers were working on emergency certificates. This number is even higher for large urban districts. In Chicago, for example, the percent of non–highly qualified teachers in 2007 was over 23% (Catalyst Chicago, 2009)! Further, the NCES research indicated that only 13% of teachers in public schools nationwide were faculty of color (Christenson & Levine, 1998). Although in Chicago the number of teachers of color is somewhat higher than the national average, the shortage of culturally compatible teachers becomes more pronounced each year (CPS, 2009; NEA, 2003; Planty, Hussar, Snyder, Kena, KewalRumani, Kemp, Bianco, & Dinkes, 2009). Moreover, large urban districts such as Chicago, New York, Cleveland, Detroit, and Chicago experience what Ingersoll (2003, p. 11) and Miner (2010) have called the "revolving door" phenomenon, where the constant transition of "inadequately prepared teachers" (¶8) disrupts not only the organizational structure of schools, but also student achievement.

Eighty percent of the U.S. public school population in urban areas is made up of students of color (National Center for Education Statistics, 2000; Planty et al., 2009) and in Chicago this number exceeds 90% (CPS, 2009). Other recent data indicate that 84% of the nationwide teaching force is White and 74% is female (Zumwalt & Craig, 2005). The very student populations in the United States in need of the most experienced and committed teachers are being taught by the least prepared educators. Further, demographic data indicate that significant numbers of teachers in urban areas are inexperienced in the communities in which they teach (see, for example, Planty et al., 2009). Unfortunately, this combined lack of academic and community-based qualifications results in substandard education, particularly for poor, urban students. Students of color are at the biggest risk because in this predicament the detrimental effects present not only in a lack of opportunities for higher education, but also in future work prospects. This alarmingly small cohort of qualified teachers in areas of high need poses a serious challenge for urban areas across the United States, and in this case, for the Chicago Public Schools specifically.

Beyond just the numbers, the discussion around "teacher shortages" ought to reflect the lack of teachers who hold the pedagogical and cultural expertise to deliver the best education to students in high-need areas. Finding, training, and supporting future educators who are committed to these particular areas is essential for the students' ongoing and future success. GYO has framed the dilemma to center around broad questions from the National Commission on Teaching and America's Future (2002): (1) How can schools in high-need districts attract, recruit, and retain academically prepared and pedagogically sensible teachers for work in their urban school contexts? (2) How do we get the teachers (especially those doing well in urban and high-need contexts) to stay in their positions? Not only do teachers need to commit to teaching in marginalized neighborhoods and under-resourced schools, but as Hill and Gillette (2005) contend, they must also ably confront the challenging work of change, social justice, reform, and renewal.

Given the dynamic nature of cultivating teachers within different environments, questions about what constitutes "a good teacher" and what sorts of skills, attitudes, and behaviors are necessary for urban environments become central concerns for colleges of education. Complex questions regarding cultural or racial parallels between teachers and their students also emerge.

Developing consistent dispositions for teachers who can teach/reach all children is one of the ways in which colleges of education work to meet the needs of students in marginalized urban classrooms. Substantial research indicates that specific defining qualities and characteristics lend themselves to successful teaching in urban areas; moreover, certain types of people are most likely to remain in underresourced schools (Delpit, 2006; Haberman, 1995; Ladson-Billings, 1994; Valenzuela, 1999). These qualities include extensive content knowledge, skills to develop and teach concepts in a multiplicity of ways, a pedagogical understanding that makes their teaching meaningful to their students, and a strong commitment to serving parents as well as students (Hill & Gillette, 2005; Payne, 2008). People who have a stake in the success of the community and are thought of as insiders are often the driving force of this commitment.

Selected GYO teacher candidates can be described as insiders in this way. Many are paraprofessionals working in community schools, parents of school-age children attending these schools, have attended these schools themselves, or have been active community members. As insiders, their lived experiences foster a shared vision of what can and ought to be in and for the community. Their investment in neighborhood schools also qualifies them as strong advocates for change. They can work effectively with parents because they live in the community, have direct and intimate experiences within it, and many are parents themselves. They personally understand barriers to success, and more important, they know what students in these particular schools need in order to achieve. Rather than a "top-down theory of change" that Barbara Miner (2010) critiques in regard to programs such as Teach for America, GYO looks to "the voices and perspectives of the communities who [are] to benefit" (¶67). Characterized in this way, this effort for "homegrown" future educators can be considered an "anti–Teach for America" reform initiative: The teacher candidates clearly "possess a more sophisticated understanding of a community's particular challenges, and therefore are better prepared to serve the children of that community" (Bomphray, 2009, ¶13).

CONCEPTUALIZING AN INITIATIVE TO GROW AND DEVELOP OUR OWN TEACHERS

Those concerned with developing competent, caring educators for hard-to-staff urban schools recognize the significance of and the challenges in sustaining "Grow Your Own" programs. One such program, Paterson Teachers for Tomorrow (PT4T), is the impetus for our conceptual framework (Hill & Gillette, 2005) at NEIU. Although the PT4T model represents collaboration between high schools and a university, many similar issues are prevalent in our community-based model. Using the PT4T framework to develop a successful GYO initiative, we have created a partnership to find appropriate ways to provide a worthwhile education to students in particular communities designated as in need.

GYO is deeply rooted in the theory of social reconstruction as an initiative seeking to change the detrimental dynamic that has become commonplace in urban schools and to challenge what has become status quo for poor neighborhood schooling. Social reconstruction theory argues that the main purpose of schools is to develop skillful individuals who are critical thinkers willing to use their talents, knowledge, and expertise to re-create a culture that perpetuates equity and social justice (e.g., Freire, 1970, 2001; Grant & Sleeter, 2008). In addition to this framework, we also rely on perspectives that derive from traditional and non-traditional epistemologies, particularly race uplift (Collins, 1991; Washington, 1901), caring (Noddings, 2005; Thompson, 1998; Valenzuela, 1999) and other mothering (Collins, 1991; Hill, 2003), critical pedagogy (Apple, 1995; Giroux, 2001; McLaren & Kincheloe, 2008), critical race theory in education (Dixon & Rousseau, 2005; Ladson-Billings, 2009; Ladson-Billings & Tate, 1995; Tate, 1996), and cultural studies (hooks, 1994) applied to intercultural communication (Beamer & Varner, 2008).

These interrelated concepts support the varying, yet shared, perspectives of the consortium members, especially those teacher educators in the Colleges of Education at NEIU, whose mission is to train urban educators wishing to teach in hard-to-staff neighborhood schools. The various members of the consortium seek to provide the guidance and nurturing necessary to foster positive, hopeful experiences for these particular students of color, as these teachers will be in turn educating similar students in the future. Endemic to working with this population in Chicago or in other urban areas around the country are issues of race, power, class, gender, and insidedness that become especially key to reaching young people. Whereas we developed this theoretical framework to aid us in implementing the GYO consortia at NEIU, examples of each theoretical construct put into purposeful action can be seen in multiple ways throughout the chapters of this book.

DARE THE SCHOOLS BUILD A NEW SOCIAL ORDER? FRAMING GROW YOUR OWN WITHIN SOCIAL RECONSTRUCTION

Social reconstructionists view schools as places where social change can and should occur. We frame the GYO initiative in the historic call by George Counts (1932), "Dare the schools build a new social order?" We certainly assert that schools need to provide the basis for justice and equity in our society and believe that the GYO effort can do just this. If we are to live up to Dewey's (1902) challenge, "What the best and wisest parent wants for his own child, that must the community want for all its children" (p. 3), we need to conceptualize education in a way that pushes unfairness and oppression within social structures to the forefront with the aim of changing the conditions that accompany socioeconomic inequality. In 1933, Carter G. Woodson posed and answered the question that succinctly describes our project: "But can you expect teachers to revolutionize the system? Indeed we must expect this very thing. The educational system is worthless unless it accomplishes this task" (p. 145). By design, the collaborative structure of GYO works toward this goal while also understanding that no teacher can attempt this alone.

We draw from the extensive work of Jane Addams (1902, 1910), who sought the betterment of the people of Hull House and of society as a whole. Partnering with the University of Chicago, community agencies, and local social service groups, Addams labored tirelessly for social uplift. Her project was not simply the transformation of individuals; she fought to ensure the opportunities promised by democratic principles. Education, then as today, was embedded in the political. While speaking of the political system in Chicago, Addams (1902) stated:

> We are all involved in the political corruption, and as members of the community, stand indicted. This is the penalty of a democracy—that we are bound to move forward or retrograde together. None of us can stand aside; our feet are mired in the same soil, and our lungs breathe the same air. (p. 112)

The goal is not only to develop antioppressive behaviors and equity through educational enterprise, but also to sustain these ideas in the broader sociopolitical milieu. There is little evidence that either traditional teacher education or alternative routes to certification have been successful in this endeavor. We believe that a (more) true social reconstructionist model must adopt an approach of school-community organizing (Warren, 2001, 2005) by partnering with community-based agencies that historically have used organizing theory and practice to promote change in the most challenged communities.

TOWARD ANTIOPPRESSIVE EDUCATION: USING A LENS OF CRITICAL PEDAGOGY

Critical pedagogy offers a theoretical focus on the relationship between educational ideas, policies, and practices, and larger oppressive political and ideological perspectives. It is grounded in the day-to-day lives of people, structures, and cultures, and pays attention to the educational perspectives and politics that serve the interests of the dominant class and silence or dehumanize students according to race, class, ethnicity, sexual identity, and gender. Critical pedagogy makes possible the critique of schooling practices in terms of social class, especially as related to oppression and the reproduction of inequality (Anyon, 2005; Freire, 1970, 1996, 2001; Giroux, 2001; Giroux & McLaren, 1989). It encourages students to resist hegemonic ideas and question dominant values while pushing participants to become readers of their world. By embracing the reality of the lived experience, especially in terms of the dichotomy of oppressor and oppressed, critical pedagogy provides a framework to challenge, problem-pose, and deliberate rather than train docile recipients.

Critical pedagogy is focused on understanding the relationship between power and knowledge (Apple, 1995). Critical pedagogues seek to develop awareness and means to help assist students in recognizing and challenging the social and cultural function of particular forms of knowledge (Kumashiro, 2002; McLaren, 2006). To this end, one aim of GYO is to bring the pedagogical expertise of the higher education faculty together with the organizing expertise of the community-based organizations to develop and return to the Chicago Public Schools a pool of committed and competent teachers who have the ability and awareness to function as educational leaders and change agents in their home neighborhoods—locations where schools have the highest need and where staffing shortages and retention issues are rampant. Inherent within this aim is the GYO teacher candidate's ability to challenge oppressive schooling experiences. The intention here is that these teachers not only have the courage and ability to act upon unjust policies and practices in public schools, but also have a deeper understanding of the power structures that exist, their relation to knowledge, and ways they can resist the perpetuation of these forms of knowledge. Through emancipatory practices, students at all levels can be encouraged to consider ways to overcome ideologies that oppress.

CRITICAL RACE THEORY AS A MEANS OF TEACHING, LEARNING, AND FRAMING CODES OF POWER

Whereas critical pedagogy informs GYO teachers in terms of power and knowledge, we look to critical race theory (CRT) in education (Dixon & Rousseau, 2005; Ladson-Billings, 2009; Ladson-Billings & Tate, 1995) to better understand why developing teachers within the communities they are from is so important. CRT during the post–civil rights era is built on the work of Dubois (1903) at the turn of the 20th century, who argues that race is socially constructed (Tate, 1996). CRT challenges the typical colorblind approach to resolving issues of equity and justice. Using the intersection of race and property as an analytical tool not only to theorize about race, but also to perceive more clearly the inequities in our schools (Ladson-Billings & Tate, 1995), critical race theory informs GYO in order to understand the embedded oppressive nature of American society.

Since most, if not all, of the GYO teacher candidates are themselves products of marginalized public schools, a framework for theorizing about their experiences in terms of race and the educational inequity can determine how they examine and experience their future roles as teachers. Using the CRT lens to go beyond the multicultural paradigm that has become mainstream in educational literature, we acknowledge the need to be informed by the persistent nature of structural inequalities that exist in U.S. society as we work to prepare teachers who are willing to teach in the same communities in which they live, and where they attended school. Since society is based on property rights rather than human rights (Ladson-Billings & Tate, 1995), we seek to draw parallels between cultivating—and certifying—teachers from historically marginalized neighborhoods and having property rights. By providing and educating this group of future teachers with this variation of property rights—namely, the ability to teach students within their community as part of the mainstream society through state-governed certification and licensure procedures—they will learn the codes of power (Delpit, 2006) and teach against inequities they experienced. We echo Ladson-Billings and Tate's (1995) concerns regarding "the difficulty (indeed impossibility) of maintaining the spirit and intent of justice for the oppressed while simultaneously permitting the hegemonic rule of the oppressor" (p. 62, parentheses original), but are hopeful that by teaching CRT as a component to and underpinning of GYO, we can promote teachers with the insight and ability to make change.

Building on critical pedagogy and CRT is a body of literature that advocates for such possibilities. Lynn (1999) refers to this framework as moving "toward a critical race pedagogy." This body of literature (Hughes, 2005, 2007; Lynn, 2004; Parker & Lynn, 2002) critiques the absence of race and racial dimensions inherent to critical pedagogy. Complementary to CRT, the potential of critical race pedagogy not only accounts for the power dynamics and the challenges to various forms of oppression, but also articulates the complexity that race, ethnicity, and class bear on our students' success in the college classroom and in their future classrooms as teachers. Grounding our GYO framework in this research, we acknowledge that our students have been repeatedly excluded from participating and matriculating to higher education because of their positionality. Hence, we expect that they will see the possibilities of instilling what Hughes (2007), building on Freire (1996), deems "a critical race pedagogy of hope" through our college courses, the additional work with community-based organizations, and our future educators' daily teaching. We latch onto this critical hopefulness, echoing Oakes and Lipton's (2007) characterization that "hope sustains the actions, and people must act or the hope turns against them" (p. 32), while acknowledging that social location needs to be integrated within coursework and activities with the community-based organizations. Our intention is to transfer this dimensionality to the future teachers' own (future) educational spaces. With an expectation that they will design justice-oriented and antioppressive curricula, we hold a strong belief that a pedagogy of hope combined with purposeful action will promote dispositions focused on justice and equity (Freire, 1996).

ELEVATING THE COMMUNITY FROM WITHIN: ADVENTS OF RACE UPLIFT AND GIVING BACK

The ideas behind the concept of race uplift are connected to social reconstruction theory. Beyond this connection, they are also linked to how we think about critical pedagogy, critical race theory, and the hopefulness for our teacher candidates. Booker T. Washington (1901) mobilized this idea as a means to challenge injustices based on race. Even though this concept is more than a century old, the tenets behind race uplift are still applicable today. These ideas, attributed to Washington's (1901) writings toward a group effort in overcoming the racialized enslavement experiences of Africans in America, are particularly relevant to the extreme situations we see in the most historically marginalized and impoverished neighborhoods. Thompson (1998) describes contemporary uses of race uplift in detailing African Americans' political and economic advancement as a group. As a group working to overcome marginalization, GYO uses this construct to overcome adversity and rise up together to become a part of the establishment (while problematizing joining the dominant culture).

GYO's interpretation of race uplift extends beyond African Americans to Latinos and other marginalized groups. Challenging sociostructural attributes of oppressed communities, common to both African Americans and Latinos, is shaping the effectiveness of the long-standing tradition of activism (Collins, 1991; de la Luz Reyes, 1997; Moraga & Anzaldua, 1983). Seeking higher education, especially in education-related areas, can be an important means to interrogate institutional racism, teach against injustice, and maintain groups' inherent culture. Also of particular importance to GYO is developing activists who will organize for reform and remain involved in grassroots community-empowerment efforts. The intimate knowledge brought to the table by community-based organizations presents a powerful model of collaborative practice that we expect our prospective teachers, having experienced it firsthand, to replicate as classroom teachers.

These attributes of race uplift are particularly critical in communities of color, since many Latinas and African American women now have greater access to careers other than teaching. Collins (1991) asserts that many African American women do not enter teaching because of the change in opportunities. The diminished prevalence of the political activism in these women's educational practices has had a detrimental effect on communities. Using the race uplift framework to foster a return to the community for people of color can have a promising effect. Training teachers of color to be critical educators can help them in uplifting and giving back to their communities (Hill, 2003) and has become a cornerstone of the GYO initiative.

As we frame such practices of uplifting for the purposes of this initiative, we cannot help but wonder how transformational it might be if national reform efforts focused on similar visions.

PROMOTING AN ETHIC OF CARE AS A PROCESS OF "OTHER MOTHERING"

The GYO initiative sees tremendous value in framing our work through an ethic of care (Noddings, 2005; Thompson, 1998; Valenzuela, 1999), reflecting Noddings's (2005) assertion that "caring is the very bedrock of all successful education and that contemporary school can be revitalized in its light" (p. 27). Using caring as a centerpiece, we seek to "suppose education" could be "planned by people primarily concerned with the kinds of relations we should establish" (Noddings, 2005, p. 44). The idea that significant adults can act as mothers to the community, or what Patricia Hill Collins (1991) calls "other mothering," therefore also characterizes the theoretical perspectives necessary for the alternative, non-traditional students who are GYO candidates. Whereas initially this may seem like an unlikely need or a method reserved for more traditional college students, we see a strong need to root GYO practices in this conceptualization. The complex and often confusing systems manifest in higher education warrant exactly the kind of supplemental guidance and nurturing associated with this authentically caring ideal, which in turn should be reflected in the relationships that our candidates develop with their students.

This ethic of care contributes to our understanding of justice and equality by suggesting that interpersonal relationships be examined as we work to build a nurturing environment within the initiative. Care theory expects that educators understand how students can best be supported. These interpersonal relationships, especially in school and classroom settings, have the potential to develop, promote, and sustain equity and justice (Hill & Gillette, 2005). This should not be understood as pejorative "handholding," but instead as instilling or embedding a structure of care, support, and guidance as GYO candidates progress, matriculate, and negotiate their higher education experiences. Further, this is similar to what Thompson (1998) describes as a Black feminist ethic of care where students are taught to be political and take action against inequalities.

Furthermore, the ethic of care readily acknowledges present structures of oppression, race, class, and gender (Hill & Gillette, 2005). An emphasis on developing a foundation for surviving and living within an inherently racist society is the basis for promoting a theory of care. Collins's definition of other mothering as an ethic of care specifically delineates Black women to innately embrace a capacity of accountability to a Black community's children and to "treat them as if they were members of their own families" (p. 5). Latinas also demonstrate this competence of care in how they see their roles within their communities (Skinner, 2005; Valenzuela, 1999). The GYO structure embraces the other mothering concept by seeing those involved in the community in capacities "as other mothers to their students" (Hill & Gillette, 2005, p. 46) and also understands that the different groups coming together to form GYO need to also act toward the candidates in an ethical, caring way. Hill's (2003) work also informs us of ways the mothering care can and should be enacted within GYO so that each consortium can best support and prepare candidates for success. These include, but are not limited to, always making sure to engage in candid, frank deliberation and exchange of ideas with the GYO candidates, and with one another in the consortium, while consistently highlighting the imperative of making community connections. The candidates' insights and ideas for ongoing program development must also be included.

Finally, the community-based organizations have been instrumental in bringing the parent perspective to the GYO program. Traditional teacher education programs often struggle with helping candidates understand parent and community perspectives (Jones, 2002). Not only are many of our GYO candidates parents themselves, but our advisory boards contain parents from the communities that GYO is designed to serve. Additionally, representatives from faith-based institutions and other community agencies regularly participate in GYO activities. The structure thus reinforces an ethic of caring by modeling a community-based approach to teacher education. Whereas we contextualize an ethic of care and other mothering for our GYO candidates, we realize that these issues are widespread, systemic concerns. We believe others can leverage the capacity of these frames to assist in the complex negotiations that many prospective teachers from historically marginalized communities face at their universities.

CULTURAL STUDIES APPLIED TO INTERCULTURAL COMMUNICATION

The GYO program brings different groups and cultures together in order to teach and develop critical educators devoted to returning to their own communities. The notion of understanding intercultural communication, especially how it relates to cultural studies, is therefore imperative. Indeed, communication and the ready exchange of information between different

groups is essential to all success. The interdisciplinary field of cultural studies examines content and subject matter in terms of the practices of groups,
particularly in their relation to power (Sardar & Loon, 2001). When applied
to intercultural communication, cultural studies reveal the complexity of the
social and political attributes that the groups maintain. This complexity can
be analyzed in an effort to better understand the different groups and, thus,
teach in order to transgress the inequalities faced within the communities in
need, and practice democratic freedom (hooks, 1994).

In the GYO consortia, varying cultural attributes define the different
constituencies and entities that have joined together to develop future educators. Intercultural communication with an eye toward critical cultural studies can allow these different groups to readily understand and work together
to reach a shared vision—namely, to develop future educators of color. Applying this concept to GYO, we believe that culture is something that can be
learned, is coherent, ranks what is important, furnishes attitudes, dictates
how to behave, and is the shared views of a group of people (Beamer &
Varner, 2008). Ultimately, by coming together and acknowledging the differences among and between groups, the GYO consortia develop their own
cultural identity and communication strategies. As we work together, we
understand the necessity of learning about and developing practices that
allow multiple entities to fully understand and work together in the best
interests of students while avoiding assimilation along the way.

CONCEPTUALIZING A GROW YOUR OWN FRAMEWORK AND SCAFFOLD FOR SUCCESS

We have worked to conceptualize GYO around what research suggests are
effective means to reach low-income and non-traditional students of color
in higher education. In order for our GYO candidates to thrive and ultimately graduate with teaching credentials, the entire structure and its components must revolve around successfully preparing this group of students
through their unique and non-traditional needs. Fortunately, NEIU has a
proud history of serving first-generation college students, especially those
who are graduates of the Chicago Public Schools, and can apply much previous knowledge and experiences with our similar student population to the
context of the GYO initiative.

Research conducted both locally and nationally indicates several key
factors that increase student perseverance and success in college (Institute
for Higher Education Policy, 2001; Light, 2001). Hill and Gillette (2005)
point out significant factors for first-generation college students and stu-

dents of color from low-income families include: academic preparation including pre-college programs and test preparation, social integration and a sense of feeling connected through non-academic social events, connections to the campus through faculty liaisons, connections to the community through community liaisons, a sense that the institution is working with and for them, forgivable loans and financial aid, assistance with child care and transportation, and support structures that include mentoring and tutoring services, in addition to components that assist students in self-reflection, community involvement, and collaboration. Therefore, the GYO structure has developed criteria and components that reflect the theoretical framework and thus help our candidates.

In order for teacher candidates to meet the demands of the GYO program, and realize "no barrier" access to teacher certification, critical components must be in place for success. Building on literature about college success has helped develop some parts, while other ideas result from working to resolve impediments that other college students face, especially those from historically marginalized groups (e.g., some struggle to pass the state-required Basic Skills test). Community-based organizations also provide critical insight into factors that prevent or inhibit success of potential and current candidates. Looking directly to the teacher candidates further helps us learn to meet their needs. Synthesizing data from these sources, we find the following to be necessary components: tuition and fee-forgivable loans, child care, academic support, assistance with applications (i.e., university, FAFSA, and so on), book stipends, transportation allowance, individualized state test preparation support, cohort meetings, dedicated advising, faculty and community liaisons, political and social activities beyond academics, course/professor selection guidance, and encouragement to take courses with fellow candidates.

As is the case with many school reform initiatives, perhaps the biggest challenge is the struggle with and development of ways to live up to our theoretical framework. Each GYO partner has other, important obligations. Our funding is currently dependent on the commitment and largesse of our state legislators. Similar to other reform efforts, we continually work to balance the academic needs of our candidates with the larger project of infusing the program with opportunities for activism. With a vision of teaching enacted as a political endeavor, the role of teacher education coursework, clinical teaching experiences, out-of-school activities, and the ideological frames from which we work constantly challenge assumptions and norms of what teaching and learning is all about. As we strive for our ideals, we need to actively discuss broad questions relating to what it means to be a change agent in an underresourced school, while addressing and sharing practical strategies for candidate success. Teaching is political in that we all have a stake. If we do not work together to be a part of a solution, then we will continue to be associated with the dire problems that our students face in school. Although we may be at the relative beginning of this initiative, we are hopeful that our emergent collaboration in GYO represents future possibilities of teacher education for high-needs schools, and perhaps, for all schools.

REFERENCES

Addams, J. (1902). *Democracy and social ethics.* Urbana: University of Illinois Press.

Addams, J. (1910). *Twenty years at Hull-House.* New York: Signet.

Anyon, J. (2005). *Radical possibilities.* New York: Routledge.

Apple, M. (1995). *Education and power* (2nd ed.). New York: Routledge.

Beamer, L., & Varner, I. (2008). *Intercultural communication in the global workplace* (4th ed.). New York: McGraw-Hill/Irwin.

Bomphray, A. (2009). Grow your own teachers: The anti-Teach for America. *Teacher, Revised.* Retrieved May 1, 2009, from http://teacherrevised.org/2009/04/13/grow-your-own-teachers-the-anti-teach-for-america/

Catalyst Chicago. (2009). Data central: Classes not taught by highly qualified teachers. *Catalyst Chicago.* Retrieved July 27, 2009, from http://www.catalyst-chicago.org/stat/index.php?item=36&cat=0

Chicago Public Schools (CPS). (2009). Chicago Public Schools at a glance. Retrieved July 3, 2009, from http://www.cps.edu/ABOUT_CPS/AT-A-GLANCE/Pages/At-a-glance.aspx

Christenson, B., & Levine, R. (1998). *Public school districts in the United States: A statistical profile: 1987–88 to 1993–94* (NCES 98-203). Washington, DC: National Center for Education Statistics.

Collins, P. H. (1991). *Black feminist thought.* New York: Routledge & Kegan Paul.

Counts, G. (1932). *Dare the school build a new social order?* New York: John Day.

Delpit, L. (2006). *Other people's children* (rev. ed.). New York: The New Press.

Dewey, J. (1902). *School and society.* Chicago: University of Chicago Press.

de la Luz Reyes, M. (1997). Chicanas in academe: An endangered species. In S. de Castell & M. Bryson (Eds.), *Radical in<ter>ventions* (pp. 15–38). Albany: State University of New York Press.

Dixon, A., & Rousseau, C. (2005). And we are still not saved: Critical race theory in education ten years later. *Race, Ethnicity and Education, 8*(1), 7–27.

Dubois, W. E. B. (1903). *The souls of Black folk.* Chicago: C. McClurg.

Freire, P. (1970). *Pedagogy of the oppressed.* New York: Continuum.

Freire, P. (1996). *Pedagogy of hope*. New York: Continuum.

Freire, P. (2001). Pedagogy of the city. In A. M. A. Freire & D. Macedo (Eds.), *The Paulo Freire reader* (pp. 231–236). New York: Continuum.

Giroux, H. (2001). *Theory and resistance in education* (rev. ed.). South Hadley, MA: Bergin & Garvey.

Giroux, H., & McLaren, P. (Eds.). (1989). *Critical pedagogy, the state, and cultural struggle*. Albany: State University of New York Press.

Grant, C., & Sleeter, C. (2008). *Turning on learning: Five approaches for multicultural teaching plans for race, class, gender and disability* (5th ed.). San Francisco: Wiley.

Haberman, M. (1995). *Star teachers of children of poverty*. Bloomington, IN: Kappa Delta Pi.

Hill, D. (2003). Womanist traditions: Black women scholar-workers in teacher education. In R. Duhon-Sells & L. Agard-Jones (Eds.), *International perspectives on methods of improving education focusing on the quality of diversity*. Lewiston, NY: Edwin Mellon Press.

Hill, D., & Gillette, M. (2005). Teachers for tomorrow in urban schools. *Multicultural Perspectives, 7*(3), 42–50.

hooks, b. (1994). *Teaching to transgress*. New York: Routledge.

Hughes, S. (2005). *What we still don't know about teaching race*. Lewiston, NY: Edwin Mellen Press.

Hughes, S. (2007). Toward a critical race pedagogy of hope. *Journal of Educational Controversy, 2*(2). Retrieved April 1, 2010, from http://www.wce.wwu.edu/Resources/CEP/eJournal/v002n001/r001.shtml

Ingersoll, R. (2003). *Is there really a teaching shortage? The Consortium for Policy Research in Education*. Seattle: University of Washington.

Institute for Higher Education Policy. (2001). *Getting through college: Voices of low-income and minority students in New England*. Washington, DC: Author.

Jones, T. (2002). Incorporating Latino parents' perspectives into teacher preparation. *Harvard Family Research Project Research Digest*. Retrieved April 14, 2009, from http://www.hfrp.org/family-involvement/publications-resources/incorporating-latino-parents-perspectives-into-teacher-preparation

Kumashiro, K. (2002). *Troubling education*. New York: Routledge Falmer.

Ladson-Billings, G. (1994). *The dreamkeepers*. San Francisco: Jossey-Bass.

Ladson-Billings, G. (2009). Just what is critical race theory and what's it doing in a nice field like education? In E. Taylor, D. Gillborn, & G. Ladson-Billings (Eds.), *Foundations of Critical Race Theory in Education* (pp. 17–36). New York: Routledge.

Ladson-Billings, G., & Tate, W. (1995). Toward a critical race theory of education. *Teachers College Record, 97*(1), 47–68.

Light, R. (2001). *Making the most of college*. Cambridge, MA: Harvard University Press.

Lynn, M. (1999). Toward a critical race pedagogy. *Urban Education, 33*(5), 606–626.

Lynn, M. (2004). Inserting the "race" into critical pedagogy. *Educational Philosophy and Theory, 36*(2), 153–165.

McLaren, P. (2006). *Life in schools* (5th ed.). Boston: Allyn & Bacon.

McLaren, P., & Kincheloe, J. (2008). *Critical pedagogy: Where are we now?* New York: Peter Lang.

Miner, B. (2010). Looking past the spin: Teach for America. *Rethinking Schools, 24*(3) Retrieved April 18, 2010, from http://www.rethinkingschools.org/archive/24_03/24_03_TFA.shtml

Moraga, C., & Anzaldua, G. (Eds.). (1983). *This bridge called my back: Writings by radical women of color.* New York: Kitchen Table/Women of Color Press.

National Center for Education Statistics. (2000). *Fast facts.* Washington, DC: National Center for Education Statistics. Retrieved January 15, 2001, from http://www.nces.ed.gov

National Commission on Teaching and America's Future. (2002). *Unraveling the "teacher shortage" problem.* Washington, DC: Author.

National Education Association (NEA). (2003). *Meeting the challenges of recruitment and retention.* Washington, DC: Author.

Noddings, N. (2005).*The challenge to care in schools* (2nd ed.). New York: Teachers College Press.

Oakes, J., & Lipton, M. (2007). *Teaching to change the world* (3rd ed.). New York: McGraw-Hill.

Parker, L., & Lynn, M. (2002). What's race go to do with it?: Critical race theory's conflicts with and connections to qualitative research methodology and epistemology. *Qualitative Inquiry, 8*(1), 7–22.

Payne, C. (2008). *So much reform, so little change.* Cambridge, MA: Harvard University Press.

Planty, M., Hussar, W., Snyder, T., Kena, G., KewalRamani, A., Kemp, J., Bianco, K., & Dinkes, R. (2009). *The condition of education 2009 (NCES 2009-081).* Washington, DC: National Center for Education Statistics.

Sardar, Z., & Loon, B. (2001). *Introducing cultural studies* (2nd ed.). Cambridge, MA: Totem Books.

Skinner, E. (2005). *Latinas in higher education: Learning from their experiences.* Unpublished doctoral dissertation, University of Illinois at Chicago.

Tate, W. (1996). Critical race theory. *Review of Research in Education, 22*, 201–247.

Thompson, A. (1998). Not the color purple: Black feminist lessons for educational caring. *Harvard Educational Review, 68*(4), 522–554.

Valenzuela, A. (1999). *Subtractive schooling.* Albany: State University of New York Press.

Warren, M. (2001). *Dry bones rattling.* Princeton, NJ: Princeton University Press.

Warren, M. (2005). Communities and schools: A new view of urban education reform. *Harvard Educational Review, 75*(2), 133–173.

Washington, B. T. (1901). *Up from slavery.* New York: Basic.

Woodson, C. (1933). *The mis-education of the Negro.* Trenton, NJ: Africa World Press.

Zumwalt, K., & Craig, E. (2005) Teachers' characteristics: Research on the demographic profile. In M. Cochran-Smith & K. Zeichner (Eds.), *Studying teacher education: The report of the AERA Panel on Research and Teacher Education* (pp. 111–156). Mahwah, NJ: Lawrence Erlbaum Associates.

3

Amalia's Quest

From Parent Mentor to Teacher

ELIZABETH A. SKINNER

My cell phone rang at around 9:30 p.m. on Thursday, April 17, 2007. It was the night of parent-teacher conferences in the Chicago Public Schools. Not even waiting for my hello, Amalia's almost breathless voice started telling me about her first conferences as a teacher and how the students had insisted that their parents meet her. Excitedly, she explained, "Even the students who only come to me for one hour a day for reading instruction. . . . My job is like a dream. I can't believe it's me teaching."

Given Amalia's status as a working-class Latina who moved to the United States from Mexico when she was 17, it may be hard to believe that she is, in fact, a teacher. For me, this sense of surprise or disbelief is not grounded in a questioning of her skills or knowledge but rather the well-documented history of a lack of educational opportunity for members of marginalized communities. Amalia is a female immigrant who speaks English as her second language and resides in a Latino neighborhood of Chicago. Her gender, class, and race are all factors that not only limit her access to higher education but also her chances for success once there.

Amalia and I met in August of 2000. At that time, she was a new student in Project Nueva Generación—the original Grow Your Own (GYO) teachers program in Illinois—and I was the program coordinator. Amalia is a longtime resident of Logan Square, a neighborhood that Chicagoans identify as distinctly Latino. Census data confirm this identity in that 65%

of the residents are of Hispanic origin and in the local schools between 83% and 92% of the students are Hispanic (CensusScope, 2010; Chicago Public Schools, 2010). Amalia and her family typify the Latino presence in the neighborhood; she and her husband own their small brick bungalow and their three children attend their local school, where Amalia worked as a parent mentor and member of the Local School Council.

Amalia's lifelong pursuit of education, including her quest to become a teacher, could be perceived as one of individual success and resilience, but it is my belief that her story—her quest—also prompts a new way of thinking about community-university partnerships. Viewing Amalia's experience through what Booker T. Washington (1901) called race uplift and her role as a community teacher as a challenge to the status quo forces teacher educators—including myself—to envision the potential in working with pre-service educators in community-based settings. We must ask: Can we cultivate a new crop of activist teachers who will work for change in their neighborhoods and schools?

FINDING SUPPORT WITH/IN COMMUNITY-UNIVERSITY BASED PARTNERSHIPS

Looking back over the years, it has become clear that Project Nueva Generación was more than just a means to a degree for Amalia. Project Nueva Generación served as the mooring that motivated Amalia to stay the course, to complete her quest to become a teacher. Further, Project Nueva Generación provided Amalia with more than the requisite academic preparation, teaching methods, and theory. Project Nueva Generación also promoted the necessary relationships that allowed her to realize her potential. Now a teacher, the relational nature of her work became clear to Amalia after she missed several days of school and one of her students asked, "Why should I be here [school], when you're not?" Confronted with that question, Amalia realized the significance of her role in the community and the bearing she will have on the children who live there.

For much of Amalia's life, education was a struggle, an individual endeavor secondary to family and financial needs. Living in Mexico, Amalia attended high school at night while working part-time jobs during the day. When her family abruptly decided to immigrate to Chicago, about a month shy of her high school graduation, she was devastated but knew that family came first. Once in Chicago, high school was painfully isolating, particularly given her newcomer status. And again, school was secondary to her family responsibilities, which included caring for younger siblings and nieces and nephews, and an afterschool job at McDonald's.

There were events, however, that propelled Amalia "to be better" and to remember "the answer was in school." In particular, when a high school teacher took her to Daley College, the local community college, Amalia envisioned herself as a college student. She remembered thinking, "If I went to Daley that would be a step toward a university, a 4-year university." This exposure to a community college provided motivation and evoked new possibility for Amalia. She began to think of herself as a student pursuing a degree in higher education.

After graduating from high school, Amalia did go on to Daley College. Her experience at Daley was completely different from what she experienced in high school; she made friends and felt like she was a part of the school community. Although she had to work nearly full-time in order to pay for school, she loved it. She recalled, "I bloomed. . . . I was finally someone important." Although the community she became a part of as a city college student ultimately could not compete with her family responsibilities, which grew to include her husband and children, the significance of community (both geographic and felt) and the relationships she developed never diminished.

When Amalia's children reached school age, she essentially returned to school along with them by working as a parent mentor. The Parent Mentor Program (see Brown and Hong, this volume), an initiative of the Logan Square Neighborhood Association (LSNA), also rekindled Amalia's desire for education. Working as parent mentor granted Amalia and other Logan Square parents, mostly mothers, access to their local schools, classrooms, and teachers. This access prompted many of the women to contemplate becoming teachers themselves, and out of this interest and desire evolved Project Nueva Generación.

Project Nueva Generación brought the university to the neighborhood and allowed participants to adjust to life as college students in the comfort of their own community. As Amalia put it, being able to jump on the bus with her kids in tow was a "small step" compared to the effort it would take to go to campus. The fact that her children could go with her and be in the care of trusted adults while she was in class also made attending easier— "How could we be in a classroom paying attention to the professor knowing that our children were not being well taken care of?"

Moreover, students found comfort among each other; they found community. When asked about the strength of the relationships formed within the cohort, Amalia most often used the word *family* to describe the experience. Including collaborative projects in coursework, forming study groups, and holding regular social events and celebrations helped cultivate this feeling of family. In addition to the program implementation, the students' sense of collegiality and community greatly contributed to the strength of the peer network. According to Amalia:

> We are like a huge family . . . if one falls down, we all help her get up. I have learned so much from all of them. We all have one thing in common, wanting to be educated. We all have children. We all have problems and we are so similar and then again, we are so different.

What Amalia conveys is much like a women's helping network described by Hondagneu-Sotelo (1994) in reference to the social ties between recent female immigrants. These social networks within the peer group provide companionship, security, knowledge, and emotional support. For the students in Project Nueva Generación, the network also provided academic help. This was illustrated when one student's husband was gravely ill and cohort members supported her by studying with her at the hospital and helping her catch up on assignments. The support network was not limited to peers, but rather it was important that students expand their network to include individuals and institutions outside of the peer group. During the second year of the program, a high-ranking official from the Chicago Public Schools, who is also Latina, taught a bilingual education course, and although it was never confirmed, Amalia believes this contact helped her land her first job in the system.

The university and the community-based organization proactively worked to strengthen and expand the network of the students but, at times, they also had to react to student needs. For example, once back in school, Amalia had to strike a balance between school and family. For the first time, she delegated household chores and responsibilities to her older children and husband and often prepared meals prior to leaving for her evening classes. Initially, Amalia's husband was not on board with the change in family dynamic, as he would have preferred to adhere to a more traditional and gender-imbalanced model. He suspected that there was a "catch" because tuition, books, and child care were all provided by the grant at no expense to the students—essentially, he felt the program was too good to be true. Amalia also thought he may have felt threatened or been jealous of the idea of her becoming a teacher because she would not only be better educated than he but also would ultimately bring home a bigger paycheck. To help in managing these difficult times, and keep in touch with the shifting responsibilities for the program participants, the education organizer at LSNA invited a family counselor to come to speak to the students about ways to manage stress related to family dynamics.

Being aware of the students' social and emotional needs and understanding the context in which they had returned to school meant that the university personnel could also reach out to students and offer meaningful support. Although she was only a sophomore, Amalia was honored at the university Spring Honors Convocation with an award typically given to an outstanding junior or senior. The award was intended to recognize her stellar academic achievement, while at the same time boosting morale. The impact it had on Amalia's family life could not have been anticipated:

> I saw my husband crying! So that changed my husband's attitude.
> Now he's being very supportive. He doesn't bother me when he sees
> me study. He says to the kids, "Let's go to the living room; Mom
> needs to rest," or "Mom needs to finish this work." He is a completely
> different person.

As family relationships evolved (some more successfully than others) and a few of the students began to conform to less traditional gender roles at home, the relationship between the university, the community-based organization, and the local schools also evolved into what might be considered a non-traditional relationship. Prior to Project Nueva Generación, the university did not have any experience placing students in Logan Square schools for field hours or student teaching. And although Amalia would have been willing to go to schools in other neighborhoods to complete field hours, the community-based nature of the program and the desire to keep the students close to home required that the university develop relationships with local Logan Square schools. Keeping the needs of the future teachers at the forefront, the university solicited advice and help from LSNA in identifying a partner school. Once the school had been determined, gaining access and forming a relationship with the administration and teachers was facilitated by LSNA, which had been involved in the school for many years. Amalia and two other students were the first student teachers at the site.

Amalia was ready. She had the desire. She had the support of her community, family, and friends. Amalia had the teacher education coursework behind her as well as the four standardized tests that Illinois teachers must pass for bilingual approval and elementary certification. She was poised to put all of her knowledge to work. Amalia was a teacher.

INNOVATIVE PRACTICES FOR TEACHER EDUCATORS WORKING IN COMMUNITY-BASED SETTINGS

When Amalia asks, "Who better than me?" to teach in her community, it is a question that merits attention. Whereas considerable effort has gone into attempting to prepare White outsiders to teach in historically underserved urban settings, Nueva Generación and the GYO initiative propose an alternative strategy, one that aims not only to increase the number of teachers of color but also to prepare them to work as change agents in schools. Much like the transformative teachers described by Greg Michie (this volume), many GYO candidates choose to enter the profession based on their own negative experiences in school and a commitment to prevent that experience for younger generations. Rather than viewing community members and parents as part of the problem in urban schools, colleges of education must look within urban communities for teacher candidates. This approach requires a core belief in the value of what candidates like Amalia bring to teaching. Meeting student needs through program adaptations while at the same time preparing them pedagogically is an approach that allows colleges of education to better meet the needs of urban schools (Sleeter, 2001).

As a first-generation college student, navigating the bureaucracy of the university system was a challenge for Amalia. Anticipating this challenge, the community-based organization and the university provided support from the admissions process through graduation. During the early years of the program, much of that support came directly from me, the program coordinator, as I dealt with the bureaucracy of the university on behalf of the students. Gradually, as the students began to go on campus for classes, they also took on more responsibility for administrative tasks such as dropping or adding classes, obtaining registration overrides from professors, submitting tuition waivers, and course scheduling. One semester, Amalia was on campus 3 mornings a week for a biology class. After class on these days, she often went to see her professor during office hours to get extra help on assignments and to discuss readings. The relationship Amalia formed with her biology professor led her to become involved in a landscaping project for the new university library. When Amalia told me about her work on the project, I interpreted that as a positive indicator not only of her comfort level on campus but also a sign of her having figured out the system to some extent.

The fact that I began to receive fewer and fewer phone calls from all of the students, including Amalia, was also a sign of their increased independence and ability to navigate the university system. So, when a few weeks into her student teaching semester Amalia told me, "I don't care if I graduate," I was surprised to learn that the cause of her frustration was, in fact, the bureaucracy. Although Amalia did get her application for graduation signed and submitted on time, this final bureaucratic hurdle reminded me to never minimize the struggle that students face at an institutional level.

In addition to the institutional barriers, for many women, family expectations and obligations pose additional hindrances when pursuing their education (Ginorio & Huston, 2001). It is not unusual, then, that Amalia's first attempt at post-secondary education was interrupted when she became pregnant with her first child. Although Amalia chose to stay home with her children, it wasn't a choice she made readily. As she put it, "My body was there, but my spirit wasn't." Understanding the dilemma faced by women returning to school and accommodating those family obligations into program implementation is critical in the community-based setting. In addition to holding classes in the evenings in the school-based community centers, with child care available, Project Nueva Generación offered a variety of support throughout the years of the program. Given that many of the students in Project Nueva Generación were the products of the Chicago Public School system in which they hoped to teach, several of them had academic deficiencies that had to be addressed (Skinner 2010). Ongoing academic support included English as a Second Language class, flexible one-on-one tutoring, individualized test preparation, academic advising, access to family counselors, and flexible course loads. Project Nueva Generación was not an alternative certification program and there was no fast track for the students; thus there was time to address their academic needs and to prepare the students for success in their courses. As the needs of the students changed, the intensity and nature of the support provided also evolved.

Accommodating family life and adapting the program to meet the needs of the students is one level of innovation to be considered in the community-based setting. However, taking a cue from community-based organizations and recognizing the inherent value in that family life requires an additional shift in perspective. The education organizing work of LSNA and other community-based organizations around the country is built on the skills and leadership abilities of parents and community members. In Logan Square, the result of engaging parents in the real work of schools has improved academic performance (Mediratta, Fruchter, & Lewis, 2002). By collaborating with a community-based organization, colleges of education not only find out what is important to community members but also learn what skills and assets to build upon when preparing teachers (Brown, 2007).

The preparation of bilingual teachers necessitates an examination of the inequities of schooling for non-English-speaking children as related to the poor implementation of bilingual education in Chicago and beyond. Bilingual teacher candidates discover early in their coursework that the research and theory supporting best practices for English language learners is clearly not reflected in policy and school-based practices. As a result, bilingual education students are inclined and encouraged to resist, as much as possible, the pressure to conform to the English-only policies and attitudes they encounter in some schools. Such resistance may include instruction in Spanish but can be less overt. Professors in Amalia's bilingual education courses taught and modeled teaching strategies and took an activist stance based on the belief that bilingualism is an asset worth fighting for in our schools. Amalia learned that well-prepared, transformational bilingual educators use children's literature that reflects the cultural background of their students, even if it means digressing from the basal reading series adopted by their school. Effective curriculum builds off what English language learners bring with them to the classroom and encourages collaboration. Bilingual teachers who create community within their classrooms understand that the language of home has academic value, and accept Spanish and English spoken in their rooms.

Amalia's culture, language, experience in the community, and prior work with schoolchildren all contribute to her funds of knowledge and are among the skills she brought with her to Project Nueva Generación (Moll, Amanti, Neff, & Gonzalaz, 1992). As an insider in the community, Amalia shares these skills and many life experiences with her students and their families. On day 1 of a science unit on water ecology, Amalia grabbed her students' attention by asking, "How many of you have been to Mexico? How's the water? How do you get your water?" In the ensuing discussion, Amalia moved around the front of a cramped classroom proudly describing and showing the students how as a young girl she had lugged buckets of water from a well to her family home. From this common starting point, the class began to construct the unit, focused on water quality and the surrounding ecosystem.

Amalia's understanding of the significance gender has played in her academic trajectory is another of the skills she brings to her work. She sees her identity as a teacher extending beyond the walls of her classroom and reaching into the community, particularly into the female community. When describing her role as a teacher, she said, "I see myself as a leader, helping all these ladies. . . ." This is an example of her "*mujerista*" tendencies or the ". . . Latina oriented 'womanist' sensibility or approach to power, knowledge and relationships rooted in convictions for community uplift" (Villenas, Godinez, Delgado Bernal, & Elenes, 2006, p. 7). After several mothers asked Amalia how she had learned to speak English so well, her response was to ask her principal about the possibility of having English classes offered in the building after school. This *mujerista* disposition, inherent in Amalia's own identity, is not taught in traditional pre-service teacher preparation programs, but it is a hallmark in Project Nueva Generación's university-community partnership. The inclination of many GYO teacher candidates to lift up their community needs to be valued and built upon through challenging, critical coursework that encourages teacher candidates to question the status quo in schools.

I believe that Amalia's teaching reflects such an approach. One hot July day, I went to visit her summer school classroom. She warned me beforehand that she was expected to adhere to the day's lesson plan as provided in the prescribed curriculum. In fact, the materials for that curriculum were the only resources made available to her that summer. I arrived just as language arts was starting and watched as her students worked in cooperative groups, reading and tackling new information together. While the students worked, Amalia moved around the room answering questions and keeping students on task. Following the group work, the students presented what they learned to the rest of the class. As Amalia facilitated discussion she prompted the students to bridge the new material with what they already knew. When we talked about the lesson after school, Amalia sighed and said, "They [textbook companies] don't know my kids." But Amalia does. That day, she demonstrated an ability to resist imposed curriculum by teaching a lesson that not only engaged the students but also valued their input and connected to their lives. Most teachers struggle to some extent with overly standardized curriculum and a lack of resources. Amalia's status as a community insider and her solid pedagogical preparation equip her to succeed with her students despite such challenges.

Now in her third year as a teacher, Amalia's challenges continue. Two days before the school year started, her teaching assignment changed. Rather than teaching 3rd grade, her principal placed her in a departmentalized 6th-, 7th-, and 8th-grade math and language arts classroom. Her chaotic schedule means different groups of students are in and out of her room all day. Further, her ability to collaborate with colleagues is limited. But she is resilient. One day, I observed her 7th-grade math students work cooperatively to solve story problems and then explain their strategies in English or Spanish. After a quick transition, 6th-graders entered Amalia's room for a 20-minute writers' workshop. She began by directing the students' attention to her own poem, which was written on newsprint hanging on the chalkboard. The poem was a heartfelt tribute to her grandmother in Mexico, and after she read it out loud, a boy raised his hand and shyly pointed out an error. Demonstrating value for the student's input, Amalia encouraged him to speak up: "Oh, you've got to correct me then. See? We all make mistakes. Thank you." By sharing both her personal life and her vulnerability as a writer through the poem, Amalia encouraged her students to do the same. Another student, too shy to read her own poem, allowed Amalia to read it out loud for the class to hear. Through such seemingly minor actions, Amalia maintains a classroom environment where her students can share their lives, opinions, and languages with each other and with their teacher.

In addition to students who come and go all day, there are five different resource personnel assigned to Amalia's classroom at different times during the week. Under the guise of providing support for Amalia and her students, the personnel only add to the mounting pressure that Amalia feels as a relatively new teacher. Is the math coach there to check her content knowledge? Is the new teacher mentor reporting back to her principal? Is the librarian noting that she speaks in Spanish? And why is the computer teacher there? Although she admits that her questions are irrational, she is keen to note that this sort of support is neither collaborative nor what her students need. Unfortunately, in a public school system threatening to lay off large percentages of teachers due to an enormous budget shortfall, a sense of paranoia prevails. Privately, Amalia admits to feeling overwhelmed and isolated, but then quickly states, "This will make me a stronger teacher." Her actions suggest that she knows what else will make her a stronger teacher. She is taking courses for a math endorsement at the University of Chicago and investigating master's degree programs in reading.

LEARNING FROM AMALIA'S QUEST

Amalia's story may be interpreted as one of individual educational resiliency, but I believe there is much more to it than that. Her success represents the potential of community-university partnerships, such as the GYO teacher movement, as a new way to think about teacher education in urban communities. Holding classes in the neighborhood schools makes returning to college more feasible for students. It solidly connects university professors and personnel to the community in ways that do not usually occur on campus. Working closely with a community-based organization in identifying individual schools for field placements also allows the university greater access in establishing a presence in the community. This results in a mutually beneficial arrangement for the school, university, and the community-based organizations.

Furthermore, the community-university partnership provides an opportunity for parents who are already involved in the neighborhood schools to participate and assume a variety of roles. In Amalia's case, she could identify and participate in a multiplicity of ways, from stay-at-home mom, to mentor, student, teacher, to activist (Zambrana, 1994). Community was clearly a significant factor in Amalia's trajectory through the teacher education program. As a first-generation college student, Amalia learned how to work within the university system, starting close to home. Taking a number of her teacher preparation courses within her neighborhood, rather than on campus, made Amalia's transition to college gradual. Additionally, the cohort model fostered familial relationships among the students, thus creating a strong sense of community.

The family that Amalia refers to when speaking of her fellow students is a critical component of a GYO teacher preparation program. Amalia recognized the significance her peers had for her, both academically and personally, and she also felt responsible for their success. As students became less reliant on the community-based organization and the university personnel, the peer-group network increased in importance. All of the students provided each other emotional support and academic support as well as friendship. This support, in the presence of personal hardships and family crises that could potentially be barriers for Amalia and the other students, improved her chances for graduating.

Project Nueva Generación and the subsequent GYO teachers movement is rooted in the communities and complements already existing, traditional models of teacher preparation, but should also promote a change in the status quo in teacher education. In order to meet the needs of a diverse school-age student body, colleges of education must diversify their own approaches to recruiting and preparing teacher candidates. LSNA and the Bilingual Education Program at Chicago State University understood and valued Amalia's linguistic and cultural knowledge. Together, the entities adapted the academic and support program not only to highlight those strengths but also to address any weaknesses. As a role model for students and parents alike and as a member of the larger community in which she teaches, Amalia uses her linguistic and cultural competencies to relate to her students and their families.

Amalia's story is an example of the "personal, collective and institutional actions" that, when combined, can create real change in community-university partnerships and teacher education (Nieto, 2001, p. 8). The realization of Amalia's quest to become a teacher and the factors that made it possible are a testament to this statement. Because she lived them, Amalia understands the inherent barriers to academic and personal success for members of her community. Just as important as her understanding of these barriers is the belief in the assets and the potential in the communities where she lives and works. Her participation in a GYO teacher program helped bring those assets to light. And unlike many new teachers who may commit to teaching in urban schools only to leave in 1 or 2 years, Amalia's commitment goes beyond the school walls and into the community—her community.

REFERENCES

Brown, J. (2007). Parents building communities in schools. *Voices in Urban Education, 17*, 26–34. Providence, RI: Annenberg Institute for School Reform at Brown University.

CensusScope. (2010). *Race and ethnicity selections, 1980–2000.* Retrieved January 20, 2010, from http://www.censusscope.org/us/print_chart_race.html

Chicago Public Schools. (2010). *School test scores and demographic reports.* Retrieved January 20, 2010, from http://research.cps.k12.il.us/resweb/ SchoolProfile?unit=3520

Ginorio, A., & Huston, M. (2001). *Si, se puede! Yes, we can: Latinas in school.* Washington, DC: American Association of University Women Educational Foundation.

Hondagneu-Sotelo, P. (1994). *Gendered transition: Mexican experiences of immigration.* Berkeley: University of California Press.

Mediratta, K., Fruchter, N., & Lewis, A. (2002). *Organizing for school reform.* New York: Institution for Education and Social Policy.

Moll, L., Amanti, C., Neff, D., & Gonzalaz, N. (1992). Funds of knowledge for teaching. *Theory Into Practice, 31,* 132–141.

Nieto, S. (2001). What keeps teachers going? *Equity & Excellence in Education, 34*(1), 6–15.

Skinner, E. (2010). Project Nueva Generación and grow your own teachers. *Teacher Education Quarterly, 37*(3), 155–167.

Sleeter, C. (2001). Preparing teachers for culturally diverse schools. *Journal of Teacher Education, 52*(2), 94–106.

Villenas, S., Godinez, F., Delgado Bernal, D., & Elenes, C. (2006). Chicanas/Latinas building bridges. In D. Delgado Bernal, C. Alejandra Elenes, F. Godinez, & S. Villenas (Eds.), *Chicana/Latina education in everyday life* (pp. 1–9). Albany: State University of New York Press.

Washington, B. T. (1901). *Up from slavery.* New York: Doubleday.

Zambrana, R. (1994). Toward understanding the educational trajectory and socialization of Latina women. In L. Stone (Ed.), *The education feminism reader* (pp. 135–145). New York: Routledge.

4

The School-Community Organizing Model and the Origins of Grow Your Own Teachers

MARK R. WARREN

The Grow Your Own (GYO) teacher program in Illinois grew out of the community organizing work of the Logan Square Neighborhood Association (LSNA). For several years, LSNA had been working to engage parents, mostly Latina mothers, in the life of the schools their children attended. As they grew in their understanding of education and their involvement in schools, these women began to ask for an opportunity to go to college and become teachers themselves. Out of this sentiment grew Nueva Generación, which became the pilot program of what emerged as GYO Illinois. But how did these parents get organized in this way? What kinds of organizing processes led them to create Nueva Generación? In this chapter, I describe what I call a school-community organizing model and show how this approach provided a foundation for the emergence of Nueva Generación and, beyond that, for GYO Illinois.

COMMUNITY ORGANIZING AND ITS TURN TO EDUCATION

Community organizing has long distinguished itself by focusing on cultivating participation and leadership by grassroots people in civic participation and political action.[1] Rather than advocating for people, organizing groups seek to engage people directly to work for change in their schools and communities. Organizers bring people together to talk about the issues they face, the values they hold deeply, and their interests and capacities to work for change. Out of these conversations, programmatic initiatives such as Nueva Generación emerge. To be sure, organizers and community leaders study the problems they face and work with experts and allies to craft solutions that will make a difference for their families and communities. But the starting point for reform is not expert-driven. Rather, programs emerge from the felt needs of people on the ground; these initiatives represent their voices and, as such, engage their passions and commitment. In contrast to many school reform initiatives that are imposed from the top and often fail to take root in local schools (Coburn, 2003; Payne, 2008), organizing approaches ensure ownership at the ground level.

LSNA drew directly from an organizing tradition developed most thoroughly in the group's home city of Chicago. Although organizing groups find their roots in several early American movements, like the populist and settlement house movements (Fisher, 1994), they draw most explicitly from the community organizing tradition codified by Saul Alinsky in Chicago in the 1930s (Alinsky, 1971; Horwitt, 1989). Alinsky sought to work with the institutions that structured community life, like religious congregations, to build leadership and power for what he termed the "have-nots." At the same time as the CIO unions were organizing workers in industry, Alinsky sought to create organizations through which working people themselves could act to create change in their neighborhoods.

Alinsky's organizing tradition went through many changes over the years and spawned a variety of styles (Reitzes & Reitzes, 1987), but its core focus on participation and leadership, if anything, strengthened (Warren, 2001). Meanwhile, the civil rights movement contributed to organizing a new appreciation for the power of religious faith and of grassroots local action (Morris, 1984; Payne, 1995), and the women's movement emphasized the relational side of organizing (Morgen & Bookman, 1988). As the movements of the 1960s and 1970s declined, organizing groups came to concentrate their work in local struggles around "bricks-and-mortar" issues of housing, economic development, and neighborhood safety. In the 1990s, however, in recognition of the increasing importance of success in schools to children's life chances, organizing groups began to turn their attention to the crisis in public education in their communities (Warren, 2005). Community organizing groups working for education reform grew to more than 200 by the turn of the century (Gold, Simon, & Brown, 2002b; Mediratta & Fruchter, 2001), and I have more recently estimated the field at closer to 500 groups (Warren, 2010).[2]

Initially, many organizing groups took the traditional approach of marshalling their base to build the political will to get schools and school districts to meet community demands. This approach followed standard organizing practice as had been applied to community development issues. In other words, most organizing groups had honed their skills in efforts to get city housing authorities to enforce codes, to get banks to end redlining and lend in inner-city neighborhoods, and to get a variety of services improved (Briggs & Mueller, 1997). They now turned to demand that schools and school districts provide better-quality education for their children.

Organizing groups quickly learned, however, that traditional approaches proved inadequate to the task. Public schools often lacked the resources—the funds, the qualified teachers, the modern school facilities—to respond quickly to demands to provide a high-quality education (Kozol, 1991). Moreover, public schools in many large urban districts struggled with the social capacity to improve, as low levels of trust and cooperation among the teaching staff—and sometimes factional divisions and outright racial hostility—undermined improvement strategies (Bryk & Schneider, 2002; Payne, 2008). Consequently, organizing groups searched for ways to collaborate with educators, to push for change but also to contribute actively to the financial resources and social capacity available for public schooling.

THE COMMUNITY ORGANIZING ROOTS OF GYO

When LSNA began to address educational issues in Logan Square in the early 1990s, it took a deeply collaborative approach from the beginning.[3] Parents and community members had identified school overcrowding as a key issue facing their community. LSNA sought out alliances with the principals of the neighborhood's schools to organize a campaign to get the district to increase classroom capacity through building annexes to existing elementary schools and opening a new middle school (Warren, 2005).

Out of these new collaborative relationships emerged LSNA's Parent Mentor Program (Warren, 2005). In this program, parents spend 2 hours each day in the classroom assisting teachers, and they receive a modest stipend for this time. In doing so, parents directly contribute to the capacity of local schools to teach; meanwhile, though, they also become more knowledgeable about schooling and better able to assist in the education of their own—and other—children. Within a few years, LSNA was training more than 100 parents across eight neighborhood schools.

LSNA brought its organizing approach to the Parent Mentor program. In contrast to typical parent involvement programs that approach parents on an individual basis, LSNA worked to form connections between parents (Warren, Hong, Rubin, & Sychitkokhong-Uy, 2009). In other words, they built a community among the parents. In a school environment that may feel foreign, unfamiliar, or intimidating to the largely immigrant group of Latino parents, relationships with other parents became a critical source of support that encouraged involvement in the school.

Meanwhile, following the emphasis that community organizing places on leadership development, LSNA offered each parent the opportunity to build skills and abilities as emerging leaders in the school and community but also in ways that responded to personal and professional goals (Warren, Hong, Rubin, & Sychitkokhong-Uy, 2009). In fact, at the beginning of the program, each parent is required to set a personal goal, such as attaining a GED or learning English. Every Friday during the school year, parent mentors gather as a group for educational and leadership training workshops on topics such as the qualities of a leader, building one-on-one relationships, improving communication with teachers, and building children's self-esteem.

As these individuals shared common experiences and concerns, they developed ideas for new programs that could meet their shared needs and desires. A group of parent mentors suggested that neighborhood schools open during the evening and provide educational opportunities for parents and community residents. As a result, LSNA worked with the parent mentors and school principals to open some of Chicago's first community learning centers based in schools.

As parent mentors became comfortable in classroom settings, many developed a passion for education. As they gained confidence through achieving their personal goals, a number of these parents began to discuss their desire for an opportunity for a college education and their interest in becoming teachers. They hoped to serve the children of their community in local schools. It was out of these conversations, set in the context of leadership development and community organizing, that Nueva Generación and eventually GYO Illinois emerged.

PUBLIC EDUCATION: ISSUE AND INSTITUTION

As the Parent Mentor Program developed, LSNA began to craft a new orientation toward education organizing. Education would no longer simply be an *issue* for the group to address, like housing or neighborhood safety. Public schools would also represent *institutions* around which to organize parents. LSNA education organizer Joanna Brown recounts the group's emerging understanding of the role of schools as a first step into public life, particular for immigrant women.

Over and over again, the women themselves speak about being transformed by the experience. Many were isolated in their homes by language, culture, and small children. For many, it is their first step out into the public sphere. This works in part because the school is the safest public institution, filled with women and children.

The Parent Mentor Program is not about involving parents in the traditional sense of the concept—that is, as supporters of the school's agenda. Rather, it became a leadership development and organizing vehicle where parents, in conversation and collaboration with educators, began to create and act around their own agenda—developing community learning centers, the Nueva Generación initiative, and later Literacy Ambassador and parent tutor programs. Even more, though, LSNA found that once parents emerged as leaders in schools, they also began to tackle community issues such as public health and affordable housing. In other words, schools became institutional sites around which to organize on education *and* community issues.

The idea of institutional organizing is not new to community organizing. Alinsky himself recognized that existing community institutions, like congregations, have resources, both financial and human, that can provide a foundation for organizing efforts (Alinsky, 1971). In particular, people are already connected to one another around churches so organizers can access these pre-existing networks and mobilize them into action. Upon Alinsky's death, the institute he founded, the Industrial Areas Foundation (IAF), came to work even more closely with religious congregations (Warren, 2001). Led by the work of Ernesto Cortes and his colleagues in IAF organizations in Texas, the IAF began to mine rich Judeo-Christian traditions that called people of faith to work for social justice and community betterment. Rooted in relatively stable networks and motivated by faith convictions, people emerged from congregations into broader public life as powerful community leaders. Many of these leaders turned out to be women who had anchored informal support networks and grassroots activities in low-income communities but had been excluded from opportunities for more formal leadership positions (Collins, 2000; Naples, 1998).

In the 1990s, organizing groups like LSNA and the IAF network in Texas and the Southwest began to experiment with schools as institutional sites of organizing (Shirley, 1997; Warren, 2001). Like congregations, public schools represent fairly stable institutions around which people connect with each other for shared purposes and thereby form networks. As LSNA discovered, schools may be particularly good places to engage women, who have historically taken the primary responsibility for children and their education.

Moreover, American public education contains rich democratic traditions going back to Horace Mann and the Common School ideal (Kaestle, 1983). Education is meant to provide a common ground for Americans across the social spectrum, however incompletely that vision is fulfilled in practice. In the Progressive Era, John Dewey reworked the common school tradition for the urban 20th century. He envisioned public schools as a vital community institution, where schools are meant to prepare children to contribute to their communities and to participate as democratic citizens in an increasingly diverse and technocratic society (Dewey, 1915, 1938 [1916]; Westbrook, 1991). Meanwhile, the civil rights and other progressive movements have continually enriched the democratic purposes of American education as they have understood education as the key to liberation (Perry, 2003). In the end, Americans continue to invest their faith in public education as what Horace Mann termed the "great equalizer," the means to provide opportunity and upward mobility to poor children (Hochschild & Scoronick, 2003). In that sense, public education is perhaps our premier instrument for advancing social justice.

In addition, public schools are located in virtually every neighborhood, and that also makes them attractive as institutional sites for organizing. Aside from schools and religious congregations, low-income communities typically lack many other viable institutions around which families adhere. In fact, public education is a universal institution in the United States. Lacking a right to jobs or housing, the right to a public education is perhaps the only social right that Americans can claim (Noguera, 2003).

Organizing in and around schools, however, does face its challenges. Many public schools, particularly in low-income communities of color, remain deeply disconnected from the families of the children they serve (Warren, 2005). Many teachers come from White, middle-class backgrounds and know little about the neighborhoods in which they work (Noguera, 1996). Meanwhile, low-income parents of color often feel unwelcome in public schools, venturing in only when there is a problem with their child; as a result, many become critical or alienated from those schools (Diamond & Gomez, 2004). Since they do not congregate around the school, low-income parents often simply do not know the parents of their children's classmates (Horvat, Weininger, & Lareau, 2003). Meanwhile, the relationships among educators within many public schools are marred by distrust and division, along racial and other lines (Bryk & Schneider, 2002; Payne, 2008). Consequently, organizers cannot rely on the same degree of pre-existing networks and trust as they might in congregations. They have to build relationships and trust among parents and between parents and educators at the school even as they are trying to activate these relationships toward a common goal (Warren, Hong, Rubin, & Sychitkokhong-Uy, 2009).

Furthermore, schools are employment organizations for their staff, not voluntary associations. This situation can disrupt reform organizing efforts, as educators might favor preserving the status quo rather than taking the risk of making change (Stone, Henig, Jones, & Pierannunzi, 2001). Meanwhile, educators have been under extreme pressure to raise test scores quickly to meet accountability standards, and that may also restrict the space for the kind of experimentation that organizing efforts require (Shirley & Evans, 2007). Consequently, in the face of pressures to narrow the purposes of education to raising student achievement in the short run, organizers have to work hard to resurrect the democratic traditions of public education and open up the space for a broader approach to the purposes and practice of schooling.

Despite these obstacles and challenges, organizing groups have increasingly turned their attention to education reform both as issue and institution, in part because the two are so closely aligned. As an issue, education cannot be addressed and improved in our most disadvantaged communities without attention to building the institutional capacity of public schools. Education is a profoundly human and relational endeavor. Groups like LSNA are realizing more and more that strategies to engage parents and teachers in building relationships will play an essential role in transforming education. Indeed, GYO itself is premised upon the idea that community members who become teachers will practice differently—and better—because of their deep connections to students and their families.

THE SCHOOL-COMMUNITY ORGANIZING MODEL
FROM A NATIONAL PERSPECTIVE

It turns out that LSNA is not alone in experimenting with a school-community organizing approach. In fact, many organizing groups have been experimenting with organizing around schools as institutions. The network Alinsky himself founded, Industrial Areas Foundation (IAF), has been a pioneer in this field.[4] The IAF takes a somewhat different approach to organizing around education than LSNA. LSNA, as we have seen, focuses its work on developing the leadership of parents. LSNA organizers and parent leaders collaborate deeply with educators—the principal and teachers at the school, but LSNA does not directly "organize" the educators. The IAF, by contrast, organizes all the adults in the school community. The network's Alliance School model was brought to more than 120 schools in Texas and then spread to local IAF affiliates across the Southwest and in California.

In this model, public schools join local IAF organizations just like congregations. IAF organizers work to develop relationships among and between parents, teachers, and all adults in and around the school. The principal typically plays a critical role in these efforts, serving almost as chief organizer in the school and working to encourage parents and teachers to become school leaders. Indeed, the IAF has taken to referring to the creation of a "relational culture" in schools as its primary goal. Then, out of relationships and conversations within and across these groups, action plans develop to improve the school. Alliance Schools do not feature a single reform agenda; rather, ideas and initiatives emerge out of local conversations. Nevertheless, the IAF holds state- and regional-level meetings at which local leaders hear from and interact with national-level school reformers. In fact, the IAF takes care to offer local school leaders many opportunities to learn from research-based policy experts. In this way, the Alliance Schools often develop a rich and vibrant culture.

For example, in Austin, Texas, as many as 18 schools have been members of the Alliance Schools network (Shirley, 1997; Simon & Gold, 2002). Through conversations and relationships built in these schools, many took initiatives to develop innovative programs such as the Young Scientist program at Zavala Elementary School. Later, Alliance School leaders across the city got the opportunity to work with University of Pittsburgh professor Lauren Resnick's Institute for Learning as a strategy for improving student academic performance. Teacher participation grew to such an extent that in some years, almost a thousand teachers have attended professional development workshops led by IAF organizers.

But all the action does not lie within the school. Just as in LSNA, as leaders develop in the school, they become active in a broader array of community issues. In fact, a key part of the Alliance School strategy lies in creating institutional connections among schools and between schools and other institutions such as congregations. In this way, the IAF brings organizing into schools but also brings schools out into organizing.[5] For example, at the Fernangeles Elementary School in Los Angeles, school leaders worked with local congregations and neighborhood-based legal and family service organizations to close a trash dump that was causing serious health problems for the school's students.

Meanwhile, other organizing groups and networks have begun to experiment with organizing around schools. The PICO network—People Improving Communities through Organizing—has emerged as another pioneer in the field of education organizing.[6] PICO's local affiliates are congregationally based, and they began to address education as a critical issue facing their families. PICO affiliates form Local Organizing Committees (LOCs) around congregations, and these LOCs increasingly took action to address the poor quality of education in their communities. Although PICO has pioneered home visitation programs by teachers and worked on a variety of other educational initiatives, it became best known for its efforts to open new, small, autonomous schools in Oakland and later in San Jose and other cities (Gold, Simon, & Brown, 2002a; Shah, Mediratta, & McAlister, 2009). Parents in member congregations of Oakland Communities Organization (OCO) had long felt disconnected from the large, impersonal schools their children attended. They began to study the situation and found that children in the large schools in the low-income "flatlands" area of the city were failing at alarming rates while children in small schools in the more affluent "hills" were achieving at significantly higher rates. Congregational leaders in OCO developed a campaign to get the district to open new, small schools that would have the autonomy to develop curriculum and other practices that would better serve low-income children of color. The district eventually came to embrace the reform and Oakland now boasts 40 new schools, constituting a dramatic reorganization of the city's educational system. Meanwhile, other PICO affiliates such as People Acting in Community Together (PACT) in nearby San Jose took up a similar initiative and campaigned for the opening of a series of small, autonomous and charter schools in the Alum Rock school district. PICO's small schools movement had deep roots in the concerns and values of low-income communities but also worked in partnership with school reform experts in the Bay Area Coalition for Equitable Schools and other nonprofits. Meanwhile, the campaigns benefited from the national discourse on research showing the advantages of small and autonomous schools and learning communities (e.g., Cotton, 2001; Wallach & Lear, 2005).

When helping to design and open the new small schools, organizing groups such as OCO and PACT found themselves building close relationships with principals and teachers and forging new ties to parents whose children began to attend the schools. Indeed, the new schools were to place a priority on engaging parents in the life of the school. Historically, PICO leaders had believed that only congregations could provide the stable networks and core values around which to organize LOCs (Carrasco, 2003). More recently, however, many local affiliates have begun to experiment with creating LOCs around schools as well. These school-based LOCs provide important support for the new schools and help keep them aligned with community priorities. Meanwhile, some PICO organizers began to see the value of schools as sites for the initial involvement of parents in civic action. Parents new to organizing could get involved in small issues that could create immediate change in school and through that process develop their leadership skills and commitment to civic participation. Parents and, to a lesser extent, teachers organized around these schools then take action on the array of community issues addressed by the PICO organizations.

ORGANIZING AND POLICY IMPLEMENTATION

Despite variations of the school-community organizing model across groups and network, there remains much in common. At its core, organizing builds relationships among people around schools and fosters leadership in a collective context. Through conversation, people develop action plans and reform agendas that are deeply connected to community needs and expressed desires. The new policies that are implemented often work to strengthen schools as institutions and provide opportunities for further leadership development, thus enhancing organizing processes. Nueva Generación provides an excellent example of a synergistic dynamic between organizing and policy implementation and between organizing around education as an issue and as an institution. As parents develop through their college education, their ability to be leaders in the school-community grows. As they graduate and enter schools, they have the potential to be change agents as teachers in the schools to which they are assigned. The organizing group—in this case, LSNA—plays a critical role connecting schools and families and serving as a catalyst for change (Warren, Hong, Rubin, & Sychitkokhong-Uy, 2009).

Other organizing groups, such as Chicago ACORN (now called Action Now), began to see Nueva Generación as a program that might meet their community's needs as well (McAlister, Mediratta, Shah, & Fruchter, 2010). GYO Illinois emerged to campaign for passage of state legislation and funding for GYO, so that other organizing groups could pursue that strategy. The coalition took care to write community organizations into the legislation so that any GYO program receiving state funding would include a community organization partner.

In essence, GYO Illinois has succeeded in "scaling up" a pilot program initially developed by LSNA, and herein lies an important tension. Nueva Generación emerged directly out of an authentic organizing process; LSNA parents feel strong ownership and commitment to this program. GYO then was offered to community organizations across the state. These organizations took care to organize internal conversations and processes to ensure that local members really wanted such an opportunity. But the level of commitment and ownership of GYO may be slightly less in those cases. Moreover, the community organizations then set out to help recruit participants into the program. These participants are parents and other community members, and they now have some tie to the community organization. In addition, GYO Illinois makes sure to include organizing training to community organization members and participants. But these new participants come to the program differently from the parent mentors of LSNA who organized and fought to establish Nueva Generación in the first place.

This situation is not dissimilar from the processes that occur in Alliance Schools or in any other case where community organizing groups adopt initiatives developed by others, sometimes adapting them to local needs. We do not want each local school-community to have to reinvent the wheel. At the same time, we do not need yet another "proven" program to be imposed on schools and communities that have no investment in them. GYO Illinois is pioneering an experiment in bringing to scale a program developed out of a set of parent leaders in a way that supports a variety of local organizing groups and works to meet the needs of a variety of communities. The more organizing can be kept at the center of the GYO experiment, the more likely we may see the programs sink deep roots and produce community-oriented teachers who will connect schools to families and communities.

THE DEMOCRATIC PROMISE OF
SCHOOL-COMMUNITY ORGANIZING

If the common school ideal represented the democratic tradition of American public education for the 19th century, and John Dewey's progressive vision reinvented that tradition for the 20th century, we might understand community organizing as working toward developing a 21st-century model for democratic education (Oakes & Rogers, 2005). This requires not only grappling with education simply as an issue, but also addressing it as an institution. Community organizing is well poised to play that role. To do so, we have to move beyond a simplistic understanding of organizing groups in which they are seen to mobilize groups of people to demand some change. In fact, most organizing groups in this country are committed to strengthening the institutions of democracy through the active participation and leadership of ordinary people. Organizers pursue long-term strategies of investment in building relationships and cultivating leaderships. At times, organizing culminates in big public actions. But the quieter, relational efforts that often happen on the inside of institutions constitute the real work of community organizing. These institutions have long included religious congregations. Increasingly, they also include public schools.

GYO itself is an institutional strategy. Its promise lies in the bet that GYO teachers can become change agents as leaders in the schools in which they teach. They are not going to be able to do that alone. They will need their fellow GYO teachers and they will need allies. Most important, they will need community organizing groups such as LSNA and Action Now that can serve as catalysts and supporters of change efforts (Lopez, Kreider, & Coffman, 2005; Warren, Hong, Rubin, & Sychitkokhong-Uy, 2009). To do so, these organizing groups have to make a commitment not just to improving education as an issue; they also have to commit to organizing around particular schools as institutions.

By conducting what I have called school-community organizing, these groups link school improvement to the broader revitalization of low-income communities. After all, what sense does it make to try to improve schools while the communities around them decline (Warren, 2005)? Improving the education of our children requires a focus on teaching and learning, but something more beyond that. It requires addressing the multiple effects of poverty and racism on families and their children so that students attend school safe, healthy, and ready to learn. By organizing parents, teachers, and community members around schools and by linking these efforts to other institutions such as congregations and community-based organizations, school-community organizing promises a holistic approach to addressing the needs of children and their families—and the broader revitalization of our democratic practice. By drawing on talents, energies, and passions, organizing creates deeply rooted initiatives such as GYO that offer opportunities for human growth and development and that foster change in schools and communities.

These are large objectives that will take greater resources and more time to accomplish. School-community organizing is just beginning to show the possibilities of this approach. Nevertheless, the model I have discussed combats the isolation and fragmentation that too often defeat efforts both at school and neighborhood improvement as it brings organizing into schools and schools out into organizing.

NOTES

1. There is a rapidly growing literature on community organizing. For a historical overview, see Fisher (1994) and Payne (1995); for treatments of the development of community organizing in the modern era, see Warren (2001) and Wood (2002); for more recent treatments, see Orr (2007) and Swarts (2008).

2. For an overview of community organizing efforts at education reform, see Warren (2010); other researchers (Beam & Irani, 2003; Gold, Simon, & Brown, 2002b; Mediratta, 2004; Oakes & Rogers, 2005; Shirley, 1997, 2002; Warren, 2005) offer detailed accounts of the education organizing work of various groups.

3. The discussion of LSNA's community organizing work draws from the author's own research (Warren, 2005; Warren, Hong, Rubin, & Sychitkokhong-Uy, 2009), informed as well by research conducted by Research for Action (Blanc, Brown, Nevarez-La Torre, & Brown, 2002) and doctoral dissertation research by Soo Hong (2009).

4. The IAF describes itself as broad-based organizing because it does not limit itself to schools and congregations as institutional sites for its work. The discussion of the IAF's education organizing in this section draws from the author's own research (Warren, 2001, 2005), as well as other accounts (Shirley, 1997, 2001; Simon & Gold, 2002). It also draws from unpublished research by the Community Organizing and School Reform research project at the Harvard Graduate School of Education, led by Mark R. Warren and Karen L. Mapp.

5. Ernesto Cortes Jr., the director of the Southwest IAF network, suggested this terminology to me.

6. The discussion of PICO's education organizing work draws from unpublished research conducted by the Community Organizing and School Reform research project at the Harvard Graduate School of Education, led by Mark R. Warren and Karen L. Mapp. It also draws from published accounts by Gold, Simon, and Brown (2002a) and Shah, Mediratta, and McAlister (2009).

REFERENCES

Alinsky, S. (1971). *Rules for radicals.* New York: Random House.

Beam, J., & Irani, S. (2003). *ACORN education reform organizing.* New York: National Center for Schools and Communities.

Blanc, S., Brown, J., Nevarez-La Torre, A., & Brown, C. (2002). *Case Study: Logan Square Neighborhood Association.* Chicago: Cross City Campaign for Urban School Reform.

Briggs, X. d. S., & Mueller, E. (1997). *From neighborhood to community.* New York: Community Development Research Center, New School for Social Research.

Bryk, A., & Schneider, B. (2002). *Trust in schools.* New York: Russell Sage Foundation Press.

Carrasco, J. (2003). Personal communication. Atlanta.

Coburn, C. (2003). Rethinking scale. *Educational Researcher, 32*(6), 3–12.

Collins, P. H. (2000). *Black feminist thought.* New York: Routledge.

Cotton, K. (2001). *New small learning communities.* Portland: Northwest Regional Educational Laboratory.

Dewey, J. (1915). *The school and society.* Chicago: University of Chicago Press.

Dewey, J. (1938 [1916]). *Democracy and education.* New York: MacMillan.

Diamond, J., & Gomez, K. (2004). African American parents' educational orientations. *Education and Urban Society, 36*(4), 383–427.

Fisher, R. (1994). *Let the people decide* (updated ed.). New York: Twayne Publishers.

Gold, E., Simon, E., & Brown, C. (2002a). *Case Study: Oakland Community Organizations.* Chicago: Cross City Campaign for Urban School Reform.

Gold, E., Simon, E., & Brown, C. (2002b). *Successful community organizing for school reform.* Chicago: Cross City Campaign for Urban School Reform.

Hochschild, J., & Scoronick, N. (2003). *The American dream and the public schools.* New York: Oxford University Press.

Hong, S. (2009). *Empowering parents, empowering schools.* Unpublished doctoral dissertation, Harvard University, Cambridge.

Horvat, E., Weininger, E., & Lareau, A. (2003). From social ties to social capital. *American Educational Research Journal, 40*(2), 319–351.

Horwitt, S. (1989). *Let them call me rebel.* New York: Knopf.

Kaestle, C. (1983). *Pillars of the republic.* New York: Hill and Wang.

Kozol, J. (1991). *Savage inequalities.* New York: Crown.

Lopez, M., Kreider, H., & Coffman, J. (2005). Intermediary organizations as capacity builders in family educational involvement. *Urban Education, 40*(1), 78–105.

McAlister, S., Mediratta, K., Shah, S., & Fruchter, N. (2010). Improving teacher quality through public engagement. In M. Orr & J. Rogers (Eds.), *Public engagement for public education.* Palo Alto: Stanford University Press.

Mediratta, K. (2004). *Constituents of change.* New York: Institute for Education and Social Policy, New York University.

Mediratta, K., & Fruchter, N. (2001). *Mapping the field of organizing for school improvement.* New York: Institute for Education and Social Policy, New York University.

Morgen, S., & Bookman, A. (1988). *Women and the politics of empowerment.* Philadelphia: Temple University Press.

Morris, A. (1984). *The origins of the Civil Rights Movement: Black communities organizing for change.* New York: Free Press.

Naples, N. (1998). *Grassroots warriors.* New York: Routledge.

Noguera, P. (1996). Confronting the urban in urban school reform. *Urban Review, 28*(1), 1–27.

Noguera, P. (2003). *City schools and the American dream.* New York: Teachers College Press.

Oakes, J., & Rogers, J. (2005). *Learning power.* New York: Teachers College Press.

Orr, M. (Ed.). (2007). *Transforming the city.* Lawrence: University Press of Kansas.

Payne, C. (1995). *I've got the light of freedom.* Berkeley: University of California Press.

Payne, C. (2008). *So much reform, so little change.* Cambridge: Harvard Educational Publishing Group.

Perry, T. (2003). Freedom for literacy and literacy for freedom: The African-American philosophy of education. In T. Perry, C. Steele, & A. Hilliard III (Eds.), *Young, gifted and Black* (pp. 11–51). Boston: Beacon Press.

Reitzes, D., & Reitzes, D. (1987). *The Alinsky legacy.* Greenwood, CT: JAI Press.

Shah, S., Mediratta, K., & McAlister, S. (2009). *Building a district-wide small schools movement.* Providence: Brown University Annenberg Institute for School Reform.

Shirley, D. (1997). *Community organizing for urban school reform.* Austin: University of Texas Press.

Shirley, D. (2001). Linking community organizing and school reform. In R. L. Crowson (Ed.), *Community development and school reform* (Vol. 5, pp. 139–171). Amsterdam: Elsevier Science Ltd.

Shirley, D. (2002). *Valley Interfaith and school reform.* Austin: University of Texas Press.

Shirley, D., & Evans, M. (2007). Community organizing and No Child Left Behind. In M. Orr (Ed.), *Transforming the city.* Lawrence: University Press of Kansas.

Simon, E., & Gold, E. (2002). *Case Study: Austin Interfaith.* Chicago: Cross City Campaign for Urban School Reform.

Stone, C., Henig, J., Jones, B., & Pierannunzi, C. (2001). *Building civic capacity.* Lawrence: University Press of Kansas.

Swarts, H. (2008). *Organizing urban America.* Minneapolis: University of Minnesota Press.

Wallach, C., & Lear, R. (2005). *A foot in two worlds.* Seattle: Small Schools Project.

Warren, M. (2001). *Dry bones rattling.* Princeton: Princeton University Press.

Warren, M. (2005). Communities and schools. *Harvard Educational Review, 75*(2), 133–173.

Warren, M. (2010). Community organizing for education reform. In M. Orr & J. Rogers (Eds.), *Public engagement for public education.* Palo Alto: Stanford University Press.

Warren, M. R., Hong, S., Rubin, C. H., & Sychitkokhong-Uy, P. (2009). Beyond the bake sale. *Teachers College Record, 111*(9).

Westbrook, R. (1991). *John Dewey and American democracy.* Ithaca, NY: Cornell University Press.

Wood, R. (2002). *Faith in Action.* Chicago: University of Chicago Press.

5

Parents Building Communities in Schools

JOANNA BROWN

On any given day, in eight public schools in Chicago's Logan Square community, about 150 parents are in elementary school classrooms tutoring children; in the evening, many of them are among the hundreds studying English or getting their GED while their children are taking part in other activities. Most of these parents are immigrant mothers or the daughters of immigrants. Their schools are part of a network serving low-income, largely Latino children, brought together by the Logan Square Neighborhood Association (LSNA) to create schools as centers of community—and to serve the needs of the immigrant students. Enter an LSNA school and you see mothers sitting in hallways with small groups of students who are intently reading out loud. A mother comfortably enters the principal's office to remind her of a meeting. Mothers meet in a corner of the cafeteria to plan a family reading night for the school. As a teacher passes by she calls, "Mrs. Hernandez, your son was looking for you upstairs; I think he's not feeling well."

LSNA, founded in 1962, is the 48-year-old community organization of Logan Square, a mixed-income, majority Latino immigrant neighborhood of 84,000 residents on Chicago's northwest side. LSNA has 45 member organizations, including churches, social service agencies, block clubs, and eight large public schools (three pre-K–8, three pre-K–6, one 7–8, and one high school). Some 8,300 students—90 percent of them from low-income Latino families, most of whom speak Spanish as their home language— study in these schools.

Since the early 1990s, LSNA has been organizing within the community to improve the neighborhood schools. In order to do so, our education committee started with some basic principles. First, as part of the 1989 Chicago school reform movement, which established elected parent-majority Local School Councils (LSCs), we knew that the Councils needed an organized community in order for their formal authority to select and hire principals on 4-year contracts to be meaningful. Second, as the place-based organization for a neighborhood with few public spaces, we developed a vision of opening the doors of "fortress" schools and helping them function as centers of community. Third, as part of an organization managed by a community board and annual meetings of as many as 1,000 residents, we were committed to listen to and value what residents wanted and to build with them on community strengths. It was also clear that disparities of education, language, and income between school staff and the students' families were only some of the many factors that created barriers to parent involvement in schools. As community organizers, we also believed that transformational learning happens through experience, by doing. We also knew that we would have to raise the money to pay for whatever we built.

BUILDING A SUCCESSFUL COLLABORATION BETWEEN SCHOOLS AND PARENTS

In the early 1990s, LSNA formed a coalition of principals, teachers, and parents to demand a solution to the severe overcrowding of the neighborhood schools. LSNA worked hard to build trust with principals, who joined the coalition because they had repeatedly asked for overcrowding solutions with no results. At a time when most community organizations focused on organizing parents to fix problems by making demands on principals, LSNA chose to seek principal and teacher allies in order to make demands on the central administration. In doing so, the organization moved from an outsider position to a more complex but productive insider-outside position. The organization was independent of the school and thus could strongly back parents, but remained a collaborator with the school administration and a bridge between administration and parents where necessary.

LSNA's new school-community collaboration was successful. By 1996, LSNA had won five large building additions and two new middle schools. In the years of meetings and advocacy, the coalition developed its community school philosophy, insisting that the new buildings be designed to serve as community centers after the school day ended. The social trust built by common struggle and victory laid the basis for the collaborative community-building efforts that followed.

PARENTS AS LEADERS: THE PARENT MENTOR PROGRAM

The Parent Mentor Program, launched in 1995, served to open the door for many parents, particularly mothers, to become involved in their children's schools. It was piloted in Funston Elementary when principal Sally Acker, who had been a leader in the anti-overcrowding campaign, asked LSNA to develop a program to involve nonworking mothers in schools and help them further their education and find jobs. LSNA recruited 15 mothers into the program and placed them in classrooms to work 2 hours daily with students under the direction of a teacher. LSNA's initial 1-week training helped mothers to see themselves as leaders, reflect on their skills, set personal goals, and commit to achieving them. It also provided the space within which to develop strong cohorts. Immigrant mothers, far from their extended families and isolated by lack of English and by staying home with small children, shared common experiences and found personal support from each other. Every applicant was accepted, regardless of education or language (many spoke only Spanish), and each was placed in a classroom where she could be helpful, but not with her own children. Mentors made friends as they attended weekly workshops on topics ranging from how to teach reading to family health to community issues. Together, they reflected on their classroom experiences and developed into strong cohorts. They wrote journals. They held potlucks. They helped one another pursue their goals, usually involving learning English or returning to school. At the end of 100 hours of involvement, they each received a $600 stipend.

The first year, in each school, only a few teachers, most of them bilingual, volunteered for the program. But in every school the number of participating teachers grew rapidly as word spread that the mothers were not spying on teachers, but in fact were helpful and respectful. "It's helpful to have another adult in the classroom," said a teacher. "And I can have her give extra attention to the five students who are most behind." The program was run with strict rules of confidentiality about what happened inside the classrooms. Rules developed by parents, teachers, and principals working together ensured that mentors did not abuse their insider position and program coordinators (themselves parents) were there to resolve slights and misunderstandings. LSNA supervisors paid close attention to the delicate informal power structures of schools and helped parents manage them.

Each mentor worked in one classroom under a teacher who taught her what to do. As they worked together, mentors and teachers developed trust and even friendships. LSNA made sure to recognize both mentors and teachers for their work, holding special events for mentor teachers and graduation ceremonies for the parents.

Teachers began to spread the word that some struggling students flourished with a one-on-one tutor, especially one who spoke the language of the family and understood cultural issues. Mentors approached teaching from their experience as parents, focused on the individual child and on his or her feelings, something many overworked teachers didn't have enough time for. Said one teacher: "My mentor brings a lot of love into the classroom, and she has the luxury of focusing on the children most in need."

As more and more mothers mentored, they became a visible and comforting presence in the school. The program helped create a more welcoming school, better relationships between teachers and parents, a greater attention to the community's culture and resources, and increased student achievement (for more on the Parent Mentor Program, see Hong, this volume). At the core of the parent mentor experience is a personal transformation from a private, often isolated immigrant or welfare mother to a person who sees herself as a school or community leader. The individual transformation of parents has led to the broader transformation of schools, teachers, and the community.

CHANGING THE FAMILY-SCHOOL RELATIONSHIP: COMMUNITY LEARNING CENTERS

The parent mentors at Funston also helped plan the Community Learning Center (CLC) that was established as a result of the successful anti-overcrowding campaign. The mentors surveyed their neighborhood door-to-door, asking more than 500 families what programs and services they needed in an evening school-community center. LSNA worked with the parents to find the funding, which initially came from pilot community development initiatives of the state of Illinois. This funding allowed LSNA to keep Funston open until 9:00 p.m. during the week with adult education and children's programming. They hired two parents to run the CLC.

The CLC helped change the way families and school staff saw Funston School. Not only was the center accessible to parents (the school was close to home, classes and child care were free, and children were tutored while their parents studied), but parents who walked freely in and out of the CLC began to see the school building as partly theirs and education as something that united their family. The CLC held events for Thanksgiving, Christmas, Mother's Day, and many other family events that served to bring the school community together. Classroom teachers got to know parents by teaching English or classes to prepare for General Educational Development (GED) tests at night, and some of the most popular classes were taught by parent mentors—including Mexican folk dance for children and sewing for adults. The CLC was overseen by advisory boards that included parents as well as principals and teachers.

EXPANDING PARENT INVOLVEMENT PROGRAMS
INTO MORE SCHOOLS

Over the next few years, the process of establishing Parent Mentor Programs and CLCs was repeated in nearby schools as parent leaders asked LSNA and their principals for the programs. Most principals who had been involved in the overcrowding fight were enthusiastic; others preferred not to join LSNA. Over time, as principals retired, new administrators have often been perplexed by the collaboration and have grown into it slowly as they began to trust LSNA and parents. Today, LSNA has CLCs in five schools and Parent Mentor Programs in eight schools. More than 1,500 mothers (and a few fathers) have graduated from the Parent Mentor Program. The majority got jobs or returned to school to get a GED, study English, or enroll in college. About 50 hold part-time jobs working for LSNA in schools, running parent programs, tutoring, or providing child care and security in the community centers. Forty have been AmeriCorps volunteers with LSNA; 10 are full-time LSNA employees—education organizers, community center coordinators, or health outreach workers; and 10 are teaching after graduating from LSNA's Grow Your Own (GYO) teacher program. At the CLCs, thousands of adults have studied English, while more than 700 have earned their GED certificates. About 700 families participate weekly in activities that range from adult education and family counseling to tutoring, recreation, music, and art for children.

The impact of the LSNA programs on the schools has been huge. Principals now hire parent mentors or CLC workers as teacher assistants or cafeteria workers when they have an opening, increasing the number of school staff who are from the neighborhood and know other parents. And most mentors are involved in volunteer activities. "We add a lot of life to the school," said one parent mentor. "We run all the activities. And the students don't feel they are alone, because their parents are there, too. And if it's not their parent, it's a neighbor, or the parent of a friend." School climates have become more positive and welcoming, and the percentage of students at level on standardized-test scores has tripled in 6 years from an average of 20% to 60–70%. The Parent Mentor Program and CLCs have also proved highly generative. Parent mentors sought a way to involve parents who couldn't visit the school during the day and helped develop LSNA's Literacy Ambassadors Program to bring parent-teacher teams to read, share food, and build bridges in students' homes with groups of families. Parents who surveyed neighbors became committed to block-club organizing and then developed LSNA's health outreach program, helping 2,100 uninsured families access affordable health care each year.

FROM PARENT MENTOR TO GROW YOUR OWN TEACHERS

By 1999, the mentor program was operating in seven schools, and it was having a positive impact for many different reasons. Some of the students had learned more and liked school better; many mothers testified to fulfilling their interrupted dreams of becoming educated and educators; teachers were relieved to have another adult in the classroom. Many mentors found that they loved working in classrooms, while some teachers encouraged their mentors to stay in the field. "Silvia really should become a teacher; she has a gift for engaging the students. They always want to work with her," said one appreciative teacher. In surveys, 90% of teachers answered yes to the question, "Some students in my class improved in reading or math because of my parent mentor." But most mentors assumed that becoming a teacher was not possible. Said one, "I love working here. I don't want to go back to the factory but there is no way I can go to college."

At the same time, principals continued to have trouble finding qualified bilingual teachers. The immigrant population kept growing, but Illinois colleges graduated few Latino teachers. It seemed there was a perfect match between the talents of the mothers and the needs of the schools. What the mothers lacked was (1) money and (2) the knowledge of how to work with the institutions of higher education to get what they needed.

TRAINING TEACHERS WHO VALUE THE COMMUNITY

It was LSNA's belief that the local schools needed more teachers who consciously promoted and respected community culture, were passionate about the academic potential of the students, and could effectively relate to the parents. If the most talented and motivated parent mentors could be supported to become teachers in a preparation program that valued their strengths (love for these children, their culture, and language), schools would become more embedded in the community, more able to draw on community resources, and less colonial in structure and feel. This meant building on the principles LSNA had developed to bring parents into the schools in the first place. These guiding principles are:

- Respect: LSNA builds on what Logan Square parents know and care about. We value them and tap their knowledge (language, culture, life experience, and knowledge about children) to strengthen the curriculum and to connect to the students. We respect their capacities (even when they doubt themselves) and challenge them to keep moving forward. Respect is a powerful idea, taking on new meanings as relationships deepen;

- Reciprocity: Respect requires reciprocity—mutual support and mutual learning. Parents learn through experience how difficult a teacher's job is, as teachers learn how much parents have to give, particularly their passion for children and strength in building relationships with them. Parents and students learn together and from each other;
- Real work: Although schools have traditionally tapped parents—as outsiders—to help with fundraisers, costumes, and the like, there is nothing as empowering as engaging in the core work of the school. Teachers are told that parent mentors must work directly with children, not make copies or clean floors.

Transformation of LSNA mothers has come from involvement in the real, respected work of teaching and learning, and they consistently rise to the challenges and achieve success. When a parent mentor tutors a failing student and that student, for the first time, is motivated and learns how to read, the parent becomes transformed and passionately engaged. Although most educators would say that parents are the first teachers and that parent involvement is key, few actually tap the resource of parents to improve underresourced low-income urban schools. Visitors from as far away as the Philippines and as close as the next neighborhood have asked: "How do you get low-income parents involved?"

Here are some practical operating principles of the Parent Mentor Program and LSNA's school work in general.

- Recruitment: We don't rely on flyers, but recruit person-to-person; we take everyone we have space for, regardless of education or language; everyone is useful in some classroom. We constantly recruit new mentors and work hard to avoid cliques and promote an inclusive "community";
- Stipends. Money (even a little) is one way to tell parents they are wanted and helps overcome their fears of the school or their feelings that they have nothing to offer. For many mothers, the stipend is their only personal income, and it legitimizes their work to their husbands;
- Bridges and spaces. A Parent Mentor Program graduate who runs the program can be the bridge across the school-community divide, backed by LSNA staff who help deal with cross-class or cross-cultural tensions. The initial training is a bridge and a space: On Day 1, mothers are shy and scared; by Day 5, they are ready, even if still anxious, to meet their teacher and enter the classroom. The Parent

Mentor Program creates a legitimate parent space inside the school, with its own rules and identities and its own cohort for support;

- Apprenticeship. Information is good, but deep knowledge and commitment come from practice. The Parent Mentor Program is structured to provide the learning. Parent mentors learn about the school as they experience it every day;
- Leadership development. The theme of the parent mentor training is, "You are leaders in the home, school, and community." Parents are challenged to be leaders—not clients. At every possible opportunity, LSNA is urging parents to take on leadership roles— working as an "assistant teacher," speaking in workshops or public meetings, testifying at state hearings, telling their story to the press or to funders, and recruiting new parents;
- Community engagement. LSNA emphasizes that schools are part of the community and that parents can make them better. At least 40 LSNA parents sit on the school councils, where they help select principals and approve budgets. Many participate in LSNA campaigns and community meetings—advocating for immigration reform, affordable housing, community safety, or access to health care. They pass petitions, march, testify, and meet with aldermen and state legislators.

Working at the school level, parents have also deepened the schools' curriculum and made it more relevant to students by bringing their cultural knowledge into the schools. They have:

- helped organize hundreds of family reading nights where mothers provide storytelling and reading games side-by-side with teachers;
- created school assemblies where mothers acted out Mexican history, displayed the variety of Guatemalan houses and food, and told the story of Puerto Rican baseball hero Roberto Clemente;
- taught "character education" to students, using bilingual books they made by hand and telling stories from their own experience;
- built Day of the Dead altars to Mexican grandparents, Princess Diana, and Mother Teresa in their school library and explained them to students;
- created parent lending libraries where mothers and fathers with small children can bring them 1 morning a week to read and borrow books while they drink coffee with neighbors;
- organized Mother's Day assemblies and Children's Day festivals to celebrate these highly popular Latin American holidays, which they felt were neglected in their schools.

SUPPORT AND CHALLENGES

This work of bringing schools and community together may sound simple, but in practice LSNA staff, from the executive director to the parents running programs in the schools, work constantly building relationships with school personnel, and mediating misunderstandings and power relationships. The work is cross-socioeconomic class and cross-cultural. Starting from a deep school-community divide that exists in most low-income, urban schools, bringing school and community back together takes time, persistence, patience, and what organizers call "disinterest"—not taking things personally.

LSNA has had to build a structure to provide support for the parents. Each parent mentor group has a paid half-time coordinator who is a former parent mentor, works out of the school, and attends biweekly meetings with the other coordinators at LSNA. At these meetings, coordinators exchange information, make joint decisions about the program, and solve problems. The coordinator's supervisor is an LSNA education organizer who is responsible for the parent programs in four schools. These organizers spend time at each school mentoring the coordinators, meeting with principals, and getting to know the parents.

LSNA's education organizers build bridges and trust in a variety of ways—from negotiating tensions to inventing programs to helping parents implement workshops and family nights. By providing parents a legitimate space within the school, and encouraging and respecting their knowledge, LSNA opens the door to many opportunities for parents to implement their ideas. For example, LSNA developed a "minigrant" program where a group of parents in a school could apply for $300 to buy food or supplies for a parent-organized event that involved parents, students, and teachers and had some educational or cultural purpose. We did that after various parents had said they would like to hold events in the school but had no resources to do so. At every level, people are mentoring and learning from each other. Supervisors try to take advantage of each leadership opportunity to help newer people develop while helping the organization thrive—running meetings, testifying at funding meetings, talking to the LSNA board, and testifying at the Illinois State Board of Education.

The work of involving parents in schools is continually breaking boundaries and subverting the mainstream paradigm of schooling. Most teachers have not been trained to place a high priority on relations with parents, much less lean on them for academic support. Most new parent mentors don't believe they can really tutor. Both groups believe teaching is primarily a technical rather than a relational act. Accountability systems have privileged the delivery of information learned in universities and evaluated by grades, rather than the less linear building of trust and connection between teacher and student which strengthens the motivation to learn.

As LSNA found when it developed the Literacy Ambassador Program to bring reading workshops into homes, many teachers are afraid to visit poor families, unduly fearful for their safety, but also of the social interactions. One teacher was too nervous to drink a cup of coffee, she told the parent mentor who accompanied her on a home visit. Families were afraid to invite teachers. "I don't know what she likes to eat, and I don't have enough chairs," said one parent who finally was persuaded to host the workshop. Some teachers asked to do the workshops in the school. But once the teachers went, accompanied by mentors, they reported back (some with a hint of surprise in their voices) that "the food was *so* good, and the people so friendly." That first step across the school-community divide was transformational for many. "Since our home visits, the parents and I have often met in the hallways where we exchange greetings and informally discuss school-related issues," said one teacher. "It makes me feel good to think that I am becoming a member of the community in which I have worked for the past 8 years." But getting some people to take the first step has required belief and persistence by LSNA staff and parents.

Some principals have balked initially at sharing their buildings, particularly in the last few years. Principals are legally responsible for the building, and while some allow the LSNA coordinator to run the building in the evenings, others require a high-level school employee to be there, just in case. Some don't see why the community board should have a voice in programming. When the CLCs first started, LSNA principals had fought for them and helped create them. But in the last decade, while there has been verbal support for parent involvement and community schools from the federal government on down, the top-down pressures to increase yearly test scores have overshadowed any focus on more long-term or holistic strategies. LSNA's parent programs have survived this pressure, as principals see the impact that the parents have on increasing test scores for the most struggling students. But for those who are not philosophically committed to strengthening school-community ties or don't feel it in their hearts, the CLC is more work, more responsibility. The process of changing the understanding of school as an isolated institution under principal control to a community asset has been contested and uneven. For some, it may take several years to feel the relevance of the community center to the mission of educating the children. It should be said, however, that some new principals get it right away and have been true allies, supporting and embracing the work as important.

The opening of community centers raised turf and power issues. Teachers and janitors may complain to principals, who are caught in the middle. Disputes can arise from minor concerns such as missing chalk and toilet paper. Principals and empowered parents may disagree. In one case, a principal did not want to keep his building open in the summer for LSNA's community center. The LSNA coordinator got nowhere. Finally, one Local School Council member (a personally fearless woman who had helped hire that principal) called a meeting of LSC parents to talk to him about it. His attitude toward the parents was quite different. He agreed to open the school, provided that LSNA hired his assistant to be there while the building was open. The complex set of interests and power relations underlying this simple negotiation (principal power, LSC power, organized parents, the fact that the principal liked the parents) are the sort of dynamics that LSNA deals with every day.

Logan Square schools have become more complex. They are no longer simply places where professionals teach poor children and the lines of power are clear. Nonprofessional parents are more present, have more power, and are becoming more educated. Students feel a greater sense of belonging and ownership. In this cross-class, cross-cultural, more democratic community, conflicts and misunderstandings arise frequently. LSNA is a constant informal mediator, always clear that families are its main constituency but that the project requires full collaboration with the schools. One of LSNA's roles has been to build the social trust that supports the complexity inside the school and the political capital to support it outside—whether at the district level, in politics, or with funders.

Funding, of course, is another constant challenge. For 15 years, LSNA has built relationships with funders and politicians to piece together public and private funding to sustain its education work, now close to $2 million a year. State funds, thanks to Latino state legislators, and federal 21st Century Community Learning Center grants have been essential, as has support from the many private funders who value the marriage of education reform, family literacy, and community organizing that LSNA has modeled. Beginning in 2009, with a state budget in crisis and funders cutting back, raising money has become an even greater challenge. Ultimately, to survive, these programs must become institutionalized with permanent public funding.

CHANGING THE PARADIGM OF SCHOOLING

With its education work, LSNA is up against two powerful national forces—the traditional isolation of U.S. urban schools from their communities and the pressures of federally mandated test-score accountability. Both paradigms view the school from the top down, and from the building out. Both devalue the many assets of low-income students and their families. Both leave community wisdom and the whole child off the agenda, restricting teaching and learning to the "qualified" who alone cannot do the job. As organizers, we know that people really only engage when they have a stake in the process and the outcomes. This is as true of parents and students as it is of teachers and principals. When collectively we fight for parent participation, for productive teacher-parent relationships, we are also fighting for motivated and engaged students.

For LSNA, GYO teachers are part of our quest to change the current paradigm of schooling. Teacher candidates from the community, particularly if experienced with children and classrooms, and if supported by universities in valuing their own knowledge, are likely to share a holistic view of education and of students.

Logan Square schools—large, urban, low-income, immigrant schools—have moved partway down the road to transformation, with organized mothers in the lead. Transformation of parents, teachers, and schools is possible, but the paradigm of schooling must change. Students must be seen not as blank slates ready to be filled by information, but as already partially formed cultural beings with their own cultural and social capital. Bilingualism and cultural complexity must be seen as assets, not deficits to be overcome.

As parents themselves, LSNA's GYO teachers understand that parents are central to the educational system, not outsiders. By treating parents as partners and welcoming what they have to offer into the classroom, teachers from the community can help create schools that engage students and increase student achievement—even more so by helping them move centrally into the educational institutions, where they can begin to shape its future.

NOTE

This chapter is adapted from "Parents Building Communities in Schools," which appeared in *Skills for Smart Systems*, Voices in Urban Education no. 17 (reprinted in *Building Smart Education Systems*, Voices in Urban Education no. 26), published by the Annenberg Institute for School Reform at Brown University.

6

Grow Your Own Teachers as Bridge-Builders

Closing the Gap Between Schools and Communities

SOO HONG

On a busy afternoon at McAuliffe School, Silvia Gonzalez is the ultimate multi-tasker. She is on the phone with her son Hector, making sure he is settled at home. She darts across hallways and rooms to make sure things are in order for the evening's community center classes. With another parent, she plans the details of a door-knocking campaign they are launching later that week. Amid the hustle and bustle of a busy day where she oversees a parent program at McAuliffe during school hours, coordinates the school's community center in the evenings, and manages the everyday details of family life, Gonzalez also participates in the Grow Your Own (GYO) teacher program in Logan Square that will prepare her to be a bilingual teacher.

This ambition to teach began during her days in the Parent Mentor Program created by the Logan Square Neighborhood Association (LSNA). The program brings parents like Gonzalez into classrooms to work as teaching assistants. The organization recruits parents with a range of school-based experiences—from those who have volunteered in classrooms before to the many immigrant parents in the community who have spent little time inside schools and classrooms. For Gonzalez, the motivation to participate was fueled, in large part, from her desire to be with her son, a child with autism, who was starting 1st grade. Over the course of her first year in the program and in her son's classroom, Gonzalez was exposed to what she describes as "a whole new world":

> I became very committed—well to be honest—attached to these 1st-graders. You get to know them and their families and you find that some are just starving for the care and attention that they aren't getting at home. And I became really committed to making sure they had a good experience in school, and I began to see how I could make a difference in their lives.

Through the Parent Mentor Program, Gonzalez became exposed to the inner world of schools and classrooms and realized the potential of her own skills and talents. The strengths and assets that Silvia Gonzalez brings to the classroom as a mother and member of the community are the bedrock bases of the GYO program. Built on the principle that teachers with a commitment to and understanding of students in many inner-city communities may be found within those same communities, GYO efforts seek to recruit individuals like Gonzalez who identify a commitment to teaching. Gonzalez's future as a teacher was "something quite unexpected," as she discovered her own commitment to teaching after her sustained involvement in schools and classroom through the Parent Mentor Program.

Drawing from a 2-year ethnography of LSNA's Parent Mentor Program, this chapter will feature the experiences of parent mentors who went on to become GYO teacher candidates. Data from this study show that when coupled with programs that bring parents into close contact with classrooms, GYO efforts may tap into a broader base of candidates who are motivated by their connections to students and teachers as well as by their commitments to the families and communities. Through this meaningful experience in classrooms, parents like Gonzalez become connected to schools and committed to teaching in ways that they had not anticipated. Gonzalez explains:

> How did I get here? Sometimes, it's hard to believe myself, but it all started in that classroom. I went in thinking that I would be helping the teacher and then I found I had some talents that were helping the students. Who would have expected that? This is not what parents do, right? We're not even expected to be in the schools. But all of a sudden, there was a seed planted. I wanted to teach.

THE PARENT MENTOR PROGRAM:
INTEGRATING PARENTS INTO
SCHOOLS AND CLASSROOMS

As Gonzalez explains, in many schools, the roles and responsibilities of parents have clear definitions and limits. Parents may be enlisted to support schoolwide activities, attend workshops or events, conference with teachers, or even volunteer in classrooms—these comprise the universally held notions of parent involvement. But in many urban schools, particularly where linguistic and cultural differences between school staff and families exist, the visibility of parents in schools may be low; these schools may claim to have little to no parent involvement (Henderson & Mapp, 2002; Noguera, 2001). Because schools have so little experience with parents and families, they may be inclined to view parents through a deficit framework and fail to acknowledge a community's resources and assets (Valenzuela, 1999). Among those who study school-community collaborations and partnerships, some researchers have argued that reform efforts will require a paradigm shift—moving from efforts that are guided by schools toward strategies that are centered on the experiences and assets of communities (Henderson, Johnson, Mapp, & Davies, 2007; Shirley, 1997; Warren, 2005). These community-based efforts that focus on parent leadership and organizing seek to address the often tense and distant relationship between schools and families that exist in low-income communities of color, engaging parents in schools in meaningful ways, providing opportunities for connection between schools and families, and working to challenge the uneven power base between school staff and parents.

Bridging the widening gap between schools and families was the primary focus of LSNA's Parent Mentor Program. As Silvia Gonzalez observed in her early experiences as a parent mentor, parent presence was not expected or encouraged. This was a common perception among many parents and staff in schools within the Logan Square community. The Parent Mentor Program was created, in part, through conversations between LSNA and a neighborhood school principal, Sally Acker, who noticed a trend among the families she encountered daily at the school. The school's surrounding neighborhood, over the years, had become predominantly Latino, and many were Spanish-speaking immigrant families. She noticed that parents rarely came into the school building beyond the quick, daily responsibilities of dropping off and picking up children from school, and she began to wonder how the school could encourage greater parent involvement, particularly for those parents who dropped their children off at school only to turn around to go back home for the day. She began to discuss the need for greater parent involvement in schools, wondering if LSNA could be of help. LSNA executive director Nancy Aardema recalls those early conversations:

> [Sally Acker] felt like the issue was that parents only came to the school when there was a problem, or they were the "good parents of the good kids," and that she felt like we had to figure out a way as a community to get just the average parents, or the parents of the kids who were struggling into the school—not in a way that they felt like they were there to be told what was wrong, not in a way that put them at a disadvantage, or put them down—but she felt they should be in the school in a very real continuous way.

To respond to the issues that school staff and organizers were seeing, the Parent Mentor Program brought parents into classrooms where they would work alongside teachers as classroom assistants, working with students to support student learning rather than completing administrative tasks. Since 1995, the program has brought more than 1,000 parent mentors into classrooms 4 days a week, 2 hours each morning, over the duration of a school year. Parent mentors work in a classroom—reading to children in small groups, working with individual students, and supporting classroom activities. Each Friday morning, parent mentors come together for training sessions as a school-based cohort, and monthly, across the community. Parents are paid a small stipend to counter the notion that they are merely serving the school, to encourage consistent participation, and to develop a sense of respect and recognition for their work. By bringing parents into schools in this way, LSNA builds a sense of familiarity with schools and the broader community among immigrant parents. In doing so, the program strives to encourage a more open attitude toward families among neighborhood schools.

According to GYO teacher candidate and previous parent mentor Ofelia Sanchez, her experience as a parent mentor provided her with an "insider perspective" that opened her eyes to the culture of school. The daily experience within one classroom throughout a school year where she became an intimate observer of teacher-student dynamics and an integral member of the community influenced her understanding of schools and her own children's experience within classrooms:

> It's not that we spend a little time here and there. We are in these classrooms every day—working with the same teachers, getting to know their habits and the way they manage things but also getting to know these students and who they are and what their families are like.

You see how they work together, how they learn, and you learn to step in when and where you're needed. It really helps you understand what your own kids are doing and what's expected of them.

As regular participants in classrooms, parent mentors become connected to the intimate details of classroom relationships, dynamics, practices, and interactions. In contrast with a more traditional parent volunteer program where parents assist in their child's classroom on a regular basis, the Parent Mentor Program seeks to bring parents into meaningful relationships with the teachers they work with. According to Anna Patock, a teacher at the Funston School who has worked with parent mentors:

When these parent mentors come in, we want the students to see them as a teacher just like me. But when this person spends two hours every day with you and your students, you become friends, you make a connection. And as individuals, we connect.

Building the relationship between teacher and parent mentor in the ways that Patock describes is a fundamental intention of the program. In an effort to break down some of the assumptions and biases that school staff and families may have about each other, the Parent Mentor Program seeks to provide each parent mentor and teacher with opportunities to engage with each other in meaningful ways. For this reason, most parent mentors are assigned to classrooms that do not include their own children. As a result, teachers and parents are free to interact in ways that do not involve expectations around their own child's experiences in the classroom.

Beyond the relationships with teachers, parent mentors also become connected to students. Working with them in the classroom, in small groups, during one-on-one sessions, parents build a repertoire of experiences with students—understanding their struggles, their families, their motivations, and their successes. These interactions, over the course of a school year, allow parent mentors to "understand how children learn, the difficulties they have to face, and the many things that happen in school and outside of school to get them where they are," according to Ofelia Sanchez. From the marital problems of parents, the violent crimes that occur on neighborhood streets, the absence of parents who work multiple jobs, to the persistent problems of poverty, Sanchez explains that her experience as a parent mentor has opened her eyes to the monumental obstacles that some students face in schools. She adds:

If they come to school and teachers don't understand why the homework isn't completed again and why they aren't paying attention, what they don't realize is that these kids are worried about bigger things—not homework and grades, they are worried about their parents, being alone, the shots they hear.

Through her relationships with students in classrooms and fellow parent mentors, Sanchez became connected to a broader community of families. For Sanchez, the school became more than a place where she sent her children; it became a community full of friends, support, and meaningful relationships. This happens, in large part, because from the start, LSNA organizers explain to parents that they will ultimately find themselves in the midst of a "web of relationships"—connected to students, their families, teachers, and their fellow parent mentors.

This relational strategy is a cornerstone of the organization's education work and originates from its roots in organizing. Jeff Bartow, the executive director of the Southwest Organizing Project (SWOP), an organizational ally that has brought the Parent Mentor Program to schools in Chicago's southwest side, has observed LSNA's approach in schools over the years and emphasizes that relationships are at the core of everything they do:

> Everything comes through the relationship first. They take time to listen and share and understand the reality of the lives of members of their organization, and there's a real deliberateness around that.

This relational approach has become a common feature of successful organizing efforts aimed at educational and school reform issues (Hong, 2011; Warren, 2005; Warren, Hong, Rubin, & Uy, 2009). By prioritizing the creation and sustenance of relationships, the Parent Mentor Program seeks to change the institutional nature of schools—moving from anonymous, rigid, tradition-bearing institutions to a community of individuals who are connected by relationships of trust and caring.

Through this relational approach fostered by LSNA, parent mentors gain a clearer, more complex view of schools. By immersing parents in classrooms and providing spaces where they can foster meaningful, close relationships with teachers and students, LSNA seeks to integrate parents into the life and culture of schools. For some parent mentors, this experience is fundamental to their decision to become teachers. According to Leticia Barrera, an LSNA education organizer and GYO candidate who is also a former parent mentor:

> When I became connected to the classroom in such a close and personal way and then I found my skill and talent is valuable there, I knew right away that I had to fulfill my dream and be a teacher here. Being a teacher—it is a part of who I am. I am thankful to have the chance to realize that.

Barrera explains that for most parents, "they don't have the chance to know what happens in the classroom, because they are there just to drop off or pick up their child." Consequently, for these parents, the Parent Mentor Program provides a rare inside view into school and classroom culture. This exposure, coupled with the relational approach of the program, provides some parent mentors with the necessary information and motivation to chart a new journey into teaching.

FROM PARENTS TO TEACHERS: THE DEVELOPMENT OF A RELATIONAL, COMMUNITY-BASED TEACHER

For many novice teachers, entry into the profession may be marked by ideals and visions about good teaching. Coupled with the harsh realities and challenges of teaching in urban schools, these early visions of teaching can be shattered as new and idealistic teachers confront the real issues of poverty, inequality, and prejudice that face urban schools and communities. Teachers often find themselves in the midst of communities and families to which they have little real connection, and these cultural differences often serve to reinforce an already existing tension or separation between the groups. Interpretive work, particularly in the field of sociology, has highlighted the structural, institutional, and ideological differences that often serve as a wedge between parents and teachers. Willard Waller (1932) in *The Sociology of Teaching* proclaimed that "parents and teachers are natural enemies, predestined each for the discomfiture of the other" (p. 68). Waller goes on to describe a chasm between parents and teachers that is fraught with tension, anxiety, distrust, and fear, and he describes schools as environments that leave little room for meaningful interactions and relationships. Further investigations have shown that the home-school relationship is one that is fraught with tension, distrust, cultural misunderstandings, and a lack of positive communication (Lareau, 1989; Lawrence-Lightfoot, 1978, 2003).

Despite the pronounced challenges in building relationships between schools and families, little has been done to promote greater awareness of school-family engagement in teacher education programs (Broussard, 2000; Morris & Taylor, 1998). Among the courses that are offered in teacher education programs, courses or class sessions on parent and/or community involvement are rarely offered to aspiring teachers (Ammon, 1999). The lack of course preparation is reflected in the many teachers who report feeling ill prepared to interact and engage with families (Foster & Loven, 1992; Graue, 2005).

Whether it is a result of cultural, structural, or interpersonal forces, there is clearly a divide between teachers and the families/communities they serve. Particularly within urban environments where the majority of students are low-income students of color and where the majority of teachers are White and/or middle-class, linguistic, cultural, and social class differences can serve as significant barriers in building communication and meaningful relationships. However, for the GYO candidates who are featured in this study, the school and home communities are one and the same—one that is full of already existing connections, relationships, and local knowledge. Rather than grooming these teacher candidates to better understand the communities they will teach, school communities can benefit and learn from their existing base of knowledge and experience.

Armed with a rich base of local and community knowledge, GYO candidates like Barrera also benefit from their years of experience in classrooms as parent mentors. These experiences provide not only the inspiration to teach but also the exposure to the realities and challenges of teaching in urban schools. Former parent mentor and GYO candidate Maricela Contreras explains:

> You become connected to each student you work with. You get to know them over a year—what they're good at, what they struggle with. And through it all, you also understand how hard the job of a teacher is. . . . What they have to manage is just impossible sometimes, so it's a reality check for me, in some ways.

While parent mentors like Contreras often confront the challenges of teaching during their experience as parent mentors, they also begin to see some of the shortcomings of the teachers they work with. It was the reality of unmet expectations that served as the basis for organizing LSNA's first GYO cohort. Parent mentors began to observe that for many of the schools in the predominantly Latino, Spanish-speaking neighborhood, bilingual education classes were often challenged by a lack of qualified teachers or the rapid turnover of bilingual teachers in schools. Some of the teachers who remained in schools had difficulty connecting with students and their families. Contreras explains, "The focus of teaching was passing along a language, not understanding a student's experiences." What Contreras describes is a common refrain in many areas of teaching—teaching becomes strictly a process of passing along skills and knowledge and lacks a sense of cultural proficiency. What parent mentors such as Contreras realized was that teaching could be a process that involved cultural understanding and individual and personal connection. Without these cultural and relational skills, parent mentors began to see how student learning could be compromised. For the parent mentors who were fully bilingual themselves, they began to see the skills they offered to students. According to former parent mentor Maria Marquez, interactions within the classroom highlighted a need for change:

I saw the necessity there was for more bilingual teachers. I saw the struggle the children have when they just come from their respective countries only speaking one language, and how hard it is for them to blend into the customs here, the way the school is taught, and the language barriers, mainly. Some of the teachers I saw were frustrated with these situations, mixing up special education with bilingual education and just generally not aware of how to teach these children in a way that respected them.

As community members and parents of children who attend the school, Marquez adds that parent mentors and GYO teacher candidates have a uniquely valuable perspective:

We know what the community needs, and what our community lacks is a lot of communication between the school and parents, and I think that as a Grow Your Own teacher, I'm going to be able to diminish that gap or that need at least a little.

By drawing individuals from the community into teaching, GYO programs have the potential for developing teachers with a community-based orientation to their teaching. In doing so, GYO efforts can work to encourage a broader dialogue about teacher education that highlights the importance of family and community engagement. In the midst of urban school environments that struggle to develop and maintain authentic and positive relationships between schools and families, GYO programs can foster teacher candidates who not only know about a community's needs but also have an interest and commitment to developing connections with families. Unlike many teachers who "just pack up and go home," Ofelia Sanchez believes her community knowledge is an asset:

I grew up in this community and I know every summer, there are certain gangs that come around and everything gets started. And a lot of times at home, a lot of the Latino children have to live with other family members, and they don't have the space or the room or the time because Mom and Dad are working and there's no one there to help.

Because of her experience in the community, Sanchez remains committed to developing a teaching style and vision that are in line with the experiences of her students and their families. Sanchez describes her own experiences as a student, feeling disconnected from teachers who neither knew nor understood the challenges that her family faced in the community. For many GYO candidates who have often experienced the shortcomings and limitations of these urban schools, these memories and experiences still profoundly shape their own motivations as teachers. According to Silvia Gonzalez, her experience as an immigrant student shapes the way she understands her own mission as a teacher in the community:

> When I came to the States, it was really hard for me, and not knowing the English language, and not having anybody lending support, period. There was nothing. There was nothing. . . . I don't want anybody to go through something like what I did . . . so I just think about this great need to understand these families better.

Teachers such as Gonzalez and Sanchez aim to develop teaching strategies and styles that are based on their own experiences in the community. For many schools that struggle with developing successful and innovative strategies to connect with immigrant parents or parents of color, they may find that with GYO teachers such as Sanchez and Gonzalez, teachers themselves are highly skilled and able to connect with students' families. This can potentially transform a school's notion of parent and community engagement from a focus on programs and strategies to a focus on individual beliefs and orientations toward families. These GYO candidates highlight the community-based assets they bring to teaching. Beyond the qualifications and credentials required of any new teacher, these teachers come with a familiarity and understanding of the community that allows them to make easier connections to students and their families. Danny Silva, a GYO graduate, argues that GYO teachers have strengths and assets that are rooted in their community experience:

> Well, for us, it is, I guess, a little easier to identify with the children since we come from this community. Our children go to school in this community. A lot of us, some of us were born and lived in this community. So we feel comfortable, and we know the needs of the community. So because, when you're talking school, we're not just talking academics. There's a social aspect to it, too. You have to be familiar with the culture, you have to be familiar with the people, you have to be familiar with the needs, and from there, you can go forward and the sky is the limit.

As a teacher in a historically marginalized community, Silva understands the importance of his commitment to providing a quality education to the students he teaches. As GYO teachers such as Danny begin to enter schools and classrooms, they will, as Silva argues, "change the dynamic within our schools." As teacher candidates, GYO teachers feel the significance of their mission and their assets. For many like Ofelia Sanchez who describe entrance into the teaching profession as a "natural step," the commitment to the families and communities they will reach is a primary motivating factor. As Silva argues, when these community-based teachers enter classrooms, they have the potential to transform school communities into ones that are more intimately connected to the experiences of students' families and communities.

TEACHERS WITH "A MIND FOR ACTIVISM"

Beyond their knowledge of families and the surrounding community, those GYO candidates who began their classroom experience in the Parent Mentor Program often have an activist orientation and more holistic understanding of community issues. Because of LSNA's roots in community organizing, the Parent Mentor Program aims not only to introduce parents to schools and classrooms as participants but also to develop them as leaders within schools. Throughout their engagement in the program, parent mentors are given opportunities to broaden their base of knowledge about schools, develop their own assets and skills, and step into leadership roles and opportunities. LSNA organizers also build in opportunities for parents to understand the broader issues of economic justice, health, immigration, and violence in the community, highlighting the connections between these community issues and the educational environments of schools. Through weekly training sessions, parent mentors are introduced to LSNA organizers working on balanced development campaigns, community health issues, safety, and immigration reform. Throughout this experience, parents begin to see the ways broader community issues influence schools as well as their own families. According to Lisa Contreras, a GYO candidate, former parent mentor, and current LSNA organizer who is based in the Funston School:

> You come to these meetings and you start to see how everything is connected. And we as a community have to be connected, watching out for each other. Safety in my neighborhood is connected to your child feeling safe walking to school and what kinds of kids she is going to connect with when she gets there. It's not just about my family or my child's classroom. It's much bigger than that.

When individuals like Contreras have a broad-based view of community issues as well as an intimate understanding of families and neighborhoods, they become teachers with a more holistic understanding of schools and communities. As Contreras explains, the experiences of families, neighborhoods, communities, schools, and classrooms become interconnected pieces that contribute to a larger understanding of how to adequately and successfully educate students whose lives are intricately embedded within many environments.

Through their work as parent mentors, GYO candidates develop a holistic and complex understanding of the environments of schools and communities. As they begin to see the interconnectedness of issues, as well as the persistent problems of poverty and inequality, parent mentors begin to see themselves as leaders and advocates in schools, working to challenge existing conditions and advocate for change. Consequently, these parents become actively engaged in promoting change rather than passively waiting for schools to change. This orientation toward leadership and activism produces teachers who understand the power and authority and their potential to advocate for change. According to Leticia Barrera:

> I think that I can make a change because I don't always agree with the school system and some of the more traditional approaches in education. But I will have the opportunity to organize for change in my school. And I don't know if the administration will always be happy with me, but I think that I have the right to do that. I don't think that the system focuses on the students in the ways that they have to grow and learn. I totally disagree with the way we use standardized tests. I more agree with assessment that sees the child as a whole, not just one part of them.

Through Barrera's experience, she feels compelled to continue her stance as an organizer, committed to pushing for change and a quality educational experience for children in the community. Through her experience with LSNA as a parent mentor, leader, and organizer, she remains committed to the role that organizing plays in her own classroom, what she calls organizing from the inside:

> I will not be disconnecting from the organizing. . . . I will put that knowledge to use in my classroom and I will organize from the inside—in my school, in my class.

Through an organizing approach in its work with parents, LSNA encourages the participation of parents who view their own skills and assets, as well as their abilities, to promote change in schools. As Lisa Contreras explains, the experience encourages teachers "with a mind for activism"—a community-based orientation to teaching that is rooted in activism and change.

BUILDING BRIDGES BETWEEN SCHOOLS AND COMMUNITIES: TOWARD THE NEXT GENERATION OF TEACHERS

GYO teacher programs have the potential to change the current dialogue on school reform—not only by encouraging us to seek alternative methods to building new teachers but also by urging us to reconsider the traditional relationship between schools and families. Through their ability to navigate both the world of school and community, GYO teachers have the potential to play critical bridging roles, mediating relationships between families and schools. In doing so, they work to address one of the most persistent problems in urban education—the disconnect and gap between families and schools.

To address this gap, policymakers and researchers have often focused the attention and blame on families, creating and implementing programs and activities to increase the school-based participation of "disinterested" parents whose lack of involvement represents a lack of caring or valuing education (Lopez, 2001). These programs are often focused on "educating" parents on the practices and priorities of schools (Valdés, 1996). Under this framework, schools assume primary responsibility and expertise for educating children. GYO Teacher programs challenge the very notion that families and communities lack the resources, commitments, and expertise to work as equal partners with school staff to educate children. Studies of local community efforts to engage in school reform have found that when schools begin to change their long-standing beliefs that they have all the answers in educating students and begin to work collaboratively with parents, schools can become places of genuine change and transformation (Warren, Hong, Rubin, & Uy, 2009).

For GYO programs to be most successful, they must work in collaboration with institutions and organizations that work to open schools up to parents and community members such as the Parent Mentor Program. Parents can overcome their own fears and misunderstandings about schools; at the same time, schools can re-create their environments in more welcoming and inviting ways. Collaboration is a fundamental feature of the Illinois GYO effort; for this reason, as Maria Teresa Garretón, professor in the Department of Teacher Education at Northeastern Illinois University, explains, these collaborative efforts allow us to explore the multiple dimensions of educational issues:

> We're trying to help teachers form relationships with parents, but if they don't understand the community, if they don't know what the issues are, it's very hard to use that lens. . . . By having the community organization at the table, we're also looking at what else is going on in the community that may be affecting this family.

Through its interactions and relationships within the community, LSNA offers schools opportunities to engage authentically with parents and families. Through the Parent Mentor and GYO programs, LSNA seeks to build a generation of parents and teachers who fuse visions of community with ideals of teaching and learning. By exposing and familiarizing parents to the relationships, interactions, and culture of schools and classrooms, LSNA's Parent Mentor Program broadens the base of community participation in GYO efforts. Through a community-based, relational approach to organizing in schools, LSNA supports the development of a generation of GYO teachers who are community-based and activist-oriented, paving the way for a teaching force that can potentially act as a bridge between schools and communities.

For the many schools in historically marginalized communities, school transformation is both urgent and necessary. GYO teachers such as Danny Silva are products of the very schools they hope to serve and transform, and they understand the sense of urgency that surrounds their mission. As Ofelia Sanchez explains:

> In some ways, it can be so frustrating, knowing that as a Grow Your Own teacher, it takes time for us all to complete our degrees. We have families, life in general, we are getting used to being back in school when school was never an easy place to be—all of this takes time, and I think sometimes that we have to hurry up and finish so we can go out there where we're needed.

There is real value in the kind of commitment Sanchez has when she reflects on her future as a teacher in her community. The GYO teacher candidates in this study highlight the invaluable strengths and assets they hold as members within the community and parents of children who attend schools in the neighborhood. Through their experience as parent mentors and in their eventual role as classroom teachers, GYO candidates have a deep understanding of schools and classrooms. At the same time, because they live in the community, are parents themselves, and send their children to neighborhood schools, they have a rich knowledge base and understanding of families and communities.

As these GYO candidates look ahead to their roles as teachers, they highlight the multiple roles and experiences they will draw upon—as teachers, parents, organizers, community residents. Their narratives emphasize the bridge-builders they promise to become. According to Ofelia Sanchez:

> Once I am in that classroom, I will understand every single student because I would have that sense of all this knowledge about how schools work, what families need, prior knowledge of the community surrounding the school as well as what's involved within the system. It's knowledge that I'm

going to take with me to better educate them and to be a better and more effective teacher. I want to give these families the knowledge that I have in how things work. That's how I see myself. I can't wait.

Teaching as bridging work between families and schools, as Sanchez suggests, becomes a benefit and resource to students and their families, as schools become more ably equipped to communicate, support, and understand their experiences as individuals and as families. As teachers, GYO candidates propose a renewed emphasis on strengthening the ties between schools and communities. For many communities that struggle with the growing gap between the worlds of home and school, GYO programs present a vision of teacher education that focuses on the beliefs and attitudes of individual teachers. Rather than merely focusing on programs and activities that seek to bring families and schools together, GYO programs emphasize that teachers must understand the curriculum of schools as well as the culture and curriculum of families. In doing so, teachers become bridges between the school and community. According to LSNA organizer Joanna Brown:

> And that's part of the point, in my mind, of Grow Your Own teachers, because if you train them right, so maybe they've acted as bridges between the school and community and so when they become teachers, they bring that experience, and they know how people think on both sides of the divide.

By calling upon the resources within a community, GYO programs emphasize the importance of meeting the needs and understanding the experiences of the communities within which schools are embedded. These GYO teacher narratives also highlight some of the shortcomings of traditional teacher education programs that may fail to emphasize the importance of family and community engagement, in effect producing a generation of teachers who remain disconnected to families. By cultivating teachers from within the community, GYO programs can potentially produce a generation of teachers who are committed to acting as bridges between the school and community, paving the way for teacher education programs that are community-based.

REFERENCES

Ammon, M. (1999). *Joining hands: Preparing teachers to make meaningful home-school connections.* Sacramento: California Department of Education Press.

Broussard, C. (2000). Preparing teachers to work with families. *Equity and Excellence in Education, 33*(2), 41–49.

Foster, J., & Loven, R. (1992). The need and directions for parent involvement in the 90's. *Action in Teacher Education, 14*(3), 13–18.

Graue, E. (2005). Theorizing and describing preservice teachers' images of families and schooling. *Teachers College Record, 107*(1), 157–185.

Henderson, A., Johnson, V., Mapp, K., & Davies, D. (2007). *Beyond the bake sale.* New York: The New Press.

Henderson, A., & Mapp, K. (2002). *A new wave of evidence: The impact of school, family, and community connections on student achievement.* Austin, TX: National Center for Family and Community Connections with Schools.

Hong, S. (2011). *A cord of three strands: Organizing parents, schools, and communities for collective empowerment.* Cambridge, MA: Harvard Education Press.

Lareau, A. (1989). *Home advantage: Social class and parental intervention in elementary education.* New York: Falmer.

Lawrence-Lightfoot, S. (1978). *Worlds apart.* New York: Basic Books.

Lawrence-Lightfoot, S. (2003). *The essential conversation.* New York: Random House.

Lopez, G. (2001). The value of hard work: Lessons on parent involvement from an (im)migrant household. *Harvard Educational Review, 71*(3), 416–437.

Morris, V., & Taylor, S. (1998). Alleviating barriers to family involvement in education. *Teaching and Teacher Education, 14*(2), 219–231.

Noguera, P. (2001). Transforming urban schools through investments in the social capital of parents. In S. Saegert, J. Thompson, & M. Warren (Eds.), *Social capital and poor communities* (pp. 189–212). New York: Russell Sage Foundation Press.

Shirley, D. (1997). *Community organizing for urban school reform.* Austin: University of Texas Press.

Valdés, G. (1996). *Con respeto.* New York: Teachers College Press.

Valenzuela, A. (1999). *Subtractive schooling.* Albany: State University of New York Press.

Waller, W. (1932). *The sociology of teaching.* New York: John Wiley & Sons, Inc.

Warren, M. (2005). Communities and schools. *Harvard Educational Review, 75*(2), 133–173.

Warren, M., Hong, S., Rubin, C., & Uy, P. (2009). Beyond the bake sale. *Teachers College Record, 111*(9), 2209–2254.

7

Overcoming Institutional Barriers to Develop a Successful Community-Based Teacher Preparation Program

MARIA TERESA GARRETÓN

In the spring of 1999, I received a surprise phone call from Joanna Brown, the lead education organizer for the Logan Square Neighborhood Association (LSNA). Joanna wanted to develop a partnership between her community-based organization (CBO) and the college of education at Chicago State University (CSU). At the time, I was involved in directing the Bilingual Education Program and felt not only satisfied in my role but also unable to take on any more projects. I was interested enough in Joanna's idea to listen, but as I listened, the prospect of developing a community-based project that catered to non-traditional students gave me pause. I was reluctant to embark on yet another partnership. I was too familiar with the time, effort, and energy that such partnerships take to develop. As Joanna spoke, I recalled having been burned by various partnerships with other institutions over the past 20 years. All had been great ideas, begun as collaborative endeavors, but became "my projects" ultimately, implemented without the partner's participation.

I suggested that Joanna contact two other universities in closer proximity to their northwest side community rather than initiate conversations with CSU located on the south side of the city, 14 miles from Logan Square. "We have tried," Joanna told me emphatically, then went on to explain that she had been regularly "calling schools of education looking for a program that could help these women become teachers," but her efforts were always brushed off or dismissed.

Joanna's insistence and persistence kept me on the phone. She described a cadre of women pushing to improve their own academic trajectory in order to impact the local schools of the Logan Square community. My initial reluctance began to fade as she detailed the profound commitment of the parent mentors, and their interest in becoming bilingual teachers. Joanna clearly believed that CSU was the only viable option for providing access to university coursework so the parent mentors could become teachers. When she asked to meet with me to discuss the potential partnership, I suggested that we met together with this group of parents instead, so I could better understand their needs, goals, and expectations.

We met on a cold fall evening in a crowded room of an old Chicago two-story house, home to LSNA at the time. Eighteen women and two men sat in a circle. They listened politely as Joanna introduced me and explained why we were all there. I could sense that many were there only because Joanna had asked them, but did not plan on staying long or participating in discussion. They sat with their coats on and their purses on their laps; others stood by the door as if ready to leave as soon as it was politely possible.

I told them a little about myself, my background, why I had come to the United States and to Chicago in particular. I switched to Spanish and began to get more eye contact; some were smiling and nodded along with my narrative as if remembering their own journeys. With some hesitation, a few women began to ask questions. Some described attempts to take college classes over the past several years. Many spoke with excitement of their dreams and described hopes for the children in their community. The more people spoke, the more the atmosphere of the room shifted from skepticism to excitement. Merely talking about the possibility of returning to school provoked true passion, even warmth. People started taking off their coats as they relaxed. Those who had been standing by the door ready to leave inched closer and sat down on the floor.

Susana pulled her college transcripts from her bag and asked, "*Los créditos de México ¿me van a contar?*" (Will my Mexican credits count?)

María asked, "*¿A qué hora serían las clases?*"(At what time would classes be offered?)

Leticia, concerned about her lack of high school degree, asked, "Will this program help me get my GED?" The noise increased and it became difficult to follow everyone's comments and questions because many spoke all at once. I left the meeting feeling energized and extremely motivated. In spite of my initial hesitation, I was hooked.

After the meeting, the possibilities for such a community-based project, rather than the barriers, surged to the forefront of my mind. As I drove home, I began to imagine ways the program could positively affect the personal lives of the community members I had just met as well as initiate change in the local schools. Such dual possibilities existed in part because the initial idea and motivation evolved out of a grassroots effort designed to challenge the status quo of the Logan Square schools grounded in and derived from the work of LSNA (Schultz, Gillette, & Hill, 2008).

Although the bilingual program had been quite successful in school-university partnerships, most fell short when it came to becoming embedded within the neighborhoods we served. Community involvement in other projects was tangential at best, and parents certainly did not have much input or significant roles to play (Skinner, 2010).

The potential of this community-based partnership provided the adrenaline rush necessary to move the endeavor from inspiration to a working program. However, the obstacles, both institutional and relational, that had prompted my initial hesitation were very real. In this chapter, I describe our efforts toward reducing and overcoming these barriers while also cultivating and negotiating an authentic collaborative partnership with LSNA. Institutional barriers included lack of funding, university admissions criteria, inflexible infrastructure, and incompatible faculty roles. As the university insider, I was responsible for navigating these issues. Developing a program that would meet the needs of this group of students and the Logan Square community, however, was first and foremost a collaborative effort between LSNA and the Bilingual Education Program at CSU. As we negotiated the parameters of the project and discussed our roles, eventually reaching a better and more nuanced understanding of each other's institutional cultures, the foundation was laid for partnership. This was no easy task. Learning to build on each other's strengths rather than carve out territories required a basic trust that was not always present.

FIRST OBSTACLE: LACK OF FUNDS

As Joanna and I discussed the realities of moving the project from an idea to a working program, we knew the first obstacle was funding. Neither the university nor the community organization had the necessary resources to carry out the program. Knowing that a request for proposals for federal funds would be announced around Thanksgiving, I considered that our best chance for finding funding. I had been successful in obtaining federal grants to support our programs in the past, so I embarked on a marathon writing project during my winter break.

The university was closed during the holiday, but my experience told me that had it been open, I would not have obtained much help in the process. I felt very confident writing the narrative. I knew the population. I knew my program. And I was very familiar with the detailed requirements of federal grants. Designing a program that would meet the needs of the students, develop partnerships with schools, and address the community's needs identified by LSNA was straightforward. The process provided me with an opportunity to truly address the connection with the community, a piece absent from our teacher-preparation program. I believe that successful schools are collaborative endeavors where teachers work with one another, and school administrators, as well as parents and community members. Our program stressed the importance of collaboration: Students had opportunities to work with mentor teachers and other staff in the school, but their interactions with parents rarely went beyond meeting them on report card pickup day. Like most traditional teacher education programs, ours did not truly prepare future teachers to work with community members and parents.

The sense of mutual excitement of a common vision and the feeling that by creating this partnership we could effect change in the schools motivated me to seek external funds and organize a team to design and implement Nueva Generación, the first GYO project. While I waited to hear about funding, I began to think about the implementation of the program and who we would find to do that. I considered the possibility of appointing a teacher as project coordinator. Elizabeth was a doctoral student, a new mom, and had contemplated leaving the classroom for the right opportunity. We met informally at her home to discuss the grant; that evening, the concepts behind Nueva Generación began to emerge.

Collaboration 101: Clarifying Expectations and Responsibilities

As it turned out, obtaining the grant was the easy part. The university was the fiscal agent and hiring the coordinator was the first task on my agenda. Although I wanted to hire Elizabeth, I hadn't yet suggested it to LSNA. First, we had a meeting at LSNA to discuss the ideal qualifications, skills, and credentials a program coordinator should have. In my view, this person would play a pivotal role in the project. Not only would the coordinator monitor and run the project on a daily basis, but he/she would also need to be the interpreter of institutional cultures. We needed someone who understood that we were very different types of institutions and would help us navigate those differences in order to meet student needs.

LSNA organizers felt very strongly that the coordinator should be recruited from the community, be housed at LSNA, and be part of the organization. Advocacy was paramount; LSNA wanted to make sure that advocating for the students was part of the job description. They did not see the university as being capable of playing that role.

I explained, however, that although this new project was designed to be a community-based teacher preparation program by design, it was very much an academic program in nature. We needed someone who knew about bilingual teacher preparation and one who could help candidates negotiate the difficulties of their university application, course selection, and program requirements. Ultimately, we reached an agreement after several meetings, and only then did I bring up Elizabeth's name as a potential coordinator. Joanna exclaimed, "She was my son's 4th-grade teacher, she is great!" Discovering someone we both knew and trusted was the first step in the development of our collaborative effort.

SECOND OBSTACLE: UNIVERSITY ADMISSIONS CRITERIA

As I had learned in my initial meeting at LSNA, several community members had made attempts at returning to school in order to pursue college course work. Joanna explained that often those students were "made to feel that they didn't belong, or that they were not the right class or ethnicity" when they dealt with staff in the offices of admissions or financial aid. The college admission application, financial aid paperwork, and advising process can be daunting for anyone, but particularly for non-traditional students returning to school. As we began to process applications, we realized that a number of transcripts from local community colleges were missing. Joanna drove to the different colleges to request that transcripts be sent to us. In order to eventually get "beyond bureaucracy," Joanna believed we needed to make sure we did the legwork so that potential students could even apply. This collaborative attitude helped us overcome the first barrier to the recruitment and admissions process.

Faculty and staff at Chicago State University are accustomed to dealing with non-traditional students who have limited availability to come to campus or who lack child care and so occasionally need to bring their children to class. Both LSNA and CSU had experience with older adults who had interrupted their education and wanted to return, but did not have the financial means, the academic preparation, time availability, or know-how to navigate college. The Bilingual Education Program students had always been mostly women, mothers, and first-generation college students whose first language was not English. Nueva Generación applicants, most of whom were LSNA parent mentors, mirrored our campus-based bilingual education students. Students who had successfully completed our program often brought siblings, cousins, spouses, and children and encouraged them to apply. Feeling supported by and understood in our program, students would feel comfortable sharing their academic and personal problems, which ranged from not knowing how to approach a professor to having difficulties with a child or spouse. As I observed LSNA organizers interacting with parent mentors, I was struck by how similar our roles were. They knew their families; they knew whose parent was sick and whose spouse was looking for work. Our similar relational approach to our work led us to agree on the kind of support necessary to ensure the success of parent mentors as college students. But first, we had to get them admitted to the university.

Given low GPAs in high school or lack of standardized-test scores, many applicants did not meet CSU's admission criteria. These potential participants had been out of school for several years and/or had completed high school outside of the United States. Scoring well on the college entrance examinations was therefore an unrealistic expectation. During the initial discussions with LSNA organizers, we had all agreed on the need for a rigorous program that would also provide support to increase the students' chances for success. What made this program both different and necessary was the great value we placed on the linguistic and cultural capital that the students brought with them. I needed LSNA staff and the candidates to understand from the outset that it was not going to be easy. Joanna and I shared similar recruitment philosophies, agreeing to admit candidates with complete applications and paperwork, and to let them "weed themselves out" during the first year. I was willing to do what I could to help then obtain admission, even those candidates who did not meet all the entrance criteria. This helped further develop the trust between us.

Admitting all applicants meant I had to convince the university administration to consider students without ACT scores. I called various innovative programs at CSU until I discovered an alternative program for non-traditional-age students (over 22 years old) who were not required to take college entrance exams. Immediately upon confirming this, I requested a meeting with the university president to discuss options for the Logan Square cohort. An exception to entrance requirements was foremost on the agenda.

In describing Project Nueva Generación, I stressed the importance of a program that had built-in room for opportunity and accountability. I assured the president that the students would meet all the standards required of the current program students. We would not lower performance standards, but we were willing to open the door and provide the necessary supports students needed in order to meet academic goals. I reminded the president of the success of our campus-based program, and explained that once these candidates were admitted, there would be no difference in program requirements for this group. Intrigued by the possibility of a community-based teacher preparation program, she agreed to waive the entrance requirements for this group and brought up the question of support. How many students would be part of this project? How many courses would we offer each semester? Who would teach these classes? She liked the fact that this was a 5-year grant, but I reminded her that it would probably take 7 to 10 years for most students to complete the program and that we would have to look for funds once this grant ran out. "You have 5 years to work on that," she told me. "You always seem to find a way," she added with a smile.

Collaboration 201: Building Trust Through Action

In addition to sharing a vision with the CBO and understanding the needs and educational goals of this group of parents, faculty involved in the project needed to earn the respect and trust of LSNA personnel. Distrust of teacher preparation programs had emerged in meetings with several CBOs where we discussed the poor quality of their neighborhood schools. Teacher quality and retention are often seen as barriers to the successful development of the community. Teacher preparation programs and universities are often blamed for the poor quality of teachers, the lack of parental involvement, and the lack of student motivation leading to high dropout rates (Mediratta, Shah, & McAlister, 2009). We knew that this trust had to be developed over time. But this process was not without tension. Ongoing communication, systematic monitoring of student progress, and respect for the individuals involved all helped develop that trust.

LSNA's early apprehension of university personnel began to dissipate as they got to know the faculty, in particular those involved in the design and day-to-day implementation of the program. Elizabeth and Joanna had weekly phone conferences to discuss student progress. I participated in monthly meetings with LSNA staff to review program decisions and keep abreast of issues that might affect program implementation. Understanding and being able to relate to the community was extremely important to LSNA. Our ongoing interactions with LSNA staff and the candidates were key elements in developing the collaborative trust between us that would allow us to make decisions that would benefit the students without having to defend those decisions at every step.

THIRD OBSTACLE: INFLEXIBLE INFRASTRUCTURE

One of the first logistical issues we faced was location. Holding classes in the community at convenient times for the participants was of the utmost importance. The LSNA organizers, our coordinator, and I met to discuss what we needed: an easily accessible location in the Logan Square community with evening availability that also came with parking, a classroom with adult-size tables and chairs, a blackboard, a projector, and other technology. Furthermore, we required that our location have a room in which we could offer child care and a place suitable for tutors, whom we envisioned working with Nueva Generación students before and/or after class.

The first site we selected for our project was one of the community centers coordinated by LSNA. It was located in a public school and met the basic requirements for our classes. Although the education program faculty was willing to travel to the northwest side of the city in the evenings to teach, this was not true of all instructors, who pointed to a lack of technology, library, and office support as drawbacks of this space. Questions were raised: "How will the students get their books?" "Where will I make photocopies?" "Can I teach this class during the day?" The College of Education faculty members were familiar with teaching cohorts or graduate programs off-campus. Our Arts and Sciences colleagues were not. In order to get them involved, we needed them to look at this project not as an additional, off-campus class, but rather as a commitment to and show of support for the mission of the university.

I had to think creatively about how to structure the program's class schedule in ways that would not conflict with the school's schedule but would meet university requirements. Classes could not start before Labor Day because schools would not be open, nor could we hold classes on days set aside for parent-teacher conferences, report card pickup, or school holidays, which did not coincide with university holidays. I worked with LSNA to find solutions to these issues as we planned the program schedule. The public library, a local coffeehouse, and other public places in the Logan Square community became alternate class sites for those off days.

Recruiting and selecting general education instructors to teach courses off-campus was more complicated than I expected. At first, following traditional channels, I asked department chairpersons to recommend instructors with experience teaching older students who were second-language learners. Administrators in the College of Arts and Sciences viewed the teaching of these required general education courses off-campus as external to their regular course offerings. Therefore, they suggested adjunct or part-time instructors who were not particularly skilled at modifying instruction. One example of a particularly bad match was the selection of a part-time math instructor who spoke Spanish but did not understand the student population and resented the suggestion that he teach the class at a different pace from his other on-campus class. As students became increasingly frustrated, the coordinator requested that tutors attend class alongside the students in order to provide help. Thinking we had hired him a teaching assistant, the instructor assigned all grading to the tutors. Eventually, we removed the instructor in the middle of the semester and hired another one to take his place.

After that incident, we learned to approach the selection of instructors in a different way. Having worked at the university for 20 years, I had a fairly good idea of which instructors were successful at connecting with students and adapting instruction to meet their needs. I approached those instructors myself. After telling them about the project and the students, I asked if they would be interested in teaching for us. Most of these handpicked, full-time instructors were intrigued by the idea of having an undergraduate cohort with characteristics similar to our GYO group and agreed to teach. Only then did I approach their department chairs, a strategy that worked very well on one level and backfired on another. Positively, the instructors connected so well with the students that they provided additional support to the students, even outside their classes. One instructor, who was confined to a wheelchair, had his wife drive him to Logan Square, and with the students' help he entered the building to teach every week. Students began to develop long-term relationships with university faculty and thanks to having such passionate teachers felt empowered to make their own connections and to look for resources on their own.

On a university level, however, this approach to the selection of instructors backfired. I had been asking professors individually to take on these off-campus classes. Learning of this, several Arts and Sciences faculty members complained, accusing the College of Education of ignoring protocol for scheduling general education courses offsite. Not surprisingly, this negatively affected the relationship between the two colleges. Ideally, I would have included the dean of the College of Education and the dean of the College of Arts and Sciences in the discussion from the beginning of the project and invited them to collaborate. The reality was, though, that neither the department chairpersons nor our deans were familiar with the program. The college administration saw our work as a separate project, unrelated to the overall mission of the university. Indeed, the president of the university understood more about our program than the very administrators running it.

Collaboration 301: Working Together to Achieve Our Goal

During the first 2 years of the program, Project Nueva Generación courses were taught in a neighborhood school that operated as a community center in the evenings. We used the school library and two or three classrooms for our classes. Although the facilities had clear limitations—food was not allowed and there was no technology available—our biggest concern was how our students were treated by school personnel. Our adult students were not permitted to enter classrooms without the instructor, which limited their ability to meet before class to work on projects or study with the program tutors. Nor were they allowed to use the teachers' bathroom because they were not teachers, and instead had to use the child-size student bathroom that regularly lacked toilet paper. Similarly, our students were forbidden to use the school elevator, which was also reserved for teachers. The teacher whose classroom we were using complained that things were moved around in her room. One evening, one of the security guards came into the library while class was in session and disconnected the phone, alleging that someone was making phone calls to Puerto Rico. Both the students and the coordinator were routinely yelled at for breaking rules, with the result that the environment became truly hostile. We were left wondering how kids were treated in that building if that was the way we were treated.

Negotiating a move to another community center was not easy. To discuss the problems we were facing, we met with representatives from LSNA, who understood that it was necessary to look for another community center, one where students felt welcome and instructors could focus on teaching rather than the problem of the day. The community center was located in a school; we needed to involve that school in our project. Invitations were in order: We needed to include the school principal, teachers, and custodians, as well as the community center coordinator. Discussing these issues with LSNA organizers was an important step in the development of our collaboration. We were all able to see the importance of the right setting to improve the effectiveness of the program.

In our quest for the right place, we met with several principals who were interested, but not for the right reasons. Some saw it as an opportunity to generate revenue; others saw it as way to keep someone employed. One principal told us that we could use his building if we hired and paid him to teach in the program. We also met principals who understood the benefit of this type of partnership and welcomed us into their schools. They understood what we were trying to accomplish and were excited about the possibility of helping to prepare teachers from the community who would remain in the community. These principals invited us to meet with their teachers to explain our program. Once teachers understood what our presence in their schools meant and the potential impact that our students would have in the Logan Square schools, they collaborated with their principal to make space available for us such as the cafeteria, teachers' lounge, and computer lab, as well as classroom space.

Principals also shared their expertise with our students. One principal served as a guest speaker in a class and talked about student data, how she used test results, how teachers used this information, and the meaning of the data in the context of teaching schoolchildren. This helped our students see themselves as part of the school community and gave them insight into the roles of the principal and teachers. One participant had an "aha" moment. "So THIS is what this score means to the teacher!" she exclaimed, finally understanding how the school interpreted test results. This student went from a parent who was upset at her son's low test scores to seeing those scores through the eyes of a teacher and then designing instruction to address the weaknesses. One of the school's teachers brought worms and compost to class in order to share her expertise in developing science projects in the elementary classroom. Creating the worm habitat together, everyone became part of the effort, not by reading about it or discussing it in the abstract, but by engaging in a hands-on experience with the teacher in her classroom.

Those examples reflect the contrast between the two settings. In the first school, both teachers and principal resented our presence, in part because they didn't always understand it. One teacher would hide all her chalk and once tried to keep our instructor's book by writing her name in it. "Why do *these people* get everything paid for?" she asked indignantly. In the second setting, where we all collaborated to plan the experience, principals and teachers became part of the project. Meeting with both LSNA organizers and CSU program faculty, this group saw that they could play an important role in this program. They understood that the school community was an integral part of the community-based teacher preparation program. Collaboration thus resulted in a much stronger program while also strengthening the relationship between the university, the CBO, and the public school.

FOURTH OBSTACLE:
TRADITIONAL FACULTY ROLES

Early on in the implementation of Project Nueva Generación, program faculty learned that we had to pay attention to student behavior in a very different way from how we typically did. Every missed class or assignment was a clue to be studied. Some students were hesitant to contact an instructor when they were having difficulty and preferred to miss class rather than admit that they were not able to do the work. Elizabeth monitored their progress and asked instructors to let her know if a student was falling behind or missing classes. Accountability for schoolwork needed to be developed jointly. The instructors, coordinator, and I had to be flexible in our roles in order to provide students with individual support. I had an administrator's role, but there were some students who related better to me, so Elizabeth would request that I call them if there was a problem. Others would go directly to Elizabeth when facing a problem. Marcial was a quiet, reserved student who during one semester stopped coming to class and would not return phone calls from Elizabeth or his peers. He would talk to me, though. I discovered that he was really struggling under the pressure of school and fatherhood. Several semesters later, when problems emerged again, this time with the university bureaucracy, Marcial trusted me enough to talk him through the problem and help him resolve it.

Similar situations with students occurred regularly. Marcial's case was just one example of how a seemingly minor barrier can become a major obstacle that students cannot overcome without the immediate help of personnel involved in the program. And program personnel need to be willing to take on multiple roles for students.

Collaboration 401: Learning to Trust the Process

As trust between us developed, our partnership with LSNA grew stronger. Faculty members felt that LSNA supported and had confidence in them in academic matters. We learned important lessons about working within the community from LSNA. There was one area that proved particularly difficult to resolve however: how to provide support for students struggling with personal problems. During the first 5 years of the program, students dealt with a range of issues, from low self-esteem to the death of a spouse. One time, when a student could not find time for homework because her husband had difficulty accepting her new role as a student, Joanna suggested that Elizabeth hold weekly meetings to discuss personal issues and conflicts. We felt, however, that this would not help the individuals with problems, but rather would create another layer of dependency, which we did not think was helpful in the long term. Yet we agreed with LSNA that personal problems could eventually become bigger obstacles, so we hired a social worker to help individual students when needed.

The underlying problem that surfaced as a result of this issue was one of strategy. We felt that it was necessary for us to build high levels of academic, social, and emotional support at the beginning of the program and gradually reduce that to allow students the opportunity to develop their own support mechanisms. To this end, we slowly withdrew supports and found that students began to build their own. As program faculty, we believed students were ready to become involved at the university. A few students started to take classes on campus and would set up carpool schedules and study groups so as not to fall behind. LSNA worried that students would get lost in the big campus: "Will there be someone available on campus to help them find their class? Will students know how to read their schedules? Who can they call if they have a problem?" We had several meetings to discuss this process. It was hard for the CBO staff to let go and have students begin to work out solutions to problems on their own. LSNA had been actively involved in the monitoring of students' well-being and it was difficult for them to trust the university to take over some of those roles. A key aspect of collaboration was learning to trust our partner but, more importantly, to trust the process.

LESSONS LEARNED

> I need to thank you because you and your incredible team prepared me very well. I know how hard you worked to make our lives easier. I appreciate everything you did for me over the last 7 years. I am a reflection of you and your team.
> —2007 Nueva Generación graduate

We encountered many obstacles in the process of designing and implementing Nueva Generación. With the help of our partners, committed faculty members, and dedicated community members, we created the "incredible team" mentioned above that helped community members become teachers in their neighborhood schools. Some of the hard work recognized by our graduate included finding funds to develop the program, being creative and resourceful during the admissions process, working around an infrastructure that was not designed to be flexible, and, finally, changing the very essence of the traditional faculty role whose priorities include research and service as well as teaching, but not necessarily making students' lives easier.

Nueva Generación taught us that for a community-based teacher education program to succeed, it must actively include all stakeholders in the implementation of the program. The university and community-based organization spent time getting to know each other's culture and priorities. Discussions about each organization's mission and how they interpret that mission, learning from each other, have been key to our project's success.

Keeping a focus on what started it all helped both LSNA staff and CSU faculty become a very strong team. We wanted the Logan Square parents to become the best teachers in order to serve the children of their neighborhood schools. The Nueva Generación future teachers taught us that giving up was not an option and that, in order to succeed, we all had to work together. They made us exceptionally aware of the importance of collaboration and teamwork.

EPILOGUE

CSU was in many ways the ideal setting for Nueva Generación. As program faculty, we had sufficient autonomy to develop a community-based teacher preparation program and the wherewithal to build in the supports necessary to ensure student success. But these same characteristics, however, prevented us from institutionalizing the program. The university never embraced the program as part of its larger mission and continued to see it as a special project, even 10 years after its creation.

When I decided to leave CSU and join another university that was working with two other CBOs in their own GYO programs, LSNA agreed to move Nueva Generación to this new home and begin a new partnership. Northeastern Illinois University made a commitment to redesign its teacher education programs, responding to community needs, and has put in place the necessary structures to institutionalize the programs. Community-based teacher preparation is not an add-on program, but rather an integral part of teacher education.

REFERENCES

Mediratta, K., Shah, S., & McAlister, S. (2009). *Community organizing for stronger schools*. Cambridge, MA: Harvard University Press.

Schultz, B., Gillette, M., & Hill, D. (2008). A theoretical framework for understanding Grow Your Own teachers. *The Sophist's Bane, 4*(1/2), 69–80.

Skinner, E. (2010). Project Nueva Generación and Grow Your Own teachers. *Teacher Education Quarterly, 37*(3), pp. 155–167

8

Community Organizing and the Evolution of Grow Your Own Illinois

ANNE HALLETT

Illinois ACORN (Association of Community Organizations for Reform Now) had a history of working in some of the lowest-income neighborhoods in Chicago. In the 1990s, they began to organize around teacher quality issues because their schools had difficulty attracting and retaining high-quality teachers. In order to begin to address this problem, they trained community members about criteria for good teachers and persuaded the local school principal to allow them to participate in interviews of teacher candidates for their schools. Thinking that the problem might be the schools' locale, they organized summer institutes to introduce the newly hired teachers—usually young, inexperienced, and from the suburbs—to the North Lawndale neighborhood. They took the new teachers on bus tours of North Lawndale and introduced them to local sights and community members so they would be more knowledgeable about their school neighborhood and perhaps feel more comfortable in the community. ACORN organizers also worked at the district level to persuade Chicago school officials to fill all teacher vacancies at their schools before the start of the school year, a seemingly obvious task but one where the district was often lax.

In spite of such efforts, the neighborhood schools continued to serve as revolving doors for teachers. In the North Lawndale schools, ACORN experienced firsthand what the National Commission on Teaching and America's Future data confirmed: High turnover of new teachers is a problem especially in high-poverty schools. The problem was not too few teachers being hired, but too many leaving (NCTAF, 2003, 2009). Although vacancies were filled, new teachers did not stay in North Lawndale schools for more than a year or two. ACORN began to understand that the problem was not poor hires or recruitment; the problem was retention. Confronted with the issue of high teacher turnover, school districts often propose solutions such as salary incentives for teachers who teach in low-income schools, hiring additional recruiters to increase the teacher supply, or reducing class sizes to make teaching in low-income schools more appealing. Community organizations such as ACORN, however, understand that in order to reverse trends and create change in their local schools, a powerful, vocal, and organized constituency is required. This constituency has the potential to create the political will and accountability to make certain that solutions extend to low-income students of color and to demand that low-income schools that need the best teachers, and whose students rely most heavily on public education, benefit from the solutions. These solutions require community organizing (Oakes & Rogers, 2006).

Community organizing posits that low-income community members are leaders who have the gifts, assets, and wisdom to help solve the issues they confront in their communities. These community members are not the problem but rather, by bringing their community knowledge and relationships to bear, are essential to the solutions. Organizers invest in community members in order to develop leaders who can research an issue, develop solutions, plan strategies, speak and act publicly, and evaluate their results. Organizers build power by developing a large constituency of people who know the problems firsthand and who turn out in large numbers to demand solutions. Organizers build relationships among community groups themselves, with school districts and higher education leaders, unions, policymakers, and legislators (Gold, Simon, Brown, Blane, Pickron-Davis, Brown, & Navarez-LaTorre, 2002). Further, organizing aims to alter power relationships and transform educational outcomes.

CHICAGO LEARNING CAMPAIGN

In 2001, Illinois ACORN, which became Action Now in 2008, assessed their organizing efforts around the issue of teacher quality. Although they had met with some success in getting their classrooms staffed before the school year began, introducing new teachers to the neighborhood, and involving community members in new teacher hires, those newly hired teachers did not stay for long in North Lawndale's schools. The new teachers gained their year or two of inner-city teaching experience and then left, leaving the schools more unstable than before. Their valuable teaching experience left with them, along with the school's investment in their teaching and any sense of professional community that they and their teaching colleagues had begun to develop. The North Lawndale schools were suffering the national trend of teacher turnover, especially acute in urban districts, where more than a third leave after 3 years and almost half leave after 5 (NCTAF, 2003).

ACORN/Action Now conducted research in 2003 on 64 of the schools in their neighborhoods and were alarmed to find just how high the teacher turnover rate was. Their research revealed that up to 40% of new teachers leave every year (Frost, 2005). Nationally, 85% of teachers end up teaching within 40 miles of where they grow up (Boyd, Lankford, Loeb, & Wyckoff, 2005), and the new teachers in North Lawndale eventually went home to teach—and home was not North Lawndale.

Action Now realized that finding qualified teachers for low-income neighborhood schools and reducing high rates of teacher turnover, with the goal of improving student achievement, required organizing strength and power beyond what they possessed as a single organization. Madeline Talbott, lead organizer, learned that there might be Ford Foundation funds to support organizing work on teacher quality and she convened a group to work together on the issue, including organizing groups and several advocacy organizations already known to the Ford Foundation. This coalition began work as the Chicago Learning Campaign. In addition to Action Now, the first organizing member of the new campaign was the Logan Square Neighborhood Association (Warren, 2007), a group headed by Nancy Aardema. While Action Now had been wrestling with various strategies to recruit and retain teachers for their schools, the Logan Square Neighborhood Association had organized the Parent Mentor Program. This project led to the development of Nueva Generación in collaboration with the Bilingual Education Program at Chicago State University. Project Nueva Generación was designed to prepare a group of community members to become bilingual teachers in their neighborhood schools. As part of the work of the Chicago Learning Campaign, Action Now's members and leaders visited Project Nueva Generación classes and spoke with participants. They loved it. They immediately realized that investing in community members to help them become teachers was a possible solution to their teacher turnover issues. They had, inadvertently, discovered the organizing model and higher education initiative that was to become Grow Your Own (GYO) teachers.

WORKING FOR A GROW YOUR OWN LAW

Having discovered this promising community solution, the Chicago Learning Campaign decided to work toward institutionalization of Nueva Generación by embedding the concept in law to provide greater legitimacy and a source of funds to develop similar initiatives throughout the state. The groups organized a GYO Task Force, made up of representatives from higher education, school districts, unions, and others in Chicago and around the state. During the fall and winter of 2003, the GYO Task Force debated the ideas and hammered out an agreement on the concepts to be included in the law. The Chicago Learning Campaign members also used these meetings to identify future partners who believed in the GYO concept and to line up allies—people who represented organizations and institutions—such as higher education institutions, Chicago Public Schools, and unions—whose legislative support for a GYO bill would be important.

As part of the preparation to fight for passage of the law, Action Now and the Logan Square Neighborhood Association invited three additional community organizations—TARGET Area Development Corporation, Kenwood Oakland Community Organization, and Southwest Organizing Project—to join the Chicago Learning Campaign. These groups were chosen carefully, with clear criteria: They were well respected; they increased representation in African American and Latino neighborhoods; they had a track record of work on improving education; they were powerful and could turn out large numbers of people in support of their issues; and each had powerful relationships with key legislators in their districts.

The community solution represented by Nueva Generación struck a chord with all of the community organizations. The community groups realized that by organizing and growing their own teachers from parents, community leaders, and paraprofessionals (their members), they could create a pipeline of qualified teachers of color who lived in and knew their neighborhoods, understood and respected the language and culture of the children in the community, and who would stay in the schools once hired. They were already home. More broadly, each group recognized that its capacity to organize in its own schools would be stronger. Through this initiative, the community organizations could also work together at the district and the state levels to influence policy related to teacher quality.

The Chicago Learning Campaign hosted the first Statewide Learning Network shortly before the legislative session in 2004, in order to promote the GYO concept, to present an outline of the law, and to attract supporters. To achieve these goals, they invited national experts to participate and speak at the meeting, including educators who had developed a similar initiative in North Carolina and had data on teacher retention from their graduates. They also invited Illinois legislators, the dean of the College of Education at the University of Illinois Chicago, Chicago Public Schools representatives, and other advocates. At the front of the room, the organizers placed an easel holding a large blank paper with the heading "We support GYO." After lunch, they invited legislators and other important guests, such as the chief academic officer of Chicago Public Schools, to come to the podium, make a few remarks, and then demonstrate their support by writing their names on the sheet in front of the 100 people at the meeting. Legislators and guests spoke to the importance of this innovative teacher preparation initiative and then stepped to the easel and signed on with a flourish. The audience roared its approval of each signature. This was the opening foray into the legislative campaign.

The next step was challenging; it involved preparing language for the bill that would describe the key characteristics of GYO to be included in the law. Together, several of the organizers drafted the language of the bill, which incorporated all of the elements that made Project Nueva Generación work. Not one of the organizers had ever prepared a bill for submission to the legislature. However, one of them knew a secretary who worked for a senator and she told them which legislative office would rewrite their draft into bill language. Because a legislator had to submit the language to this office, they had to find a sponsor for the bill. Logan Square organizers approached their newly elected senator, Iris Martinez. She agreed to sponsor the bill in the state senate. Other organizers then met with their own legislators and encouraged them to sponsor the bill. Several legislators agreed to sign on as sponsors and the bill was introduced.

The process of supporting a bill to passage was also new to the organizers. Chicago Learning Campaign leaders determined who would be influential in this process. They set up meetings with their own legislators, chairs of committees, and legislative leaders. They met with the governor's staff to discuss the bill and enlist support. In one case, they showed up at the restaurant where a key policy person was having dinner to meet her by chance and to introduce her to the GYO concept. At the end of the 2004 legislative session, the hard work of the Chicago Learning Campaign paid off and the GYO Teachers Education Act was passed into law (Illinois Public Act 094-0979). Because the state was facing a fiscal deficit, the Chicago Learning Campaign agreed to remove the appropriation that had been attached to the bill in order to get it passed. But savvy legislators knew that GYO would be back for funds the following year.

THE GROW YOUR OWN TEACHERS EDUCATION ACT

The 2004 law states the purposes of the GYO Teachers Education Act: to reduce teacher turnover; to create a pipeline of teachers of color, thus increasing the diversity of teachers by race and ethnicity; and to prepare teachers for hard-to-staff positions and hard-to-staff schools in areas serving a substantial percentage of low-income students. The goal of the law is to prepare 1,000 GYO classroom teachers by 2016.

The law defines the partners that make up a consortium as a community organization, a 4-year higher education institution with an accredited teacher preparation program, and at least one school district or a group of schools. Community colleges and school employee unions may be included as well. In recognition of its organizing roots, the law defines the community organization as an organization that has a demonstrated capacity to train, develop, and organize parents and community leaders into a constituency that will hold a school and school district accountable for achieving high academic standards. In an effort to gain support from the unions and an advocacy group, a parent organization, including one of special education or bilingual education parents, or a teachers' union may qualify as a community organization, as defined in the law.

Parents and community leaders who are active in their schools as well as paraprofessionals, school clerks, teacher aides, and school-community liaisons are all potential GYO teacher candidates. According to the law, candidates must have a high school diploma or equivalent, but cannot yet have earned a bachelor's degree. Additionally, candidates must be eligible to receive federal financial aid, which means they must be U.S. citizens or permanent legal residents. Teacher candidates who are selected from this target population are expected to progress through the program together as a cohort to the extent possible, taking into account that they are often at different academic levels and may attend classes at different campuses (community college or the 4-year higher education institution). The cohort is an important support group for the candidates. A cohort coordinator helps the candidates develop bonds and friendships. The coordinator ensures that supports are in place, including tutoring, child care, transportation, help with class scheduling, and navigating higher education's bureaucracy. Additionally, the coordinator helps to schedule courses at convenient times for the candidates, usually in the evening, recognizing that most of them work full-time.

The law targets neighborhood schools that serve a substantial percentage of low-income students. The community organizations suggested a definition of substantial that would include as many schools as possible. They proposed that substantial be defined for a pre-K–8 school as one that has 35% or more students eligible for free or reduced-price lunch and for a high school, 25% or more eligible students. These definitions balanced a focus on low-income students with an understanding of the great variety of size and student populations in Illinois' schools.

The Illinois State Board of Education is the agency responsible for administering the GYO law, and in considering consortia to be awarded funding, the agency looked for proposals that included the following:

- The experience of the community organization in organizing parents and community leaders to achieve school improvement and a strong relational school culture;
- College classes accessible to candidates in terms of both time and location;
- Articulation agreements between the community college and the 4-year institution;
- A plan for use of existing financial aid resources before using GYO forgivable loan funds;
- Availability of support services such as counseling, child care, and tutoring;
- Inclusion of community organizing strategies in the teacher preparation program; and
- Support for graduates for at least 2 years following graduation.

The law provides forgivable loans for candidates to pay tuition and other direct college expenses that are not covered by financial aid. These loans are to be forgiven when a graduate has taught for 5 years in eligible low-income schools. In addition to funding forgivable loans, the law allows consortia to use GYO funds to cover costs such as child care, tutoring, classes held in the community, and the salary of the cohort coordinator(s). Funds must be used to supplement, not supplant, the average per-capita expenditures that higher education institutions spend on students.

In 2005, the year after the law passed without funds, the Chicago Learning Campaign once again organized, this time for funds to implement the program. In 2005, and every year since, the organizers prepared a GYO appropriations bill that specified the funds needed for the coming fiscal year and lined up legislative sponsors to introduce the bill in both the Senate and the House of Representatives. An individual appropriations bill of this kind serves only as an organizing tool since all approved appropriations are, in fact, included as part of the entire fiscal year state budget. However, having an individual appropriations bill enables the organizing groups to ask legislators to take visible action in support of GYO by requesting that they co-sponsor the bill. Also, an appropriations bill is typically passed by the appropriate legislative committees, giving the groups and their supporters opportunities to testify before the committees about the importance of the program, thereby both making the case for funding and raising the visibility of the initiative. In addition to public testimony, the organizers made as many contacts as possible with legislators and the governor's office, and ultimately, the legislature approved a $1.5 million appropriation for fiscal year 2006 for planning and developing GYO statewide.

In 2006 and again in 2007, the organizing groups used the same strategies described above. However, they now could employ an additional and highly effective strategy—having GYO teacher candidates themselves speak on behalf of the program. In both years, the legislature approved $3 million to support the implementation of a growing number of GYO initiatives statewide. In 2008, the initiative received an increase of $500,000, resulting in an appropriation of $3.5 million, a modest increase but a major win in a year when the state of Illinois was staggering under a deficit of billions of dollars. However, since 2006, GYO has annually and unsuccessfully requested an appropriation of $4.5 million that would allow GYO both to expand into additional high-need communities and to recruit new teacher candidates into existing GYO cohorts.

GROW YOUR OWN ILLINOIS

In 2005, after the legislature approved the $1.5 million planning grant, the Illinois State Board of Education issued a competitive Request for Proposal for a contract to help implement GYO statewide. The Chicago Learning Campaign competed for this implementation contract against two other bidders whose identities were kept secret. The Chicago Learning Campaign wanted to win the contract to ensure that the initiative stayed true to their vision as founders, to help organize the initiative around the state, and to develop a close working relationship with the Illinois State Board of Education. The Chicago Learning Campaign won the contract in the fall of 2005, and it has since been renewed four times. After winning the state contract, the Chicago Learning Campaign officially changed its name to GYO Illinois. Since the initiative was now state law and would be implemented statewide, members wanted a name that was more descriptive of the work they would be undertaking and that reflected the state, not only Chicago.

In addition to consulting on implementation with Illinois State Board of Education staff, GYO Illinois' work under the contract was to provide assistance to all of the GYO consortia in the state. This began as the community groups in GYO Illinois helped organize new consortia in high-need communities around the state and continued as ongoing support with organizers acting as troubleshooters and advisors. The assistance now includes helping consortia prepare their annual proposals and budgets for the Illinois State Board of Education, advising on issues that consortia partners may be having with each other or with the State Board, answering questions about the specifics in the law or about candidate selection, facilitating communications among consortia, and making consulting support (such as a public relations firm) available to all consortia.

GYO Illinois also provides support for the independent GYO evaluation conducted by a research firm hired by the Illinois State Board of Education, coordinates informational activities with policymakers, carries out strategic communications, presents GYO at conferences locally and nationally, and organizes an annual conference, the Statewide Learning Network meeting, that enables representatives of all of the consortia to share experiences and learn from each other. They have also helped establish partnerships between consortia so they can develop stronger relationships.

When GYO first received the contract in the fall of 2005, members began to organize the initiative around the state by conducting research to identify high-need areas, school districts that had high rates of teacher turnover, large numbers of hard-to-staff schools or positions, high percentages of low-income schools, and significant disparities between the numbers of students of color and teachers of color. Members then prepared how-to documents that described the steps needed to develop a GYO initiative, such as how to develop a GYO consortium and strategies for recruiting a cohort of candidates.

Once high-need communities and school districts were identified, GYO Illinois organizers traveled to those communities to generate interest in and to help develop a GYO consortium. They sought a lead organization or institution with a preference for a community organization and helped identify other interested potential partners, such as higher education institutions, both 4-year and community colleges, as well as school districts. The lead organization then convened representatives from each of these institutions to begin planning. In several communities, such as East St. Louis and Springfield, the school district took the lead to organize a GYO consortium. The higher education institution took the lead in several others.

In fiscal year 2006, funds for the new GYO initiative were available and the emerging consortia wrote and submitted planning proposals to the Illinois State Board of Education. These proposals resulted in the award of $40,000 planning grants to support the start-up work. The planning grants enabled the new partners to figure out how they were going to work with each other and which entity would take responsibility for which tasks. They used the planning time to determine and carry out their strategies for recruiting candidates. As the final step in the planning process, the consortia wrote and submitted a GYO implementation proposal to the Illinois State Board of Education.

By June 2006, the end of the planning year, 11 new GYO consortia had been organized. Each of the five community organizations that originated the GYO initiative developed its own consortium and recruited candidates. By June 2007, another five consortia had been developed, for a total of 16. The unique partnerships among community organizations, higher education institutions, and school districts continue to be fruitful, although the relationships between these very different entities are sometimes challenging. As of spring 2010, the 16 GYO consortia in Illinois include 16 community organizations, eight out of 12 of Illinois' public universities, three private colleges or universities, 11 community colleges, 23 school districts, and two unions.

GROW YOUR OWN TEACHER CANDIDATES

The teacher candidates are the heart of the Grow Your Own initiative. With a particular interest in increasing the numbers of teachers of color, Grow Your Own recruits candidates who have deep ties to the neighborhoods in which they will teach and a track record of working with children and in the schools (Young & Berry, 2007). Together, candidates form a cohort, go through the program together, and provide academic, social, and emotional support for each other. Whenever possible, they take classes together, study together, commiserate together, celebrate together, and build strong friendships and bonds. Candidates often say that their cohort becomes like family.

The GYO initiative incorporates key elements of effective education of adult learners: good screening; strong academic instruction; a cohort for mutual support; a full-time coordinator to help navigate the challenges and celebrate the successes; strong community connections; and supports, such as tutoring and child care (Young & Berry, 2007). The community organizing groups also support the candidates' participation in community activities, helping them to grow as leaders as part of their being educated to become teacher change agents.

As of spring 2010, statewide data reveal that 415 GYO candidates are on their way to becoming teachers and that:

- 84% are people of color (51% African American; 33% Hispanic);
- 85% are working full-time while attending college;
- 66% are between the ages of 30 and 50 years old;
- 84% are women;
- At least 59% entered the program with some college credits;
- Half of the candidates have taken the Illinois Test of Basic Skills, a requirement to enter Colleges of Education, and 60% of those have passed the test; and
- 43% are preparing to be bilingual or special education teachers, hard-to-fill positions.

As of March 2010, 20 GYO teachers have graduated, and close to 100 candidates are in their final year or two of college.

GROW YOUR OWN AS AN ORGANIZING CAMPAIGN

GYO Illinois is a community organizing response to specific conditions that organizers were working on in their neighborhood schools. Originally, in Logan Square, it was developed to provide the logical next step for Parent Mentor Program participants. In Action Now's North Lawndale community, it was developed as a promising solution to high rates of teacher turnover and to create a pipeline of new teachers of color. These solutions are part of larger campaigns for equity and social justice, and the organizing work they represent are part of building the power necessary to ensure that improvements benefit the lowest-income students and the neighborhood schools in which the organizers work.

GYO Illinois was founded on the belief that teachers who have high expectations for students and connections with the families, their culture, and the communities in which they will teach will be more successful in improving student achievement, especially in low-income schools. GYO candidates are encouraged to play active roles in the community, both as part of their leadership development and to help them learn, firsthand, about the challenges that their students-to-be and their families face on a daily basis.

Jeff Bartow, the executive director of the Southwest Organizing Project (SWOP) explains:

> There are analogies between learning to become teachers and
> many of the skills learned through participation in public life:
> specifically relational skills that require the development of trust and
> accountability and diagnostic skills related to breaking a problem
> down into actionable solutions.

GYO consortia throughout the state of Illinois are working to capitalize on those skills that their community members already possess and to support them to become agents of change in their neighborhood schools.

THE NEXT STEPS

Since 2006, two more community organizations, Enlace Chicago and Organization of the North East, have been added to the community organizations that make up GYO Illinois, making a total of seven groups. The groups recently established a collaborative decision-making structure for GYO that includes representatives from school districts, community colleges, and 4-year higher education institutions, both from Chicago and downstate.

This group, the GYO Partners Council, meets quarterly to discuss policy issues, including data collection, data use, and the ongoing struggle for state funding.

As of 2010, the funding level of $4.5 million that would allow Grow Your Own to expand remains elusive. Illinois has the second largest fiscal deficit in the country, which makes even sustaining the current level of funding difficult. In 2009, Grow Your Own members carried out their strategies by submitting appropriations bills, enlisting legislators as sponsors and supporters, testifying before committees, holding a large GYO rally in the state capitol building to give 150 candidates from across the state the chance to meet with their legislators, and spending countless hours phoning, meeting, writing, and rallying both for the GYO funds and for a revenue increase for the state overall. The funding decision was still a cliffhanger, with funding for GYO first cut in half and then restored to 90% by the governor, in the final hour, a full month into the new fiscal year. One month later, GYO Illinois organizers were already preparing to testify at the first hearing for the 2011 budget. Because legislators pass the Illinois state budget annually, advocacy for funding is a very time-consuming process.

Although work for funding at the state level takes a great deal of time and energy, one of the many benefits of the GYO initiative is that it provides a platform for community organizations and their partners to work on other educational issues in their low-income neighborhood schools. The community organizations with their school and higher education partners are beginning to plan for strong mentoring and induction programs at their schools, so GYO teachers, when hired, will be well supported. Organizers are working with local school principals to examine effective teaching in their schools and piloting multiple ways to help GYO candidates gain experience in schools, working directly with principals and effective teachers. Since the number of GYO graduates is beginning to increase, the community organizations are designing a data collection project that will allow them to create a baseline to assess the strengths that new GYO teachers bring to teaching.

The community groups launched the GYO teachers initiative and the related work, such as the mentoring and teaching effectiveness work mentioned above, to improve teaching and student achievement in their low-income neighborhood schools. This is and will continue to be organizing work—building strong grassroots constituencies, growing teachers who will be leaders in the school and in the community, and developing the power and relationships that will ensure that the improvements benefit low-income schools. The unusual GYO partnerships and the GYO teachers-to-be have great potential to make this innovative strategy a national model.

REFERENCES

Boyd, D., Lankford, H., Loeb, S., & Wyckoff, J. (2005). The draw of home: How teachers' preferences for proximity disadvantage urban schools. *Journal of Policy Analysis and Management, 24*(1), 113–132.

Frost, S. (2005). *Here one year, gone the next: Summarizing the teacher turnover data for 64 ACORN neighborhood schools, 2002–2003 to 2003–2004.* Chicago: ACORN.

Gold, E., Simon, E., Brown, C., Blanc, S., Pickron-Davis, M., Brown, J., & Navarez-La Torre, A. (2002). *Strong neighborhoods, strong schools.* Chicago: Cross City Campaign for Urban School Reform.

National Commission on Teaching and America's Future. (2003). *No dream denied: A pledge to America's children.* Washington, DC: Author.

National Commission on Teaching and America's Future. (2009). *Learning teams: Creating what's next.* Washington, DC: Author.

Oakes, J., & Rogers, J. (2006). *Learning power.* New York: Teachers College Press.

Warren, M. (2007, February/March). Community schools and community building. *Our Children.* Retrieved December 7, 2010, from http://www.pta.org/2219. htm

Young, V., & Berry, J. (2007). *Grow Your Own Illinois.* Independence, OH: The Center for Collaboration and the Future of Schooling.

9

"I Went to This School . . . I Sat in Your Seat"

Teachers of Color as Change Agents in City Schools

GREGORY MICHIE

Like many teacher educators at colleges and universities across the United States, I typically look out on undergraduate classes filled with young, White women. But as I scan the faces around me on the first night of a class I'm teaching for a Grow Your Own program on Chicago's South Side, the picture is far different. The students look to range in age from their late 20s to their late 40s. Except for me, everyone in the room is African American or Latino. And I feel a nervous excitement and sense of purpose in the air that I rarely encounter on the first day of class with my undergrads.

To begin, I ask the students to introduce themselves to the group and recount a memory from their own elementary school experiences. I listen and take notes.

Mario is a jet fueler at O'Hare Airport and a proud father of three. When he performed well on a standardized test as a 7th-grader in Chicago Public Schools (CPS), his teacher wanted him to retake the exam because she thought he'd cheated.

Joan has worked as a teacher's assistant in CPS for 20 years. She's always struggled with math, and she's never forgotten her elementary school math teacher, who went out of her way to help Joan understand difficult concepts.

Alex graduated from high school in Mexico before immigrating to the United States as a young man. He has worked as a paraprofessional in CPS for 6 years, and remembers having a crush on his 4th-grade teacher.

Teresa is a mother of three young children who loves to spend time at the park with her kids. She says she has only one positive memory of a teacher from her elementary school days in Chicago: Ms. Jordan, a substitute who made school fun and made Teresa feel smart.

"None of your other teachers stand out?" I ask.

"No," she says without hesitation. "Not one."

As we proceed around the room and other students narrate parts of their stories, it's clear that each has traveled a singular path to this point. But they also share common bonds, similarities in their backgrounds, and a unified goal: All plan to become teachers in Chicago communities much like the ones in which they grew up or currently live.

I leave class later that night feeling inspired. I know these students have a challenging road ahead of them—working full-time, taking care of their families, and adding a steady academic-year course load and summer classes on top of that. But I also know that if they can make it through the program and into teaching positions in Chicago schools, their future students will benefit greatly from their presence. They can become what Peter Murrell (2001) calls "community teachers"—teachers who possess "contextualized knowledge of the culture, community, and identity of the children and families" they serve (p. 52), and utilize this grounded understanding to connect with their students and positively impact their learning.

TEACHING FOR CHANGE IN URBAN SCHOOLS

I witnessed several "community teachers" in action when I undertook a year-long study focused on the experiences of young teachers of color who were "working for change" in urban schools (Michie, 2005, 2007). Although none of them had gone through a Grow Your Own program, several had returned to teach in neighborhoods much like the ones in which they'd been raised. The purpose of the research was to learn more about how these teachers understood their experiences, what motivated and sustained their work with children, what they believed about teaching and learning, and how they managed to teach against the grain of the prevailing educational climate of hyper-accountability, standardization, and top-down decision-making. I wanted to find out how they enacted the commonly heard phrase *teaching for change*, and what practical meaning it had for them.

One of the teachers I observed that year, Nancy Serrano, was the sixth of nine children born to a fiercely determined Mexican immigrant mother.

Nancy grew up in Chicago's Back of the Yards, a poor/working-class port-of-entry community on the city's South Side, and after graduating from DePaul University with a degree in elementary education, returned to her neighborhood—and to the grammar school where she'd spent 9 years as a student—to teach. On the first day of her first full year as a classroom teacher, she stood in front of a group of 7th-graders who walked the same sidewalks she'd walked as a kid, shopped at the same cramped corner stores, and attended mass at the same Catholic church. "I went to this school," Nancy told her students that morning. "I was in these classes. I sat in your seat."

In a school district where only 15% of the teachers are Latino—even though Latino children comprise 41% of the system's student population—the power of Nancy's presence, to borrow Alice Quiocho's and Francisco Rios's (2000) phrase, would be difficult to overestimate. But her return wasn't only of statistical significance. More important than Nancy coming back to the neighborhood was what she'd come back to do. While in college, she'd been pushed to question the inequities she saw around her, and she now had words to wrap around some of the ideas she'd long felt but couldn't always express. She knew the children in her community were struggling in many ways—against poverty, racism, lack of opportunity, feelings of inferiority—and she felt an intense passion, maybe even a calling, to help them better understand these obstacles, and to strategize ways to surmount them. Nancy saw teaching as a way to make a real difference in the lives of kids who were growing up much as she had. She wanted to change the world, and she wanted to begin in her own backyard.

I knew from personal experience that Nancy wasn't alone in her conviction. Through my association with Golden Apple Scholars, a Chicago-based scholarship and teacher preparation program, I'd worked with diverse groups of undergraduate pre-service teachers who were committed to teaching in what the program terms "schools of high need." One thing I observed over several summers in the Scholars program was that many of the students of color, especially those who'd grown up in urban areas, came into teaching with an already awakening sociopolitical consciousness, and with the belief that issues of equity and justice should be central to a teacher's work. Many hoped to teach in communities like the ones they'd grown up in and felt committed to working with students with whom they shared racial or cultural backgrounds.

This is not a new phenomenon, of course. Cultural critic bell hooks (1994), in describing her schooling experience as a young Black girl growing up in the apartheid South, remembers that at that time, in that place, teaching was about "giving back to one's community." hooks writes:

> For black folks teaching—educating—was fundamentally political because it was rooted in antiracist struggle. . . . Almost all our teachers at Booker T. Washington were black women. . . . We learned early that our devotion to learning, to a life of the mind, was a counter-hegemonic act, a fundamental way to resist every strategy of white racist colonization. . . . Teachers worked with and for us to ensure that we would fulfill our intellectual destiny and by doing so uplift the race. My teachers were on a mission. (pp. 2–3)

In a similar vein, Michele Foster's *Black Teachers on Teaching* (1997) provides compelling oral histories of 20 African American teachers from across the United States, many of whom view education as an essential vehicle for bringing about not only individual uplift but also collective social change. More recently, Yvette Lapayese (2005) examined the "oppositional acts" of five "insurgent" Latino/a bilingual teachers in California who refused to simply go along with their schools' English-only policies. Instead, they enacted classroom practices that honored their students' home languages and lived experiences, providing "a more just learning experience for [their] language minority students" (p. 6).

The teachers of color who participated in my study (see Table 9.1) didn't label themselves as insurgents, but they all worked purposefully to provide "a more just learning experience" for the young people who came through their classroom doors each day. Each of the women animated the notion of teaching for change in her own way, enacting a rendering that was deeply personal and shaped by her own history, values, and beliefs. Still, when looking at their work in classrooms as a whole, it becomes clear that the teachers shared certain motivations, commitments, teaching approaches, and ways of seeing children, schools, and the world. Although their stories don't provide a recipe for becoming a change agent in an urban school (and who would want one?), they do point toward a number of possibilities. What follows are several themes that emerged from the teachers' narratives, with illustrations of each culled from one or more of their portraits.

USING UNSATISFACTORY SCHOOLING EXPERIENCES AS MOTIVATION

In my undergraduate teacher preparation courses, where nearly all the students are White females, I sometimes do an icebreaker activity on the first day of class called "Stand Up." The purpose is to help students recognize things they have in common that they might not have suspected, and to notice ways they differ from one another as well. One of the statements I always read is, "Stand up if you loved school as a kid." Invariably, almost

Table 9.1. Participating Teachers in Study

	Identifies as	Grades Taught	Subject Area	School Type
Nancy Serrano	Mexican/Latina	7–8	Language arts	Neighborhood K–8
Liz Kirby	African American	9–12	History	Neighborhood H.S.
Freda Lin	Taiwanese American	9–12	History	Neighborhood H.S.
Cynthia Nambo	Mexican/Latina	6	Science	Charter all-girls
Toni Billingsley	African American	6–8	Spanish/reading	Charter middle/H.S.

every person in the room stands. What's clear at these moments, and during the discussions that follow, is that school worked well for most of these students. Not only did they learn, but they felt embraced, affirmed, and respected.

For the teachers of color I studied, memories of elementary and high school were more complicated. Each of them looked back on her own schooling experience with a degree of dissatisfaction or, in some cases, outright bitterness, and used those feelings as motivation to reach toward something better for her own students. Nancy Serrano, for example, had been placed into regular-track classes in high school, where one of her teachers routinely spent entire class periods with his head buried in a newspaper. Feeling bored and disconnected, Serrano spent much of her freshman year ditching classes. Her grades, not surprisingly, bottomed out, which she believed led many of her teachers to write her off as a troubled kid.

Serrano knew she wanted to go to college, but since none of her older siblings had done so, she had no idea how to apply or how she would afford it. About midway through her sophomore year, she went to visit her counselor in hopes of finding out about scholarships. "He didn't give a crap," she remembered. "He was just like, 'Well, what's your GPA? Oh, well, it's not too high.' He was all nonchalant, like he didn't care. He got out a box and gave it to me, and he's like, 'Well, look through these and see if you find anything.' Talk about a mess—it was just a bunch of papers about colleges and scholarships, not even organized or anything. And that experience made me think, 'You don't give a shit about us. If I wouldn't have come down to the office on my own, you wouldn't have done anything for me!' I was really upset."

Although Serrano had entertained thoughts of teaching as far back as she could remember, her interest waned somewhat during her early teenage years. But the indifference she experienced from some adults at her high school had, perhaps paradoxically, given her a renewed purpose. "I realized that they weren't doing their job," Serrano said. "And when you realize that, you become angry. You want to change it. When I graduated, only 25% of the seniors went on to college, and only a few of us went on to universities. And it was mostly because we weren't getting the support we needed. A lot of the teachers and counselors didn't really care. So that's why I decided to become a teacher. It wasn't for the fake, little kid, 'I wanna be a teacher' reasons. It was more. I wanted to change things."

This echoes work done by Elizabeth Sugar Martinez (2000), who writes of a cohort of Latino bilingual teachers she studied who, at least partially in response to being "mauled" by schools as children, committed themselves to creating classroom environments where students felt culturally validated and cared for in genuine ways. Similarly, Zhixin Su (1998) noted that a high percentage of the minority teacher candidates she interviewed—especially those who perceived their early school experiences as negative due to their racial identity or language difficulties—were committed to teaching as a means of struggling for social change.

Of course, although that may hold true for many—maybe even most—teachers of color, it's important to note that there isn't always a correlation between one's skin color (or gender, or social class, or sexual orientation) and one's politics. I worked with a Mexican American bilingual teacher who, when asked what she thought about the school's uncritical celebration of Columbus Day, responded: "I don't know why everybody has a problem with Columbus all of a sudden—I like him." The way she said it made it sound as if he were a contestant on *The Bachelor*, and the lesson her words reaffirmed was this: There's nothing automatic about who teaches with an eye on social justice.

Still, common experiences of "exile and struggle" (hooks, 1990) do characterize the daily lives of groups in this country—people of color, women, gays and lesbians, the poor—and the strength that individual teachers draw from this can be formidable. Prospective teachers who have had pleasant, affirming schooling experiences themselves—like many of my White undergraduates—may, as teachers, be more likely to view their practice through an uncritical lens. They may not push for change because, from their perspective, the system appears to function pretty well. Serrano and the other teachers of color I studied, however, due at least in part to their own experiences of "exile and struggle" in schools, committed themselves to critiquing and re-imagining their own practices in the classroom.

NURTURING RELATIONSHIPS CHARACTERIZED
BY "AUTHENTIC CARING"

Building strong relationships with students was a key for all the teachers as well, but as I saw it, their caring involved more than just an emotional connection. They nurtured relationships characterized by what Angela Valenzuela (1999) calls "authentic caring," which involves not only getting to know kids as three-dimensional beings, but also developing a keen awareness of the societal barriers they face. In her ethnographic study of U.S.-Mexican youth at a Houston high school, Valenzuela notes that the school's teachers (most of whom are White or African American) and students (most of whom are Mexican American) have vastly different conceptions of what it means "to care" about school. Teachers expect students to buy into ideas or behaviors that will supposedly lead to school and future success (abstract or "aesthetic caring"), while students want genuine and reciprocal relationships with their teachers ("authentic caring"). When students rebel against or resist teachers' expectations, their actions are often read as evidence that the young people "don't care" about getting an education.

But Valenzuela suggests that it is an unsavory schooling experience, not education, against which the youth are rebelling. More important, she asserts that although authentic caring as previously conceived—"premised on the notion that individuals need to be recognized and addressed as whole beings" (p. 108)—is necessary, it is also insufficient unless it is linked to a concern for social justice. "Students' cultural world and their structural position must also be fully apprehended" by teachers and other school-based adults, Valenzuela writes. "A more profound and involved understanding of the socioeconomic, linguistic, sociocultural, and structural barriers that obstruct the mobility of Mexican youth needs to inform all caring relationships" (p. 109).

Although Valenzuela's focus is on Mexican youth, her notion of a politically infused, contextually rich conception of caring was essential for all the teachers I studied. Toni Billingsley's personal knowledge of the struggles many of her low-income African American students faced helped her understand why some didn't display an "aesthetic caring" toward school. But rather than write them off, she worked hard to show them that "there's somebody else outside their family who cares about them." Cynthia Nambo, too, forged genuine relationships with her middle-school-age girls, and she was driven by the notion that most of the girls she taught, because they were of color, would "have to work twice as hard as other people—maybe three times as hard—to achieve [their] dreams." For Nancy Serrano, authentic caring meant affirming her students' cultural identities and not making excuses for them—both of which, for her, were connected to an awareness that the kids she taught were playing against a stacked deck. "I'm not going to tell you 'I love you,'" she'd tell her students, most of whom came from Mexican immigrant families. "I'm not going to hug you all the time and say, 'You did an excellent job.' . . . But when I'm hard on you, or I'm lecturing you, you need to see that as an example of my caring."

As skilled as these teachers were at developing authentic relationships with the kids they taught, though, they all experienced their share of resistance from students as well. Although they seemed to be viewed as "cool" teachers, as adults who made efforts to understand their students' lived experiences and could be trusted, that didn't give them a free pass when it came to dealing with discipline problems or student misbehavior. It's difficult not to take such opposition personally, and sometimes these teachers did. When you believe you're doing your best to provide students with a more humanizing and meaningful education and they still push against you, it can be tempting to throw your hands up in despair. But more often than not, I saw these teachers use their students' resistance as an invitation to reflect on their own practice, and I sensed, too, that each, deep down, welcomed the challenge of trying to engage her most difficult kids—even if it sometimes drove her crazy as well.

Too often, teachers in struggling schools misread student opposition as a sign that kids simply don't care about their educations. Being a change agent in such a situation means keeping in mind that for young people struggling against feelings of powerlessness and alienation, resistance can be a palpable sign of life.

BRINGING STUDENTS' LIVES, EXPERIENCES, AND CONCERNS INTO THE CLASSROOM

Valuing students' knowledge and experiences—and making space for them in the classroom—has been cited by numerous educational scholars as crucial for any teacher seeking to challenge the business-as-usual realities of public schools. Gloria Ladson-Billings (2001) writes of using "student culture as a basis for learning." Ana Maria Villegas and Tamara Lucas (2002) advocate "build[ing] on what students already know while stretching them beyond the familiar." The editors of *Rethinking Schools* insist that classroom practice must be "grounded in the lives of our students" (Au, Bigelow, & Karp, 2007).

This emphasis on making connections, on bringing students' cultures, lives, and experiences into the classroom, was integral to the work of all the teachers I studied. Sometimes it was evident in spontaneous, even silly, moments that demonstrated a willingness to acknowledge or embrace youth culture: Toni Billingsley referencing rapper "Snoop PerroPerro" in her Spanish class, Freda Lin comparing the "adopted identities" of Hitler and Eminem with her U.S. history students, or Cynthia Nambo allowing her all-girls classes to "do science" backed by a Christina Aguilera soundtrack.

Other times, teachers took more extended detours from their planned lessons to take advantage of teachable moments that they believed were connected to students' concerns or interests. When a 19-year-old unarmed Black man was shot and killed by a White police officer in Cincinnati and public protests followed, Liz Kirby shelved her class's study of *The Autobiography of Malcolm X* for 2 days to focus on the issue of police brutality. Kirby knew it was an issue that resonated with her students—many said they'd experienced or witnessed police misconduct firsthand—and she thought it was important to help them process what had happened and think about possible responses. "We've been talking a lot about old-school resistance," she told the class, referring both to their study of slave rebellions and to their examination of the tactics employed by Malcolm X and Martin Luther King Jr. in the 1960s. "But I want us to look at how we can create some new-school resistance. What can we do in our own lives to resist injustices?"

Even more substantively, though, curricular connections to students' lives came as the result of planned lessons or strategies. Toni Billingsley, for instance, chose the novel *Drive-By* (Ewing, 1997) for the 6th- to 8th-graders in her reading class for three reasons: It was a well-crafted narrative, the vocabulary was simple enough that her students wouldn't get frustrated reading it on their own, and it addressed issues that she knew concerned them. Its story centers around Tito, a 12-year-old who is pressured to join a gang when his older brother Jimmy is killed over stolen drug money. The lure of "quick dollars," according to Billingsley, was one of the most critical issues facing the kids she taught. "They see kids their age who aren't even in school making big money," she said. "So they're thinking, 'You're telling me to stick with this school thing, which means I have to not only finish grammar school and high school, but also possibly college if I want a career. That's a long way off. And here my 7th-grade friend is selling drugs and he has all this money in his pocket, and next year he's going to buy a car.' So when they see that, they're like—'What is all this for? My family is struggling, we can't pay the rent. I need the money now.'" Using *Drive-By* gave Billingsley the opportunity to help her students examine and question these real-life dilemmas in the context of their reading class.

In Liz Kirby's African American studies classes, she initiated an ongoing autobiography assignment with her high schoolers: a year-long project in which students wrote personal essays that pushed them to examine who they were, what they believed, and what paths they were choosing. "I want them to see that their lives and histories are as important as other histories," she told me.

Kirby typically came up with the writing themes, but after the students completed several chapters, she decided that they should have more input in deciding on topics. To kickstart their thinking, she listed on the board all the autobiographical assignments they'd already completed, followed by a list of six future possibilities:

- My Greatest Fear and How to Overcome It
- In Five Years
- My Contribution: How I Will Change or Impact the World
- Who My Friends Are and How They Are a Reflection of Me
- What Lesson Would I Teach the World If I Could?
- What I Value Most in Life

"So what do you think about these suggestions?" Kirby asked the class. It was a simple question, but a brave one. Based on my experience, opening one's ideas to student critique could be a humbling exercise.

"Number one—that one's too personal for me. I think you need to get rid of that one."

"And number three—that's a kindergarten one. That's little kid crap."

"I understand what you're trying to do, Ms. Kirby," said Ebony, caramel-skinned with long beaded braids. "You're trying to give us some kinda direction and help us find our purpose in life, but—"

"Don't nobody know they purpose in life," Charles interrupted. "Do you know your purpose, Ms. Kirby?"

Kirby leaned against a table. "I think I do. I think part of my purpose is to educate."

"But Ms. Kirby, I don't just learn from you," Kevin said. "I learn from Ebony over here, I learn from Kentrell, I learn from Shanice. We all educate each other. So in a way, we're all educators."

"I agree," Kirby said. "We're all teachers and we're all learners." She walked over to the desk of a kid who wasn't participating and casually took away the *XXL* magazine he'd been reading. "How about number five? What lesson would you teach the world?"

"Or how about, 'What lesson is the world teaching me?'" asked Warren.

"Oooh yeah!" Charles said. "I'm feelin' that one!"

Kirby wrote it on the board. "I like that, too. What else? Other ideas?" The suggestions came faster than she could write them:

"Does the music you listen to reflect your life?"

"Is your father really a role model for you?"

"How can I change society's outlook on my generation?"

"Why are some people's lives so unfair?"

The kids were off and running with ideas—their questions driving the process and, in turn, the curriculum itself. It was a wonderful example of what Peggy McIntosh and Emily Style (1999) say the curriculum should be: both a "window" and a "mirror" for students, allowing them to look out on worlds previously unknown to them while also seeing their own experience with new eyes. With students whose cultural, economic, or linguistic backgrounds differ significantly from those of the mainstream, holding up such mirrors can be particularly powerful practice.

MAINTAINING HIGH EXPECTATIONS—
AND HELPING STUDENTS MEET THEM

A recurring refrain with all the teachers I interviewed and observed was the high expectations each held for her students. "I push them—I mean, I really push them," Cynthia Nambo remarked of her 6th-graders. Toni Billingsley wasn't satisfied with simply giving her students "an experience" with Spanish—she wanted them to have the power that came with fully acquiring a second language. In Liz Kirby's African American studies classes, the atmosphere of academic rigor was unmistakable from my first visit: "It's going to be an intense quarter," she told her students that day. "So please prepare yourself for that intensity." Nancy Serrano said she saw herself as an older sister to her students. "I don't let them get away with things," she told me. "I'm hard on them. Academically, I'm hard on them because of my own experience. I went to college unprepared."

It is important to remember, however, that at least initially, kids may not appreciate being pushed beyond their accustomed limits. When Serrano asked her 8th-grade students to write evaluations of her language arts class during her first year, one boy scribbled a vehement protest. "I think this class is a piece of good for nothing class," he wrote. "I don't know why we have to do so much writing. People ain't going to look at how we write. DON'T THINK WE LIKE TO BE CHELLANGED!"

Serrano told me the letter made her question the tough demands she had placed on her students and scrutinize her motivations. "But most of all it just made me sad," she said. "Somehow this kid has been going through his education and getting by without being challenged, and he's gotten to the point where he's fine with it. . . . It's just sad to see that some kids are conditioned to expect less of themselves, and they get mad when somebody asks them to expect more." In the end, Serrano decided to relent only slightly: Instead of three or four pages of writing a night from her students, she agreed to settle for two.

In large part, Serrano felt she was paying the price for the low expectations of others, for years of students being granted what Gloria Ladson-Billings (2002) calls "permission to fail." According to Serrano, too many teachers at her school—and in other schools that served the urban poor—focused too narrowly on discipline as a measure of their success: If the halls were orderly and the classrooms quiet, it was assumed that all was well, that learning was taking place. But how could all be well, Nancy wondered, when so many students were coming to 7th grade lacking the most basic of skills? "A lot of the kids, at the beginning of the year, don't know how to capitalize, they can't write a paragraph," she told me. "They've never written an argument, never analyzed anything—in 7th grade!" Serrano believed most teachers at her school genuinely liked their students, but liking them, she said, didn't translate into believing in them.

Serrano knew from her own college experience that the world outside the neighborhood would demand a lot of the kids she taught, and she wanted them to be ready. "I don't even see myself as a 7th- or 8th-grade teacher," she told me. "Everything I do, I do it as if they were already in high school and I was trying to prepare them for college."

Students in the classrooms I visited that year typically did rise to meet the challenges their teachers set before them. In fact, one of the most profound realizations I had while observing in their classrooms was that while I thought I had set high standards for my Black and Latino students during my years as a Chicago teacher, I had not pushed nearly hard enough. Too often, I had let my students' tough circumstances reduce my expectations, consciously or not, to more realistic ones—an all-too-common response of well-meaning "progressive" teachers. Of course, being aware of students' outside-school challenges is essential. But feeling sorry for them and allowing them not to learn is something educators must actively guard against. The teachers I studied worked hard to understand the forces that constrained the kids they taught and to show compassion for their situations, but they worked just as hard to help their students acquire the tools to push against those constraints with all the force they could muster.

HOLDING ON TO A VISION OF CHANGE: EDUCATION FOR WHAT?

While the teachers I studied all had a solid understanding of what some believe are the essentials in a teacher's toolbox—curriculum, methods, classroom management strategies, child development—they also brought a key additional understanding into the classroom: a sociopolitically infused conception of teaching. They recognized that to teach well in city schools, they needed not only an understanding of how to design engaging lessons, but also of what it means for families to live in poverty. They needed to know not only how to utilize multiple means of assessment, but also how current immigration policies can limit students' college options, or how living in a "food desert" impacts the health prospects of a community. They took account of the broader contexts that impacted their students' lives, and used this knowledge to help frame their philosophical approaches and their day-to-day work in schools. They responded to the question "What are we educating kids for?" with answers that transcended rhetoric about raising test scores or preparing students for the workforce of the 21st century.

"Education for African Americans has always been about liberation and liberating," Liz Kirby told me. "But somehow that message has gotten lost." She added:

> If the purpose of schools is just to keep kids off the streets or help them get jobs, that's one thing. But if we're educating kids so that they can develop critical minds and really engage in society, so that they can affect the community and demand things of their government and develop initiatives themselves, that's a completely different vision of what schools could be.

Reflecting on her work with her Mexican immigrant students, Nancy Serrano put it this way: "I want to be honest with these kids. I want them to see a bigger picture, because when I was growing up, my sense of the world was isolated and narrow. I want them to question, to understand themselves in this world, to understand why things are the way they are, and to be able to use that to overcome whatever they need to overcome. I want them to understand the system so they can look at it and say, 'You know what? That's not right.' I want to let them know that a better future is possible."

Taken together, Liz and Nancy's conceptions of education as a "liberating" force that helps students "overcome whatever they need to overcome" reflect a keen awareness of the societal inequities that continue to impact poor students and students of color in our nation's cities. And Liz's call for "a different vision" of the purposes of schooling in a democratic society makes clear that the status quo of underfunding, low expectations, and test-driven curriculum in too many urban schools is unacceptable. Teaching for equity and justice, these teachers believe, necessarily means teaching for change.

Of course, as mentioned earlier, it's not a given that teachers of color who emanate from urban communities will be predisposed to teaching with an eye on equity and social justice. But that's where Grow Your Own can play an important role. In partnering with community-based organizations, GYO aims to infuse its teacher preparation with a commitment to teacher activism, and to prepare more teachers like Liz and Nancy: "community teachers" who have a deep understanding of the contexts of their work, who see possibility and vibrancy in the faces of their students, and who recognize that "a defining characteristic of good teaching is a tendency to push on the existing order of things" (Rose, 1995, p. 428). Bringing more such teachers to communities that desperately need them is one of the most daunting challenges facing teacher educators, and it is both the hope and the promise of Grow Your Own.

REFERENCES

Au, W., Bigelow, B., & Karp, S. (2007). *Rethinking our classrooms* (Vol. 1). Milwaukee: Rethinking Schools.

Ewing, L. (1997). *Drive-by.* New York: HarperCollins.

Foster, M. (1997). *Black teachers on teaching.* New York: The New Press.

hooks, b. (1990). *Yearning: Race, gender, and cultural politics.* Boston: South End Press.

hooks, b. (1994). *Teaching to transgress.* New York: Routledge.

Ladson-Billings, G. (2001). *Crossing over to Canaan.* San Francisco: Jossey-Bass.

Ladson-Billings, G. (2002). "I ain't writin' nuttin'": Permissions to fail and demands to succeed in urban classrooms. In L. Delpit & J. K. Dowdy (Eds.), *The skin that we speak: Thoughts on language and culture in the classroom* (pp. 107–120). New York: The New Press.

Lapayese, Y. (2005). Latina/o teacher insurgency and No Child Left Behind. *Penn GSE Perspectives on Urban Education, 3*(3). Retrieved September 18, 2007, from http://www.urbanedjournal.org/archive/vol3issue3/index.html

Martinez, E. (2000). Ideological baggage in the classroom. In E. Trueba & L. Bartolome (Eds.), *Immigrant voices: In search of educational equity* (pp. 93–106). Lanham, MD: Rowman and Littlefield.

McIntosh, P., & Style, E. (1999). Social, emotional, and political learning. In J. Cohen (Ed.), *Educating hearts and minds: Social emotional learning and the passage into adolescence* (pp. 137–157). New York: Teachers College Press.

Michie, G. (2005). *See you when we get there.* New York: Teachers College Press.

Michie, G. (2007). Seeing, hearing, and talking race: Lessons for white teachers from four teachers of color. *Multicultural Perspectives, 9*(1), 3–9.

Murrell, P. C. (2001). *The community teacher*. New York: Teachers College Press.

Quiocho, A., & Rios, F. (2000). The power of their presence: Minority group teachers and schooling. *Review of Educational Research, 70*(4), 485–528.

Rose, M. (1995). *Possible lives*. New York: Penguin.

Su, Z. (1998). Becoming teachers: Minority candidates' perceptions of teaching as a profession and as a career. In D. McIntyre & D. Byrd (Eds.), *Strategies for career-long teacher education* (pp. 179–198). Thousand Oaks, CA.: Corwin Press.

Valenzuela, A. (1999). *Subtractive schooling*. Albany, NY: SUNY Press.

Villegas, A., & Lucas, T. (2002). *Educating culturally responsive teachers*. Albany, NY: SUNY Press.

10

Teaching and Learning in a Beloved Community

KATHLEEN McINERNEY

We just want teachers who respect us, our culture, our lives, and our experiences.
—Rosa, Grow Your Own teacher candidate

Usually, respect is seen as involving some sort of debt due people because of their attained or inherent positions, their age, gender, class, race, professional status, accomplishments. . . . By contrast,. . . respect [can create] symmetry, empathy, and connections in all kinds of relationships, even those, such as teacher and student, doctor and patient, commonly seen as unequal . . . arising from efforts to break with routine and imagine other ways of giving and receiving trust, and in so doing, creating relationships among equals.
—Sara Lawrence-Lightfoot, *Respect: An Exploration*

Introduction to Linguistics takes place in the school library. The bright covers of *Azul y Verde* (Ada & Campoy, 1999), *Harvesting Hope: The Story of Cesar Chavez* (Krull, 2003), and *La Velita de los Cuentos* (Gonzalez, 2008) lean upright against the walls as if encouraging presence, silently supporting our work and drawing us to history, to stories of family, pride, struggle, and love. The windows, open on this late afternoon in May, let in the sounds of the vendors selling ice cream and *elote*, their cart bells ringing lightly like wind chimes. My college students enter the elementary school/community center, passing classrooms filled with other parents and community members here tonight for English, citizenship, and immigration rights classes.

Talking and laughing, the students enter the library in twos and threes. Plastic containers emerge. Although food is not officially allowed in this space, students value the ritual and significance of eating with others, the care and respect shown by feeding others. Having stowed homemade food in canvas bags, the students now produce potato flautas, salads, tinga, chips and salsa. Like other GYO classes, this evening begins with hugs, checking in, and food. A lot of food.

As a professor of bilingual education and applied linguistics within GYO for the past 5 years, I am no longer surprised by the strength of the relationships within this small learning community. Yet the endurance and the students' unwavering stewardship toward each other continues to astonish me. Class never begins quite on time. The exchange of personal, academic, and community issues and events initiates our entrance into this learning space and echoes the transition that occurs for these students the moment they enter the classroom. From the train ride over, to dropping off children at the evening child care the program provides, to the extra dinners prepared and left at home for their families, these students come prepared to check in with each other through the exchange immediately upon entering this learning space. For GYO students, stepping into the classroom is both substantive and symbolic, a spiritual endeavor.

As I unpack my handouts and books for this evening's class, Marisol arrives and plants herself in front of me. "Doctora! Why do you make us suffer so much?"

I look at her, alarmed. "Marisol?" She has a twinkle in her eye but I can see she's also upset.

"Chomsky! I do not understand everything he is saying!"

It's my turn to smile. "It's okay! No one understands everything Chomsky writes!" She looks at me sideways, doubtful. I say, "Let's talk. Are you free to meet me at the coffee shop tomorrow at 4 or so?" My office hours on campus are not helpful to GYO students who live far away from the university, so I hold extra hours at a café in their neighborhood. Marisol smiles, drops her shoulders a bit with relief, and agrees to meet with me tomorrow afternoon. I look to see if the community-based liaison, Grace, has arrived to discuss community issues with the class. I overhear Julia telling a few other students about her struggle getting help for her child with special needs. Manuel is arranging bowls of food and reporting to others his experience of being laid off at the public transit center.

A few moments later, Grace pops her head into the doorway. I wave her in: "Come on, come on. Great to see you!" As we hug, she promises she won't take more than 10 minutes of class time. "Whatever you need," I assure her. More hugs all around among Grace and the students. Grace then provides background on a proposed controversial zoning ordinance in the community that is driven by developers' interests and will increase housing density. She passes around a sign-up sheet for door-knockers to help defeat the referendum. There is 100% participation from the students; some commit to multiple shifts.

Maria says, "Elvia, can you watch my kids while I do this on Saturday morning?"

Elvia responds, "Sure! And on Sunday we can meet at my house to work on our projects for music class." It is common practice among GYO students to help each other with family as well as school responsibilities.

The spirit of this community resists institutional boundaries and imagined lines associated with school. GYO students frequently refer to each other as "family," and say that they are "connected," that their relationships with each other and the group as a whole sustain them through the most difficult personal and academic challenges, losses of family members, exhaustion, and wanting to give up. This familial community that the GYO insistently created and re-created in classrooms and meetings echoes hooks's (1990) notion of homeplace, where "all that truly mattered in our life took place—the warmth and comfort of shelter, the feeding of our bodies, the nurturing of our souls. There, we learned the dignity, integrity of being; there we learned to have faith" (pp. 41–42).

This homeplace is characterized by collaboration and intimate conversations. So, too, are the voices and dialogues in this study textured by the familiar register of homeplace. Interviews with and observations of GYO faculty and GYO teacher candidates showcase themes that point to classroom practices and professors' attitudes as contributors to GYO student success. These themes include: (1) envisioning a beloved community typified by respect and mutuality; (2) knowing good teachers: developing successful classrooms in GYO through listening, availability, and accommodation; and (3) "non-traditional, non-traditional students" who bring valuable perspectives to the classroom. When faculty members describe the dedication of GYO students, they respectfully point to this as what strongly differentiates them from those in typical on-campus classes. Professors also speak of their own growth, both personal and professional, gained through interactions with GYO students. The faculty recognizes the "funds of knowledge" (Moll, Amanti, Neff, & Gonzalaz, 1992) students possess as well as their potential to transform classrooms and communities as future teachers. Such ideas emerge as recurrent motifs when professors discuss their work.

Although based on personal experience, our GYO stories are supported by observations of and interviews with professors and students in the program. Such narratives depict the strong relationships among members of the GYO community, bonds capable of ensuring the learning, persistence, and success of students in the program. Sharing these narratives, I characterize the teaching practices of this GYO program with the aim of informing other programs with kindred goals.

ENVISIONING A BELOVED COMMUNITY

It's 6:00 a.m., and I am preparing for work. I remember that the GYO group is on school buses, somewhere along the interstate, going to the state capitol to speak against budget cuts aimed at GYO. I call Claire, the academic liaison for the group. "Tell everyone how proud I am of them," I say. She shouts to the students on the bus, who yell back energetically, "Good morning, *Profe! Abrazos!*" I'm glad to show my solidarity, even if only through an encouraging phone call.

Although not all of the students could get away for the 16-hour day to lobby, more than half rearranged commitments in order to voice their support for funding the program, demonstrating their collective dedication to saving their chance to become teachers. Eliana, one of the spirited volunteers, was chosen by her peers to address the legislature. Later on, she reflected on what she gained as a member of GYO, saying, "It gave me life. I found myself. I know who I am now. I am a teacher. This is what I was meant to do and will do for the rest of my life." The sense of identity and belonging to a group sustained Eliana through to graduation. Recognizing the sacrifices students make to be part of the GYO group, professors often speak of their respect for this kind of commitment. One professor notes, "What keeps me teaching in the program is the students—their drive, their spirit, their stories." For this teacher, the dedication of the students is not only an energizing element of teaching in GYO, but also demonstrates the mutuality between students and professors in the program.

The opportunity to attend college to become teachers has inspired students to create a network akin to Ella Baker's "beloved community" (Ransby, 2005, p. 344). In the tradition of participatory, supportive organizing groups of women, this GYO cohort hopes to improve community schools through culturally responsive, transformational teaching as well as community activism. Beloved community to them means faculty and students working in unity to reach program goals—preparing underrepresented candidates for the teaching profession who will return to their neighborhood schools with the aim of improving their schools and communities. Together, faculty and students are engaged in this cultural work that is GYO.

After an evening history class, John, the professor, leans forward and speaks to me with intensity. "GYO students are positive, dedicated, and focused—the most resourceful students I have ever had. They rely on each other; everyone is concerned about everyone else's success." During a break earlier, we had watched students collect money for Marta, a fellow GYO student. Marta's husband had just suffered a heart attack and the medical bills and household expenses were rapidly adding up. John and I contributed as well, demonstrating the faculty respect for the students' commitment that also crops up again and again in interviews with other professors. John values the students' beloved community and the way that they take care of each other and each other's families. He recognizes that their journey through school is more challenging than that of the typical college student or even, as discussed later, a typical non-traditional student. John says, "They are making real sacrifices to do this, and for some of them, English is not their first language. I think this is amazing. I can't imagine going to school in some other culture, especially to college, in another culture." He pauses, raising his hands as if holding up the weight of the students' efforts: "All their sacrifices—it all makes me just really like the students a lot." To John, the high degree of dedication and focus of GYO students is atypical student behavior.

I ask John about his sense of the students' commitment to teaching. He sits up and begins to speak louder: "Somebody's going to do 10 years in school? Who's going to question their commitment? They want to make their neighborhood schools the best they can be." He shakes his head, disturbed that anyone might not perceive the students' efforts to be as worthwhile as he does. John's commentaries on student commitment and character point to the importance of knowing, supporting, and forming good relationships with students. Faculty members believe that learning content is predicated upon good relationships and a recognition of the strengths of the GYO community.

Another GYO professor, Mark, expresses similar respect for and personally meaningful connections with the students. A burly math professor with a quick smile, he promised students that he would attend an upcoming end-of-semester celebration. A group of about 30 students gathers in the back room of a neighborhood restaurant alongside the GYO cohort coordinator and five faculty members. The state representative for the district is on her way. These kinds of gatherings are unusual within communities of non-traditional students. I see Mark arrive and gesture him over to my gift-wrapping table, saying, "I'm glad you made it!"

Mark responds, "Unfortunately, I can only stay for a short time." Simply by being there, Mark demonstrates his willingness to go beyond the classroom in order to foster strong relationships with students.

Engaged with many aspects of the GYO project, effective professors are flexible, responsive, respectful, and open to learning. Faculty members do not just arrive for class, teach, and return to their own lives; rather, they take on an active role in the GYO community. They write letters of support, attend meetings and rallies, collaborate with program tutors and social workers, and support GYO activities outside of the classroom. Playing the role of teacher and student advocate, effective instructors foster mutual respect. Multiple gatherings, including stroller marches and celebrations, are a defining aspect of this cohort's felt life, and faculty members demonstrate their respect by taking every possible opportunity to honor their students and the community.

KNOWING GOOD TEACHERS AND
MODELING GOOD TEACHING

Mark's classes are active and hands-on; tonight, students work in cooperative groups with multicolored manipulatives, speaking to each other in Spanish and English. Although he commutes well over an hour from home to the GYO course site, Mark welcomes every chance to teach in the program. Having taught math in the program for 7 years, Mark is very aware of the competing claims on the candidates' lives, and as a result, his classroom policies are flexible, more so than his policies for on-campus classes. I ask him about the presence of a 4-year-old girl who is sitting near her mother. He shrugs. "Students have to find a way to make classes fit with their lives," he says. "Maria called and said I have to bring my child to class tonight, and I said that was fine." Mark wants students to be in class. Their success, he feels, is deeply predicated on bridging boundaries that require students to check the rest of their lives, including children, at the door. "If a small thing like this helps the students to be in class," he continues, "then fine." Judging by the high level of engagement of the students in the class activities, along with 100% attendance, Mark's accommodating policies are working.

Students express an appreciation for teachers like Mark and John who travel to their community to teach classes. Additionally, Mayra speaks of the encouragement she receives from instructors and how she makes connections between course content and her cultural identity. "If it had not been for the teachers' support, we would not be here. My professors made me believe in myself and really got me going . . . especially in understanding my roots." For Mayra and others, an instructor's ability to listen and understand students is essential to success in class.

I've learned to tap into this spirit of community that GYO students bring with them by always beginning courses with a powerful writing activity. The exercise invites participants to acknowledge the events and people that bring us to the classroom and sets the tone for classroom interactions based on collaboration and trust. We write poetry based on George Ella Lyon's (1999) *Where I'm From*, which creates a space for the students to honor the many experiences, memories, and debts we carry with us, which include the sacrifices our families have made to provide students with the time to learn and teach in college.

On the first night of a children's literature class, rather than beginning with the usual introduction to the syllabus, I start with "Where I'm From" poems and read a poem written by a Peruvian American to the class. After we read two more examples and discuss their structure, I pass out a template and ask the students to compose their own. At first, they look worried, but I tell them to take their time and that I will be writing one, too. We write for 30 minutes, and then share. This is not a quick classroom activity, or a brief icebreaker, but a sounding of the depths of our identities. We write of rich family lives, gratitude to parents and grandparents, persistence, dreams, loss, and multiple roles, contextualized by two, or more, cultures. In an excerpt of her poem, Sylvia describes her journey to the GYO program:

> I am from San Luis Potosí and Guadalajara
> I am from gorditas en el horno to pozole blanco
> I am from grandma saving all plastic bags to grandpa collecting
>   every single can to crush them
> I am from holding off on college and getting a full-time job
>   because parents got separated
> I am from becoming a hard worker to get things on your own
>   to be independent
> I am from becoming a bilingual teacher to saying it is never too late!

There are many laughs and some tears as we read our poems. Ximena weeps with grief for a brother whom she was unable to see before he died. Angela writes of her journey into the United States, with little food or water and no documentation. Susana opens her poem with a statement of personal power: "I am from you have to be as strong as a man, and don't take NO shit from no one." Consonant with the transformational practices and routines of community organizing groups, teachers, and beloved community, this teaching approach affirms identities, heritage, joy, and pain.

In Mark's math class, transformation occurs through a variety of learning styles, which reduces student anxiety. This approach is especially important for students who have been out of school for some time ˙ who have long histories of being told by teachers that they aren't good at something.

On the first night of class, Mark immediately addresses math anxiety: "I know most of you have had bad experiences with math classes in the past," and he pauses to look around the room at heads nodding and eyes rolling in confirmation. "But I'm going to create opportunities in this class for you to succeed." Mark's got their attention now. "I'm going to present math concepts auditorially, visually, kinesthetically. Just the way I want you to do when you are teaching. I'm going to tie math to real-world events. And we will succeed together—all of us." The GYO students need instructors who will help them see a usually dreaded subject, such as math, differently. Students need to be able to learn not only so that they understand the concepts, but also so that they can continue this practice as teachers.

John explains that he would advise other instructors to remember that not all members of the group are the same and that learning about each student is critical. He takes a deep breath, as if punctuating his next sentence. "The *most* important thing that the program has taught me is not to take assumptions into the classroom." John notes that there can be both surprising richness as well as gaps in students' knowledge. Given the diversity of educational backgrounds that the students bring with them, including schooling in other countries and in learning environments "a hell of a lot harder than ours," John endeavors to become a student of his students, through discussions and student writing, in order to be the best teacher possible for them. John believes that this is a critical principle of good teaching in GYO.

As examples, John and Mark provide a glimpse into what ideal professors in GYO provide for their students. They are skillful at modeling engaged, authentic, transformational teaching practices. They structure their lessons in culturally responsive ways and strive to develop democratic classrooms that will guide their students' future roles as teachers. One program graduate, Josefina, who now teaches upper-level social studies in a dual-language elementary school, illustrated this point. I ran into her in the school hallway, dodging children on their way to recess. She described learning teaching methods from her professors even in classes not focused on teaching methodology: "I learned from the way in which the professors implemented their own classroom strategies that worked for us. . . . I've used those strategies. . . . They worked perfectly." Within such a learning environment, the teacher candidates can see, in action, teaching that demonstrates value for student experience and the importance of a personal connection. Good teaching requires not only respect for and connections with students, but also the modeling of pedagogical practices that teacher candidates can internalize and use in the future.

As demonstrated through their relationships with students, effective GYO instructors care about candidates and the program. Ultimately, the effective GYO professor listens to students' needs and accommodates them, even if doing so is inconvenient for the instructor. This practice, however, is not always the norm. GYO students, as teacher candidates, parent mentors, and school volunteers, are experienced observers of teaching behaviors, and they recognize practices and attitudes that fail to support learners. Julio recounted his experiences with a professor in an on-campus classroom, telling me, "The professor refused to explain answers. He just told us to 'figure it out' and said that the material was 'easy.'" The professor suggested that course content was too basic to merit class time. Julio shook his head and continued in a low voice, "He yelled at us and said, '*You people* are unprepared and would be failing at any other university.'"

Laura, another student who had also been in that class, overheard our conversation and nodded her head, saying, "He never answered our emails. He didn't even have office hours and wouldn't meet with us for help!"

I shared these comments with Mark, who responded, "It's a type of mindset: thinking about the students or thinking about yourself. A lot of profs who are not ed-based profs think about content first and students second." Although this construction of best practices in teaching and learning is not particular to GYO, both John and Mark believe that without a student-first approach, the GYO program would not be sustainable. Students need instructors who can model student-centered learning not only because their neighborhood schools need teachers with exactly these skills, but because their experience as students themselves also necessitates these approaches.

GYO professors also rely heavily on program resources, including two GYO tutors who have been carefully chosen and trained to work in the program. These tutors, June and Maya, sit in on classes. They also provide consistent support through reliable and responsive email and telephone communication with students and professors. Both June and Maya, young women with backgrounds in education themselves, arrange to meet students at a coffee shop in the neighborhood. On one afternoon, Maya convenes with a group of three GYO students and begins probing for any challenges that the students may be having in class. "So tell me about your next assignment," says Maya, "and let's look at your class notes for art while we're here." Maya is demonstrating the organic nature of the program's effective teaching practices: meeting students where they are—intellectually, socially, and physically—and connecting with them individually to support their academic success.

"NON-TRADITIONAL NON-TRADITIONAL STUDENTS"

The presence of experienced teachers and tutors in the GYO program is a key element of student success. Both Mark and John report feeling reassured about their students' academic progress thanks to the tutoring and other supportive elements built into the program, including responsive administrators, vigilant coordinators, child care, and the availability of a social worker who assists students with a variety of issues from learning difficulties to achieving school-life balance. Although these program features can be valuable to any student, particularly non-traditional students, John feels they are critical to GYO because of the students' "non-traditional non-traditional" status—a description that emphasizes the degree to which GYO students are atypical college students.

In Mark's class tonight at the community center, I observe as he creates a classroom climate specifically designed to support his students. Although this is a pre-service teachers' math education class, Mark is reviewing fractions as needed, recognizing that students may not have some of the requisite skills. Without stigmatizing any particular student, Mark says, "I know we've gone over fractions before, and you have learned the process in other classes, but sometimes we have to back up and reinforce our skills when we try a new problem." As the students participate in a pair-share activity, Mark encourages them to use their dominant language, banking on the students' linguistic assets. Coming to the back of the room where I sit, Mark says, "They can transfer back to their linguistic comfort zone. Code-switching allows them to understand and explain to each other the nuances of what I have said that could escape a non-native English speaker." He also attempts some Spanish a little later on in the class, saying, even though he's not fluent: "I try to show them I respect their language." Mark feels that one of his strengths as a teacher is to create a comfortable climate appropriate to his "non-traditional non-traditional" students, incorporating their funds of knowledge while also encouraging risk-taking: "It's not about the math . . . we set up this environment that is open and honest and appealing and it's okay to make mistakes and we're going have fun, we're going to laugh, and we're going to do some hard work." He suggests that other GYO professors implement these approaches as a way of increasing student engagement and achievement.

Recognizing and affirming candidates' cultural and intellectual assets are central to transforming educational practice and policy (Moll, Amanti, Neff, & Gonzalaz, 1992). Not only do GYO professors connect content learning to students' life experiences, but they also connect with students by creating a climate that challenges traditional constructions of professors as transmitters of knowledge, distanced from students. Professors feel involved with the transformative aims that set GYO apart from traditional teacher preparation programs. Mark says, "They're bettering themselves but they are [also] bettering their neighborhoods and trickle-down effect is going to be incredible." GYO candidates serve as models to their families and communities. Moreover, their engagement in educational activism through acts of community organizing, such as protesting closures of neighborhood schools and the reduction of services to students with special needs, will serve them in the future as teacher advocates for their students and schools.

John also recognizes the collaborative power unique to this group and exploits it for deeper learning, telling me: "These students talk to each other in and out of class. A lot. I'm really after critical thinking and engagement with ideas rather than memorizing, and this interaction between students helps them." The students' widely varied educational backgrounds, their relationships with each other as well as their professors, and their investment in education for transforming their communities combine to create a powerful trinity that distinguishes the GYO students from more typical non-traditional student groups. John's teaching practices have evolved to be more responsive of the "non-traditional non-traditional" qualities of the cohort, capitalizing on the depth of the students' relationships with one another, encouraging multilingualism, and individualizing instruction as much as possible through program tutors.

Mary, a GYO program evaluator, confesses that she did not believe GYO would work because the students struck her as unusual potential teacher candidates. She was concerned about their skill levels coming into the program, telling me, "When I first saw the [GYO] proposal, I thought, there's no way this is going to work, so it's thrilling to see the student growth." Mary also advises, "Each project is unique. Understand what is unique about your community, see this as strength, and use it." It is important to focus on the elements of such uniqueness and strengths of this teacher recruitment and preparation project.

A TEACHER'S GRATITUDE TO THE GYO STUDENTS

One summer evening, a member of my family became quite ill just before I was leaving to teach a GYO class. Our class was off-campus, but without a secretary or any of the students' phone numbers with me, I ended up calling another family member to take my place at the hospital. I left the emergency room, deeply torn between my family and my teaching responsibilities. I made it to the community center on time, but there was no hiding my distress from the students. I apologized for needing to leave my phone on and told them that class would end early tonight.

Lorena rushed up to me, her face perhaps 2 inches from my own and her hands tightly on my arms. She said, "*Profe*, something is terribly wrong. What is it?" My eyes welled with tears and I explained that one of my children had been hospitalized. By now, Sylvia and Ana had joined us, and there were more hands supporting and consoling me. "*Profe*, we are mothers, too," said Lorena. "We know. You need to go. We will be fine. We will work here. Go." In that moment, I knew that the students' concern and love for me was as strong as my own family's. I left soon after, but the students stayed to work on projects in that classroom for 3 more hours. Teaching GYO students takes us all down a "non-traditional non-traditional" path and we are indeed richer for it. The themes of best practices for teaching and learning in GYO—"beloved community," responsive teachers, and honoring students' cultural and intellectual assets—deepen our understandings of our own and other communities of practice. Through envisioning a beloved community, discovering good instructors, and valuing "non-traditional non-traditional" students, GYO programs support as future teachers students who are extraordinary assets to their neighborhoods, colleagues, and the profession.

REFERENCES

Ada, A., & Campoy, I. (1999). *Azul y verde*. San Diego, CA: Del Sol Books.

Gonzalez, L. (2008). *La velita de los cuentos*. San Francisco: Children's Book Press.

hooks, b. (1990). *Yearning: Race, gender, and cultural politics*. Boston: South End Press.

Krull, K. (2003). *Harvesting hope: The story of Cesar Chavez*. New York: Harcourt Children's Books.

Lawrence-Lightfoot, S. (1999). *Respect: An exploration*. New York: Perseus Books.

Lyon, G. (1999). *Where I'm from, where poems come from*. Spring, TX: Absey and Co.

Moll, L., Amanti, C., Neff, D., & Gonzalaz, N. (1992). Funds of knowledge for teaching. *Theory Into Practice, 31*, 132–141.

Ransby, B. (2005). *Ella Baker and the Black Freedom Movement*. Chapel Hill: University of North Carolina Press.

11

On a Grow Your Own Journey

The Teacher Candidate Experience

CHRISTINA L. MADDA & MORGAN HALSTEAD

Magdalena hurried down the long, familiar corridor toward the principal's office. She glanced at her watch; it was nearing the end of the school day. She only had a few minutes to meet with the principal before she had to return to the classroom to assist the teacher with student dismissal. As she continued, Magdalena rehearsed the speech in her mind. This would be the fourth time this month she had gone to the principal to address her son's academic struggles and discipline issues. Magdalena had been a parent volunteer at Harrison Elementary for 3 years and was no stranger to the issue of bright and enthusiastic kids in her community failing to perform well in school. She was convinced that if only she could communicate what she understood about her community's children to the school staff and administration, things would be different.

Upon entering the main office, Magdalena encountered a room full of parents, who were also there to see the principal. Frustrated, she turned to leave when a yellow flyer taped to the wall caught her eye. "Do you want to be a teacher?" it read. Magdalena turned toward the room again, where she met the faces of parents desperate to find someone or something that would help them lead their children toward success in schooling. She sighed. "Do you want to be a teacher?" Magdalena grabbed the flyer and left.

Across town, Chantelle had just finished up with her mentoring group; three 15-year-old girls attended that day. They had spent their time talking about some of their classmates and friends who were pregnant. Chantelle had wanted to give the girls an opportunity to air their feelings, while also addressing the realities of life that accompany teen pregnancy. As she was packing up her things, there was a soft knock at the door. Chantelle turned to see one of the girls' mothers, a young woman herself, slip through the door. "Hey, Trina! Good to see you!" Chantelle said, giving her a big hug. "Is everything okay? I talked to your daughter today and she was . . ."

"Oh no, girl, she's fine. I came to talk about something else." Chantelle was always willing to listen to parents; she thought they were the best support in the world. "Listen, you know how I think what you're doin' here is amazing. All of us parents feel so blessed to have you working with our girls. But I wanted to talk to you because . . ." Trina paused. "I really think you should be a teacher." She whispered this last part as if sharing a secret.

"Oh lord," Chantelle responded as she resumed packing up her things. "I wish, but I tried college once and it wasn't for me."

"No," Trina continued. "I heard about a program that's all about the neighborhood—our neighborhood." Chantelle looked up. Trina had gotten her attention.

As individuals who have spent much of their lives giving back to their communities, Chantelle and Magdalena are in many respects already teachers. Their commitment and dedication toward improving and empowering the lives of young people have earned them this title. However, as current participants in the Grow Your Own teachers (GYO) program, these particular women now have the opportunity to become teachers in a more formal sense—through the completion of a college degree that will lead them to state teacher certification.

As GYO Academic Coordinators, we (the authors of this chapter) have had the privilege of working closely with Chantelle and Magdalena from the time at which their recruitment with GYO transformed them into teacher candidates. The role of the Academic Coordinator is to ensure each student's successful matriculation from application and coursework to certification. In this capacity, we work to provide or connect students with a range of financial, academic, and social support mechanisms necessary for their success. We spend countless hours with students navigating the terrain of their college educations, celebrating accomplishments and negotiating obstacles along the way. Within the university setting, we see ourselves as critical advocates for the students and for GYO. In addition to cultivating a professional relationship in which we help to guide Chantelle and Magdalena through the maze of higher education, we have forged a personal bond that extends beyond the walls of the university. We have visited their homes, shared meals, and played with their children. On this GYO journey, we have been both the students' challengers and allies, and they have been our inspiration.

The experience of the GYO student typically does not resemble what might be considered the traditional college experience. In most cases, GYO teacher candidates begin or return to college after many years away from school while entrenched in the responsibilities that accompany adult life. Moreover, as members of communities that historically have been shut out of schools at all levels, these non-traditional students often face a unique set of personal and academic challenges as they navigate university life. However, individuals such as Chantelle and Magdalena also distinguish themselves from traditional students seeking teacher certification by bringing a history of community involvement and activism, as well as an insider perspective to teaching in urban schools.

In this chapter, we present the stories of Chantelle and Magdalena to bring to life the experiences of GYO teacher candidates. Drawing upon interviews and informal discussions, as well as our knowledge of these impassioned women as we have come to know them over several years, we provide a window into each student's unique path toward teacher certification. We begin by discussing Chantelle and Magdalena's commitment to neighborhood advocacy as a backdrop to their involvement with GYO. Next, we highlight the personal and academic obstacles these candidates identified as complicating factors on their journey toward becoming certified teachers. Last, we share Chantelle and Magdalena's visions for their future practice as teachers working to transform schools and communities.

COMMUNITY ROOTS

Both Magdalena and Chantelle began their commitment to community and education long before their involvement with GYO. As a high school student with a passion for working with children, Magdalena began volunteering in an afterschool program. Assuming the role of teacher was familiar to Magdalena, who grew up playing school with her three siblings. "We had a huge blackboard that our mom bought us, so we used to pretend that we had a classroom and took turns being the teacher," she remembered fondly. The sense of fulfillment she experienced during her high school years as a tutor and role model for younger kids stayed with Magdalena, and in many ways was the catalyst for her long-standing commitment to neighborhood schools. In the years to come, she continued to seek out opportunities where she could give back to her community by working with its youth.

After marrying and becoming a parent, Magdalena joined her neighborhood association, where several initiatives involving local schools were taking shape. She became involved in the Parent Mentor Program (see Brown and Hong this volume) designed to promote parental involvement in schools by training and employing parents as teachers' classroom assistants. "I always volunteered at the schools, but now I get to be active at my son's school," Magdalena explained excitedly. For Magdalena, becoming a parent mentor was a natural transition from her years of volunteer work with afterschool programs. Only now, she was able to combine her enthusiasm for helping children in her community with her dedication to strengthening her son's school.

While Magdalena started out volunteering at neighborhood schools, Chantelle's community involvement grew out of participation with her church, where she founded a faith-based mentoring troupe for teenage girls. After noticing a growing epidemic of teen pregnancy within her congregation, Chantelle decided to take action. She and a friend established a non-profit organization to provide mentoring for girls ages 13 to 19. As someone who had always been, as she put it, "Passionate about youth, and advocating for youth," she took to this work easily. Before long, other churches started asking about the program. Local schools also began contacting Chantelle in hopes of integrating her program into their school curriculum. "Principals were telling us 'we need this in our school 'cause our girls are acting up,'" she said, "so, it ended up being bigger than we expected." Today, as she nears completion of a bachelor's degree in elementary education, Chantelle's fervor for what she describes as "empowering young people" endures. "I want my life to be able to change somebody else's life. And I'm willing to fight for everybody's child." Earning state certification and returning to her community's schools to teach is the way she will do that.

Chantelle's readiness to fight for everybody's child struck a personal chord when Jenna, her eldest daughter, began to struggle at one of the city's magnet schools, and shortly after was labeled learning disabled. Jenna soon began to slip through the cracks. Chantelle described feeling livid over the neglect of her daughter's academic and emotional needs by what she felt was an underprepared, apathetic school staff and administration. "Jenna was sinking," she recalled, "and once I realized they weren't helping her, I thought to myself, they aren't helping any of the children." As a parent and mentor, Chantelle feels that many teachers in her community's schools struggle to relate to their African American students, thereby fostering low expectations for academic achievement. She believes that a lack of cultural competence, the ability to relate to the history and experiences of students, has contributed to an educational system in which kids are simply shuffled along without acquiring the academic foundations necessary for success in high school. Chantelle reflected on the implications of this situation for students. "So where do these students go? They drop out of high school and they end up being 'Michael' on the corner—the people you're running from in my neighborhood."

Individuals such as Chantelle and Magdalena bring a commitment to teaching in urban areas derived from a personal awareness of the challenges and barriers facing students of color. As members of historically marginalized communities, many GYO teacher candidates come equipped with an understanding of the need to uphold high expectations for students in urban settings. Their insider status, coupled with a vested interest in improving their communities, creates the potential for acting as agents of change within their neighborhood schools. "I feel a commitment to give back to where I came from," Chantelle explained. "I was really encouraged that there was a program right here that actually felt that people in the community could come back and serve the community, 'cause that's what I'm about."

As both community insiders and advocates, Chantelle and Magdalena embody the potential to challenge and disrupt what has become status quo for public schooling in impoverished neighborhoods. However, simply staffing classrooms with community insiders or teachers of color does not ensure a progressive agenda for schools. Instead, it requires teachers who also engage in social and political activism, and exude agency both inside and outside the classroom. As participants within local community-based organizations, GYO teacher candidates like Chantelle and Magdalena are involved in ongoing grassroots organizing efforts around issues such as housing, immigration policy, and education. Magdalena serves as the community representative on her Local School Council (an elected group of teachers, parents, and community members) where she works to connect the school with community-led efforts around housing reform. Last year, she gathered parents and students in the auditorium of a local school to speak with city aldermen about transforming a nearby abandoned building into low-income housing units.

In addition to the work connected to her nonprofit organization, Chantelle has served as president of the Parent Teacher Association (PTA) and vice president of her Local School Council. She is currently the student director of her neighborhood's community center, where she assists in the planning of children's summer camps as well as ongoing charity events and fundraisers to benefit local residents. Engaging in community-based activism facilitates the ability of teacher candidates like Chantelle and Magdalena to view themselves as change agents and helps to foreground the importance of instilling this activist spirit within their future students so that together they can work toward uplifting the community. "I feel like I can make a change," Chantelle emphasized. "I'm not saying I'm a savior or whatever, but I do feel that I have a lot to contribute."

The potential for confronting, infiltrating, and disrupting a school system that has perpetuated the status quo lies within GYO teacher candidates such as Chantelle and Magdalena. Their history of community advocacy and insider knowledge offer the promise of a lasting commitment to effecting change not only in struggling schools, but in their broader neighborhoods. However, for these individuals, rich backgrounds of community involvement are coupled with complicated educational histories that impact on their GYO experience. In the next section, we delve deeper into Chantelle and Magdalena's stories, by highlighting the dreams deferred and false starts that have shaped their pathways to higher education.

COMPLICATED PATHWAYS

For many students who come to participate in the Grow Your Own teachers program, attending college did not always seem to fit into life's equation. As Magdalena recalls, "There was never a huge push in my family to go to college. My parents never went to high school; they just did middle school and that's it. So I was just always really focused on finishing high school." Upon earning her high school diploma, Magdalena had surpassed her parents' level of education, achieving a milestone in her family. This celebrated event elicited pride and admiration from family members and friends. Although she had often imagined taking the next step toward a college degree, she typically dismissed such thoughts. Going to college wasn't something she or other women in her family were raised to set their sights on. "My mom had always wanted to teach," Magdalena told us, "but my grandfather never let her go to school."

Struggling against the current of traditional gender roles was not all that made a college education appear beyond Magdalena's reach. The barrier of being able to pay for college seemed to trump all others. Growing up as part of an immigrant family that often struggled to pay the bills despite their hard work, Magdalena knew that she could not ask her parents to put what scarce financial resources the family did have toward continuing her education. Going to college would mean not only an added expense, but also a reduction in the number of working hours that Magdalena could contribute toward the collective family income. This reality, coupled with little knowledge of or guidance with potential scholarships or other financial aid programs, left Magdalena believing student loans were her only option. Reluctantly, Magdalena gave up her dream of pursuing higher education since, as she put it, "I just never wanted to get to a point where I owed thousands and thousands of dollars—I didn't want that."

Family encouragement and guidance from high school counselors led Chantelle to pursue a college education straight out of high school. As an academically strong and outgoing student, her application for admission to a well-respected Midwestern university in a neighboring state was readily accepted. Despite the ease with which she had become college bound, Chantelle also felt the weight of paying for school heavy on her shoulders. Having decided to take on the burden of student loans, Chantelle was ever more determined to succeed. "I had the good grace to be admitted to the university, and believe me, I was committed! Not only had I taken a student loan, but I was going there all by myself!" she said emphatically. Chantelle recognized the gravity of taking on substantial debt while venturing into unknown territory on her own. "Unfortunately," she continued, "I totally went through culture shock, so I came back home." As the only Black woman in classes with more than 100 students, Chantelle felt alone and overwhelmed during her first few months away. "I didn't know how to connect," she explained, "and my instructors didn't really reach out. I was on my own." Chantelle's academic prowess and determination were not enough to combat feelings of isolation that left her ill-prepared for adjusting to and navigating the complex demands of higher education. After accumulating credits for 1 semester, Chantelle returned home, and from that point, struggled to maintain her path toward obtaining a college degree. "I went to a community college on and off, and just goofed around," she explained. "After that, I got married and life just happened."

As adults, with families of their own and bills to pay, the prospect of earning a college degree was fading from life's landscape. For Magdalena, the dream had never gotten off the ground, while for Chantelle, it had crashed shortly after taking flight. However, for these particular individuals and many others, becoming part of the GYO program presented a second chance—an opportunity to rewrite a college education back into life's equation. For Magdalena, GYO offered an opportunity to pursue a path that she had previously been denied. As she put it, she would "finally get a chance to do it." For Chantelle, participation in GYO provided an opportunity to pick up where she had left off after what she referred to as her "20-year sabbatical." For both, a new chapter in life was about to begin. For nontraditional students, however, the road to success is often fraught with challenges. As we continue to detail the stories of Chantelle and Magdalena, the personal and academic struggles of these candidates as well as those of the GYO program, come into focus. By elaborating on these struggles, we aim to reveal the complexity and often messiness that characterize the journey of the GYO teacher candidate.

FAMILY MATTERS

Adjusting to student life can be both exhilarating and exhausting for many GYO teacher candidates. In many cases, it requires a shift in identity and a redirecting of one's attention. Changes must occur and sacrifices must be made—not only on the part of the student, but also on the part of his or her family members. As Magdalena explained, "My biggest concern was, 'How am I going to balance everything?'" As a working mother and wife with aging parents to care for, the commitment to becoming a college student held uncertain consequences. "I knew it was going to be ridiculously hard," she told us. Even her mother, who had once dreamed of becoming a teacher herself, questioned Magdalena's decision to continue her education. "At first, [my mom] was like, 'You're crazy! What are you going to do with the kids? How are you going to keep your job?'" Despite some doubt from family members, Magdalena moved forward with her decision. She was ready to "go for it."

As predicted, adjusting to the demands of schooling proved difficult for everyone involved. "At first, the transition was rough for my husband," she recounted. "He kept saying, 'You're spending too much time out of the house!'" Despite being enrolled part-time, the hours Magdalena now dedicated to attending class, studying, and completing homework complicated life in new ways. Orchestrating day care and transportation for her children became more difficult, as did keeping up with everyday household duties such as shopping, cooking, and cleaning. Magdalena shares a home with both her parents and her brother's family, so there is a history of familial support. However, managing the added responsibilities of school within an already full life required new and additional help from family members. Despite their initial misgivings, Magdalena's husband and mother in particular encouraged her studies by creating a space for her to study in the dining room and tending to the children while she completed homework. "There were times when it was hard," Magdalena explained. "We were all tired."

When Magdalena became pregnant with her third child, support at home wavered. Her mother said, "Maybe you shouldn't do school anymore." For weeks, Magdalena agonized. Was giving up school the right thing to do for her family? In the end, Magdalena persisted. "I told them no, no, no, no, no, I'm going to do this." With the arrival of her new daughter, Magdalena again questioned whether she could manage her burgeoning responsibilities. Moreover, she worried about the toll her schooling might be taking on her loved ones. "I didn't want to leave the baby too much with my mom," she explained. "It was burning her out. And on the days I really needed her, I wanted her to be able to help." In order to alleviate some of the demands on family members, Magdalena decided to quit her job so that she could stay home with the new baby and have more time to keep up with household obligations. "Now I just don't do any school work until my husband gets home. If the baby takes a nap, I'm doing something for the house, like cleaning."

Chantelle confronts similar struggles when balancing her life as a community leader, mother, wife, and university student. Her family was most affected financially by her decision to return to school. GYO subsidizes college-related expenses through financial provisions such as tuition and fee forgivable loans and book stipends. Allowances for transportation and child care, in addition to providing school supplies and laptop computers, also help to reduce some of the financial demands typically experienced by college students. However, many GYO families that already subsist on a narrow income, profoundly feel the economic ramifications of a household breadwinner returning to school.

Chantelle and her husband jointly decided that she would pursue her education full-time. "We just felt that it was better to power through. That way, I would have a real paying job sooner rather than later," she said. As a consequence, Chantelle was forced to give up her steady line of employment. As might be expected, this decision severely impacted her family's finances. In order to make up for Chantelle's lost income, her husband began working a second job. Although this softened the loss of Chantelle's earnings, she and her husband still struggled to meet the basic expenses of day-to-day living. Additional hidden expenses associated with Chantelle's decision to return to school full-time began to surface. For example, her transportation costs increased. As the result of her cross-city commute to campus 6 days a week, Chantelle was driving more frequently and considerably longer distances. Although the GYO transportation stipend awarded to students each semester provided some relief, Chantelle found that it typically was not enough. With rising gas prices and the ongoing need for general car maintenance, transportation costs associated with school quickly added up.

Child care for Chantelle's two children also became an issue as she and her husband found themselves available less and less during afterschool hours. Chantelle's classes often stretched into the evening, and her husband often didn't return home until late at night due to his second job. Without extended family to help care for the children, Chantelle was forced to seek out an appropriate child-care provider. Again, the cost of afterschool care was alleviated somewhat by the allowance provided by GYO. However, some months Chantelle incurred large out-of-pocket child-care expenses, further exacerbating the struggle to make ends meet.

Meeting the demands of school while attending to their family's needs remains a delicate balance for Chantelle and Magdalena. Despite their commitment to becoming teachers, there are times when they inevitably second-guess their decision to embark on this path. Nevertheless, with each semester that brings them closer to accomplishing their goal of earning college degrees and becoming fully certified teachers, their faith and determination to succeed are renewed. Their resolve and resilience are central to weathering the personal struggles they face as non-traditional students. However, beyond the difficulties that exist for GYO teacher candidates outside of school, additional challenges present themselves as part of life within the university. As we continue to peel back the layers of complexity that envelop Chantelle and Magdalena's lives as GYO students, we explore the struggles they face, as well as the support mechanisms they rely on within higher education.

SCHOOL MATTERS

Higher education poses specific challenges for students of color, particularly those who are first-generation college students. Low retention and completion rates speak to the difficulty with which non-traditional students adapt to and navigate university life. For many GYO students, a lack of academic preparedness, limited knowledge of collegiate culture, and minimal experience operating within university bureaucracies are obstacles to success. In order to combat these challenges, GYO support structures facilitate the cultural, social, and academic transitions necessary for student achievement.

For many GYO teacher candidates, getting (re)acclimated to the expectations within college-level coursework proves to be a significant challenge. Coursework can be very demanding, according to Chantelle, and keeping up with weekly readings and assignments is a difficult task. "I just assumed college was going to be super hard," Magdalena told us. As a Spanish-dominant speaker who had been out of school for several years, Magdalena was particularly concerned about developing the language and literacy skills necessary for performing well in her courses. GYO addresses such concerns through systematic and customized support such as established study groups and tutoring. For instance, in support of students such as Magdalena, professional tutors specializing in working with bilingual students were hired to maintain regular office hours and appointments at a local coffee shop. These tutors, available exclusively to the GYO teacher candidates, understand the unique challenges that non-traditional students may face within their academics. "Having tutors available after hours and in places that were convenient for us has definitely helped," Magdalena explained. For Magdalena, GYO's ability to provide access to academic support that was flexible in terms of time and location was huge in terms of building her capacity for academic success. "If it weren't for GYO, it would be, 'Here's your assignments; if you need help, find it yourself,'" she remarked. "I mean, who else gets people to tutor evening hours and weekend hours? It's great!"

In addition to academics, many GYO students face uphill battles when it comes to institutional gatekeepers such as college entrance and exit exams and the tests required for teacher certification. For example, the Illinois Basic Skills Test, a 5-hour examination of reading, writing, grammar, and math, often acts as a roadblock to students' admission to colleges of education. Although some GYO students, such as Chantelle, are able to obtain a passing score on their first try, it is not uncommon for students to have to repeat the test multiple times in order to pass. Magdalena, for instance, did not receive a passing score on her first try. Despite consistent high grades in her coursework, the language arts (grammar) section of the Basic Skills Test in particular proved difficult for her as a non-native English speaker.

In other cases, a long history of low performance on standardized testing often experienced by individuals from historically marginalized communities can be a source of battered confidence and extreme test anxiety. As a result, concerted efforts must be made to create test-savvy students who are confident not only in their math and language skills, but also in their ability to succeed in a testing environment. Preparatory classes designed specifically for GYO students help to familiarize students with the testing genre while also providing a forum for students to discuss and work toward overcoming any past negative experiences with standardized tests.

Navigating the bureaucracy of higher education can also present a challenge for non-traditional students. Cultivating a basic knowledge of processes and norms associated with post-secondary institutions is therefore key. As indicated by Chantelle, having a circle of advisors with whom trust can be established is critical to meeting the demands present in a university setting. As GYO academic coordinators, it is our responsibility to help orient students to relevant procedures and expectations associated with college life. For example, when first starting out, students need to develop an understanding of registration requirements and processes. Learning to navigate the university electronic portal through which students can view their current transcript, check on the availability of courses, and add or drop classes is critical. We also provide assistance with the College of Education application process as well as the mountain of paperwork required in advance of completing clinical hours and student teaching.

As trusted liaisons to the university, we can help acquaint our GYO students with the necessary procedures and resources available for cutting through what often seems like excessive amounts of red tape. This personal attention helps to reduce the anxiety that GYO teacher candidates may experience as non-traditional students functioning within institutions where historically they have been outsiders to. The purpose, however, is never to hand-hold but rather to promote students' independence over time by equipping them with the knowledge and skills necessary for success. The end goal is to empower students so that they can assume ownership of their educational trajectories.

Beyond developing an understanding of the bureaucratic inner work-
ings of the university, perhaps the most significant challenge to overcome
is feelings of outsiderness. For many non-traditional students, getting ac-
climated to a college campus can be overwhelming and produce anxieties
or feelings of discomfort. Magdalena and Chantelle credited the sense of
community and family derived from their participation in GYO as central to
their ability not only to adapt but also to succeed in a college environment.
Magdalena regards her participation within a GYO cohort as a particular
source of strength and inspiration. Some GYO consortia such as the one
Magdalena participates in choose to implement a cohort model in which
students progress throughout their coursework as a group and may take
some classes off-campus at a community-based site such as a neighborhood
school. Magdalena attends some of her college courses at a local elementary
school. These classes are taught by an instructor from the partnering university, and are limited to the enrollment of GYO teacher candidates only. This
cohort approach provides opportunities not only for the GYO teacher candidates to engage with each other around academic content, but also helps
to create safe classroom spaces where the students can take part in candid
discussions about the challenges that currently exist in their communities
and how they might address them as future educators.

Magdalena believes her membership within a GYO cohort was vital to
helping her transition into school; yet she was surprised initially by the extent to which she bonded with other students. "I didn't think we were going
to be as connected as we are," she explained. "I thought it was just going to
be a bunch of us going to school together, but it's not like that. Everybody
kinda connects, and I've made some best friends here." The sense of connectedness that Magdalena garners from her cohort of GYO peers provides
an ongoing source of motivation and support in her schooling. "It's more
than making friends or having people you can talk to. It's having somebody
you can call and feel comfortable with," she explained. Being able to reach
out to individuals with whom she has a shared experience makes school
easier and less stressful for Magdalena. "I can't imagine what my experience
would have been if I had just been thrown into a college classroom without
anyone to relate to," she said.

That trauma of being thrown into a college classroom was what characterized Chantelle's first attempt at college. The comfort, support, and sense
of belongingness described by Magdalena were absent from Chantelle's initial experience with higher education immediately following high school.
What Chantelle experienced then, and now refers to as culture shock, was
enough to send her packing for home despite the fervor with which she set
out for college. The network of GYO coordinators, faculty liaisons, and
students to which Chantelle now has access has helped abolish the feelings

of disconnect or cultural isolation that she faced in her previous college experience. "I love the relationships and support system that I've developed within GYO," she told us. "GYO is different. It's like a sense of community to me. If I just enrolled at some college or if I went back to [my previous university], I would have nobody."

However, instead of taking classes exclusively with other GYO students, Chantelle attends classes on campus with the broader student population. She feels that the absence of a cohort model within her GYO experience has limited the degree to which she has been able to bond with other students. "Had we started out as a true cohort, you know, all taking classes together, things would've been different," she explained. Chantelle believes that she was "unable to establish a relationship with a lot of the other students" early on, simply because they were enrolled in different courses. "We were all on different pages," she said. "I managed to build relationships eventually, with some of them, but I think it's better when the students start together as a cohort. That way the support system is there amongst the candidates from the beginning."

Chantelle's words shed light on some of the programmatic considerations that need to be made when designing and implementing a program geared toward non-traditional students. Why was the cohort model not implemented within her particular consortium? If utilizing a cohort model is not possible, what steps need to be taken to ensure social cohesion among teacher candidates? GYO promotes community and connectedness through regular meetings and other social outings that allow students to come together and reflect on their schooling experience. Magdalena, for instance, attends GYO monthly student committee meetings where students organize year-end celebrations and fundraisers for student scholarships. GYO also facilitates solidarity through its belief that teachers need to be active in public policy. Chantelle, Magdalena, and other teacher candidates regularly participate in GYO rallies for funding and lobbying the state legislature. These shared experiences of democratic participation provide opportunities to act politically while also strengthening the students' relationships. However, there is an ongoing need to engage students both off and on campus. Chantelle's experience in particular speaks to the need for bridging support structures across contexts.

FUTURE DIRECTIONS

As parents, community leaders, and activists, GYO students such as Chantelle and Magdalena embody the potential for bringing a high level of commitment and insider perspective to teaching and learning in urban schools. Moreover, as non-traditional students from historically marginalized communities, they recognize the importance of a nurturing and supportive schooling environment. In reflecting on her future as a state-certified educator, Chantelle indicated that she wants her practice to be culturally relevant and fulfilling for students. "I want my teaching to be empowering," she asserted. "I want my students to feel a sense of self, and feel better about themselves. That's what I've gained from my own education." The empowerment that Chantelle has experienced through her own schooling has shaped her vision of the kind of educational experience she hopes to create for her future students. "I come from a very impoverished neighborhood, but you can't let that define who you're going to be," she told us. "We can achieve. Kids need to know this." Similarly, Magdalena's experience as a parent and community activist has contributed to her distinct outlook on what she hopes to accomplish as a teacher. She intends to give parents a better understanding of what goes on in schools by increasing their level of involvement. "I think a lot of teachers feel sole ownership over the classroom," she said, "but I want parents to feel ownership, too."

Earning a college degree and becoming state-certified teachers challenges the status quo not only in Chantelle and Magdalena's communities, but also within their families. While they have long worked to inspire individuals in their neighborhoods, they have also begun to motivate those closest to them in new ways. Like many GYO teacher candidates, Magdalena was the first to attend college in her family. She believes that her involvement with GYO has inspired her immediate family members to view college as a serious possibility in their own lives. "My daughter, who is 5, says, 'I want to go to college, too.' My sister asks me for advice on going back to school, and now even my husband wants to go to college!" she exclaimed proudly. Chantelle, who hopes to one day also earn a master's degree and Ph.D., described the impact her return to school and participation in GYO has had on her family. "My husband and kids just love it. They go around calling me Dr. Robinson," she laughed. "I'm just so happy they see my perseverance. And I always tell them, 'If Mommy can do it, you can do it.'"

Today, Chantelle is only months away from realizing her dream of becoming a state-certified teacher. She is currently completing her student teaching assignment in a Chicago public school 5th-grade science classroom serving predominantly African American students. Upon fulfilling this requirement, she will graduate from Northeastern Illinois University with honors. Beyond graduation she looks forward to going home to teach by securing a position within one of her neighborhood's schools. Magdalena also continues to make steady progress toward meeting her goal of elementary and bilingual teacher certification. Despite a difficult year afflicted with family health issues, she has stayed the course, managing to maintain a 3.6 grade point average. With 45 credits left until graduation, there is still plenty of work to do. However, her determination and will to teach keep her looking forward.

Magdalena and Chantelle's stories represent just two of the more than 500 GYO journeys currently under way. Although each faces his or her own unique set of challenges, GYO teacher candidates are united in their dedication to bettering themselves *and* their communities. The personal and academic experiences that GYO students will bring to their work as classroom teachers afford special insight into the needs of students and families of color in urban schools. As they progress toward teacher certification, their desire to impact children's lives and make things better will continue to light their paths.

12

Doing It Better Together

The Challenges and the Promise of Community-Based Teacher Education

MAUREEN D. GILLETTE

In 2005, Grow Your Own Teachers Illinois won a competitive grant to scale up Nueva Generación, the successful Logan Square–Chicago State University (CSU) partnership. The monumental task of "growing" community-based teachers through a series of partnerships in urban and rural communities across Illinois began and is now a network of consortia whose first graduates are currently entering classrooms as "teacher insiders" (Hill & Gillette, 2005, p. 43) for high-need schools.

Scaling up a small teacher education program to one where Community-Based Organizations (CBOs), Colleges of Education (COEs), a school district, and sometimes a community college work together in a state as large as Illinois has had its challenges. GYO has quickly expanded to include 16 CBOs, 11 universities, 21 school districts, and 11 community colleges. In promulgating the legislation, its founders promised to produce 1,000 diverse, community-based, and well-prepared certified teachers committed to teaching in low-income communities by 2016. As of March 2010, GYO Illinois is on track to graduate a little more than half of that number. Troubled by a reduction in state funding for adding new candidates and partnerships, the consortia have also struggled with candidate attrition due to the issues that face many older-than-traditional-age, working adults who entered or returned to college a number of years after high school (e.g., balancing work, family, and school; relearning academic skills and content). Additionally, as CBO and COE personnel learned to work together, their "bumpy road" sometimes impacted recruitment and retention.

This chapter examines some of the problems and issues that have arisen during the scale-up, placing them in the context of recent critiques of traditional university-based teacher education and the promise inherent in authentic community-based, collaborative teacher education as a significant means to school reform.

The issues and analyses presented herein are framed in light of my own experiences as a teacher and a teacher educator, as well as my involvement in GYO where, at Northeastern Illinois University (NEIU), we house five GYO projects. Committed to cultivating community-based teachers, our faculty has actively taken on more partnerships. As COE dean and a member of the statewide GYO steering committee, I have been involved in discussions with various CBO partners regarding GYO components. Additionally, as a member of the Consortium of Chicago Area Deans of Education (CCADE) and the Illinois Association of Deans of Public Colleges of Education (IADPCE), I have participated in discussions about GYO with deans from institutions that have or are interested in GYO programs as well as with the staff at the Illinois State Board of Education who manage the state GYO initiative. I have been fortunate to sit in two worlds as we struggle to bring together organizations that have heretofore had different primary missions and different primary constituencies, but the same overarching goal—educational equity for all students. If we are to meet the goal of preparing community-based teachers with strong content and pedagogical expertise who know their community and who will use their insider knowledge of the community to enhance teaching, learning, and educational reform, then we must work together to improve our own practice in several areas.

Following a brief discussion of the current state of university-based teacher education, I will address four areas that I believe were underdeveloped in the scale-up and appear to be at the root of some of the problems that GYO currently faces. My participant observations and meeting notes, the literature on community organizing and effective practice for urban schools, and my direct work in our own five consortia have helped me to identify four factors that are foundational to the challenges we now face in sustaining reform-oriented consortia that can graduate successful candidates: building commitment, building trust, building deep collaborative structures, and building cross-institutional expertise. Finally, I will address the reform-oriented possibilities in GYO through the use of some examples culled from NEIU's GYO work with our partners, and present instances of GYO's promise as a reform model through Murrell's (2001) framework for urban partnerships.

THE NEED FOR AND PROMISE OF GROW YOUR OWN

Teacher turnover in high-need neighborhoods is a severe impediment to student success, staff morale, and school reform and renewal. The quality of the teacher is the single most important factor in student achievement, and it is almost impossible for a student to academically recover from having three consecutive years of an ineffective teacher (Darling-Hammond, 2010). Thus, recruiting and preparing excellent teachers for high-need schools—teachers who will stay in the classroom and hone their pedagogical skills while making connections to students, families, and the community—should be a national priority.

Others in this volume have documented the problem of teacher turnover in the schools served by GYO candidates. This is a nationwide issue, not a problem that is unique to Chicago (Darling-Hammond, 2010). The continual turnover of teachers in any school places the educational progress of students at risk, but the high rate of new teacher turnover is especially troubling. Since even the most talented beginning teacher needs supports to increase professional knowledge and skills, students in schools where the novice teacher turnover rate is exceptionally high will have few opportunities to have a teacher with a well-developed level of expertise.

Rarely do students in our nation's most challenged neighborhoods have an opportunity to learn from a teacher who looks like them and who understands the challenges of growing up in their neighborhood. A recent Illinois Board of Higher Education (2010) report indicates that in 2008, 50 Illinois institutions produced 6,394 graduates with education degrees. Only 419 (7%) were Latino, 399 (6%) were African American, and 164 (3%) were Asian American. Seventy-three percent of the candidates graduating from the two institutions that prepare the largest number of candidates are White and come from locations far from the communities served by GYO.

Data on the effectiveness of teacher education institutions in Illinois in preparing teacher candidates for work with families, communities, and in multicultural settings with students whose first language is not English indicate that we have much work to do. Statewide data (IADPCE, 2009) collected from 1st-year teachers indicates that only 21% of the almost 1,200 respondents believed that they were "extremely" or "mostly" well prepared to teach English language learners, while 56% reported that they had English language learners in the classroom. Sixty-one percent believed that they were "extremely" or "mostly" prepared to address issues of socioeconomic diversity. Less than half felt "extremely" or "mostly" prepared to work with parents, to utilize community resources in the classroom, or to foster community relationships.

GYO presents a unique opportunity not only to impact the teaching force in our most challenged neighborhoods, but to change the way that all teachers are prepared. COEs and CBOs have the potential to co-create a model that could lead to more effective teacher education for all candidates. In GYO, candidates and organizers are insider experts in their community who hold the power to teach what they know to university faculty and peer outsiders. Teacher education could be underpinned by and embedded in a model that, by design, leverages organizations with deep community ties to assist in developing the methods, materials, and experiences that would ensure an understanding of school/community context and the importance of authentic parent/community involvement for student success. Although GYO did not intend the model to serve the general pre-service population in this way, GYO alone cannot produce enough teachers for economically distressed communities. We must undertake this task together.

The promise of GYO as a national reform model lies in the possibilities that arise when the intimate community knowledge of the CBOs and their expertise in organizing for change is combined with the professional, pedagogical expertise of the COEs. To fulfill this promise, GYO must hold fast to the mission and vision of the original design. The model has great potential, but the scale-up occurred quickly, with GYO brokering consortia without a structure in place for ensuring that the CBOs and the COEs attended to what they know are key elements of a successful organizing campaign or an effective good classroom: building commitment, trust, deep collaborative structures, and cross-organizational expertise. The next section argues for attention to these four elements across all consortia.

BUILDING COMMITMENT TO COMMUNITY-BASED TEACHER EDUCATION

The lack of a coherent vision among participants about the mission and moral purpose of the work is an issue troubling GYO today. We must confront one of the problems with any voluntary change model, the assumption that teachers and reformers are working with the same epistomologies (Payne, 2008). The rapid rate of scale-up and the diversity of partners in each consortium have understandably resulted in differing expectations and assumptions about the work.

Importantly, theoretical foundations underpin the work we do in preparing school and community professionals at NEIU and specifically in our GYO projects (Schultz, Gillette, & Hill, this volume). Without these foundational discussions, consortia members can easily move forward without a common understanding of the GYO project as a social justice movement.

This is especially important since we are not working with service-oriented CBOs such as the Boys & Girls Clubs of America. Our CBOs are advocates for equity and action-oriented reform, organizations that were built on the traditions of activists such as Saul Alinsky (1946, 1971).

The original founders of GYO may have clearly defined its mission, vision, and moral purpose when they undertook the campaign to win GYO legislation. However, as GYO leaders moved around the state soliciting partners, there was no consistent means to ensure that all participants understood and agreed to the reform mission of GYO. As I listen to conversations from consortia members around the state, it is clear that a multiplicity of ideas about the purpose, goals, and outcomes of the work are in play. As Barber and Fullan (2005) state, it is not possible to "substantially move toward sustainability in the absence of widely shared moral purpose" (p. 33). One clear example of this occurred at a meeting of GYO board members and COE deans called to discuss what some deans felt were significant problems with GYO (e.g., distribution of funds). As one CBO member commented on candidates' participation in a local community action, a COE administrator interjected, "The GYO teacher candidates don't have time for this social justice stuff right now. They need to concentrate on their courses. They can do that other stuff when they get a teaching job." Advocating the uncoupling of the work of CBOs and the work of the COE is the antithesis of GYO. Such thinking demonstrates how difficult it can be to alter the status quo.

Another example of an absence of shared vision occurred during a discussion at a GYO Steering Committee meeting about how to reach the goal of 1,000 GYO teachers by 2016. As the participants debated thorny issues such as candidate attrition and the inability to add new consortia or GYO candidates due to lack of funding, some suggested that current consortia recruit candidates with loose or nonexistent ties to the community but who had a strong commitment to teaching in urban schools. Others argued that this means of increasing candidate numbers would violate the spirit and purpose of GYO Illinois.

The discussions presented in these two examples illustrate that GYO participant institutions bring differing philosophical commitments to the work. In many settings, these comments go unchallenged. Given the vision of GYO, should each consortium define, within the context of the GYO theoretical frame, how they see the work of their consortium? Without these discussions, one can logically question whether a true partnership exists, whether the key elements of GYO will be lost, and whether there will be lasting change in the teacher education programs should state funds for GYO no longer exist.

One promise of GYO is that COE faculty and CBO staff members learn together as they jointly prepare teachers for challenged communities. As philosophy becomes practice, the results of ongoing lessons should manifest themselves in a reexamination and revision of teacher preparation programs that are more closely aligned with community needs and priorities. Without commitment to the goals of GYO, it could end up as another program whose promise goes unfulfilled, the valuable partnerships between CBOs and COEs lost, and the lessons learned from GYO never realized in teacher preparation programs nor manifested in local communities.

BUILDING DEEP COLLABORATIVE STRUCTURES

The second hurdle we face as a group is the challenge of creating the type of "inside collaboration" or consortia togetherness necessary to building capacity for the type of continuous improvement that Fullan (1999) has described. This type of deep collaboration may not be understood in the same way or desired by all. For example, in one NEIU GYO consortium, each partner hired program coordinators without the input of the other, despite our having openly discussed the necessity of working together. Ironically, after each partner hired a person who was not a good fit for GYO, we collaboratively hired a person—who was not a good fit for our consortium! The difference was that the third time, we both owned the error and collaborated to rectify the situation. Finally, working together on a new hire, we got it right.

In two of our GYO projects, we have begun to discuss the idea of deep collaboration and consider what this might look like in practice if we are to call each other partners. Fleshing this out in each consortium entails exploring and mining the expertise of other members; learning about and acknowledging the social, political, economic, and bureaucratic landscape of each partner; and helping each other navigate that terrain to accomplish our goals. We must jointly own our problems and work together toward solutions.

Building deep collaborative structures is no easy task. Teacher education programs have often utilized the resources of various CBOs in addressing the school-community connection issue (see Boyle-Baise, 2005). Scholarly literature abounds with lessons learned in such collaborations, generally exhorting the university personnel to consider the needs and perspectives of the people in the community. CBOs have a long history of advocating for reform in urban schools but rarely have their efforts evolved into partnerships with traditional, university-based teacher educators (Mediratta, Shah, & McAlister, 2009). A search of the literature turned up no examples of CBOs and COEs working closely on a project like GYO. Despite considerable attention paid to the partnership between the Logan Square Neighborhood Association (LSNA) and CSU (Gold, Simon, Brown, Blanc, Pickron-Davis, Brown, & Navarez-La Torre, 2002; Skinner, 2005; Warren, 2005) the collaborative aspect of this work remains unexplored.

In order to effect change, the work of GYO must develop what Michael Fullan (1999) calls "collaborative cultures for complex teaching" (p. 33). Fullan's work focuses on what occurs inside of schools and districts, but he also calls for "deep inside collaboration" to connect to "deep outside collaboration" (p. 33), which offers an appropriate parallel. GYO consortia must create "Collaborative cultures to 1) foster diversity while trust-building, 2) provoke anxiety and contain it, 3) engage in knowledge creation, 4) combine connectedness with openness, and 5) fuse the spiritual, political, and intellectual" (Fullan, p. 37). Already evident in some GYO consortia, ideally these key tenets would manifest themselves throughout GYO. A continuum of collaboration currently exists, with some consortia developing close reciprocal partnerships while others appear to operate with fewer connections. It is hard work to build deep collaborative structures. All consortia across GYO might consider asking what effective collaboration looks like and focus on supporting consortia to develop such structures.

BUILDING TRUST

GYO Illinois ramped up quickly, moving from planning to implementation within a year. The rapid pace came at the expense of key elements that may have been assumed or bypassed in order to form consortia and recruit candidates. CBOs and COEs have traditionally operated fairly autonomously, the former working primarily outside of the system and the latter working within a complex bureaucracy. Each entity typically enjoys local control over operations and has developed a range of expertise in specific areas. Bringing two such groups together is bound to be fraught with issues of trust. Indeed, the authors of the report *Strong Neighborhoods, Strong Schools: The Indicators Project on Educational Organizing* (Gold et al., 2002) argue that one point of frustration for community organizers is that their work is largely invisible to outsiders. One reason for this is that "many educators see urban communities as part of the problem. Second, public officials and professional educators who actually carry out the program for which the community organizing groups campaigned, end up receiving the credit" (p. 9).

If the GYO organizers fear that university partners will claim credit for their work, or if the university partners see the CBOs as part of the community's problem, then trust is immediately undercut. For example, at one meeting, a university administrator referred to the community organizers' work as "rabble-rousing" as opposed to advocating for equity. At another meeting, one CBO spoke at length about their project as if the CBO were working alone. Ultimately, the university partner reminded the organizer that the university, too, was part of the process and deserved to be acknowledged as a partner.

Unless we find a way to see GYO as "our" work, and together decon-struct the issues that are inherent in our assumptions about the other, we will not build a foundation of trust. Currently, many consortia exist as loosely coupled entities where CBO and COE personnel have varying degrees of knowledge about each other. At almost every statewide meeting, incorrect assumptions, inaccurate statements, and patterns of behavior surface, signi-fying our continued entrenchment in the general practices of our respective organizations. If transparency is lacking, if democratic decision-making is not practiced, and if we cannot find a way to interrogate the beliefs, prac-tices, and assumptions of each other in a just and humane manner, we com-promise our ability to transform the status quo and we risk perpetuating a business as usual model.

BUILDING CROSS-ORGANIZATIONAL EXPERTISE

The promise of GYO as a school reform effort lies, in part, in the potential to transform teacher development through the collaboration between candidates, parents, school personnel, CBOs, and COEs. Each group of partners brings significant expertise to the table that other partners need, but success depends on the willingness of the partners to demonstrate the basic characteristics of a good community organizer and a good teacher (Alinsky, 1971; Fullan, 1999), the ability to listen to, teach, and learn from each other. Building cross-organi-zational expertise is not possible without these sensibilities.

Early in GYO, several organizers voiced the sentiment that traditional teacher educators did not know how to prepare teachers for urban schools. They reasoned that if we did, high-need schools would be populated by community-oriented teachers even if those teachers did not live in the com-munity. NEIU and CSU GYO leaders began meeting regularly with CBO members to share perspectives. We shared teacher education syllabi and dis-cussed our conceptual frames while CBOs shared the theoretical constructs for organizing. Over time, a deep respect for the knowledge and experience of the other took shape.

Working in their respective neighborhoods for decades, community or-ganizers have intimate knowledge about the culture and character of the community. They also have a structure for working with community mem-bers to identify problems, brainstorm solutions, and create a plan of action that involves wide participation. Importantly, they have well-developed po-litical strategies for addressing pressing issues at the highest levels.

Faculty and administrators in COEs bring a wealth of experience in P–12 schools, as teachers and researchers. Professors at NEIU have expertise in working with candidates of color. Our students mirror the GYO population, and we have faced academic hurdles and developed structures for success. Recently, the NEIU GYO staff and candidates met with representatives from a philanthropic organization to discuss our collective work and to describe our scholarly practice in order to potentially secure funding for NEIU GYO. The organization knew of GYO from its inception but had dismissed it as a possibility for grant-making because the CBO that approached them had no track record with university partners. As one graduating teacher candidate described her commitment to the community, the funding possibilities took shape. In this instance, our university work provided a sense of legitimacy for the partnership with the CBO, whose work had been derided during the 2008 presidential election. Together, we can be a force for change.

CAPITALIZING ON THE PROMISES OF GYO— DOING IT BETTER TOGETHER

The GYO model has the potential to significantly alter traditional, university-based teacher education in ways that have not historically been documented. For example, while innovations such as Teacher Corps (Corwin, 1973) and Training Tomorrow's Teachers (Gamble, 1989) attempted to address the need to train teachers in the community, such models were implemented separately from what was happening in the traditional teacher education programs at the institutions where they took place. As a result, only vestiges of the programs remained once funding disappeared. Traditional preparation programs have never truly embraced community-based teacher education. The successful model developed by the LSNA with CSU provides convincing evidence that such partnerships can result in a pipeline of community-based teachers. Even at CSU, however, GYO remained separate from the regular teacher education programs.

GYO began with a vision of a one-way program, recruiting neighborhood-based candidates for teacher certification. Yet, at the current pace, GYO will not be able to produce the number of teachers necessary to have a significant impact on neighborhood schools for quite some time. But in the process of collaboration in our own consortia, the CBOs have found justice-oriented teacher educators, and we have found allies in the struggle to prepare all candidates as excellent teachers for the children who need them most. We have learned that we can implement GYO while simultaneously and collaboratively developing a wider vision for the education of teachers through the partnership between our COE and the CBOs. Our work is shaping a new vision of teacher preparation based on the institutionalization of aspects of the GYO model, especially embracing the COE-CBO partnership in teacher development.

What are the benefits of GYO if we never get beyond the model as designed? GYO provides NEIU with outstanding candidates who teach professors and peers as much as they learn from them. Although we tire of assuring funders and legislators that our GYO candidates meet the same rigorous standards that all of NEIU's teacher candidates must meet, we revel in their accomplishments on the campus and in the community. Our candidates are on the dean's list, in honor societies, and members of academic research communities. They can just as easily testify before a congressional panel or speak at a political rally as they can successfully teach 3rd-graders. In other words, our collaboration is resulting highly skilled, socially responsible, and politically active teachers who know how to advocate for their students.

GYO has created a space for new relationships that enable all of the partners to work more effectively. Together, we have affected high-level policy discussions, challenged state education department mandates, and provided each other with a renewing sense of support when the work seemed overwhelming. GYO has forced us to co-create a data system, curricula, assessments, and innovative practices. It has demonstrated the potential for building a model of teacher education that balances the acquisition of bonding social capital with bridging social capital (Putnam, 2000) to develop the strongest possible teachers for the schools that need them the most.

THE PROMISE OF GYO: THE SOUTHWEST ORGANIZING PROJECT (SWOP) AND THE NEIU COE

In 2006, NEIU began a GYO partnership with SWOP, a CBO that is part of a 28-member coalition whose work takes place on the southwest side of Chicago in the Chicago Lawn/Marquette Park neighborhood. SWOP's community development work focuses on anti-violence, education, housing, immigration, and leadership development. Together, Executive Director Jeff Bartow and I began addressing the four essential components of a successful COE-CBO partnership that were described earlier: building commitment, trust, deep collaborative structures, and cross-organizational expertise.

Our work with SWOP can be seen as a developing example of what is possible. Placed within the framework described by Murrell (2001) in *The Community Teacher: A New Framework for Effective Urban Teaching*, our work speaks directly to the nine suggested perspectives for effective school-university collaboration. Each of the perspectives will be described through examples of our work with SWOP:

- Quality of education
- Collaborative, multilateral partnership

- Positionality
- Community development agenda
- Scholar-teacher
- Relationships over bureaucracy
- Expanded roles
- Community as a network of relationships
- Joint responsibility and accountability

Although Murrell (2001) does not specifically address the CBO-COE possibilities, his proposed qualities aptly depict what a successful GYO consortium might look like. Our partnership with SWOP, though a work in progress, embodies parts of all nine aspects. Each year, we work to deepen and strengthen our commitment to each other and to the goals of GYO.

A "quality of education" perspective requires that we build "a conception of quality education formed from the perspectives of the communities, students, and families" (Murrell, 2001, p. 29) that each project is intended to serve. SWOP has created an education team comprised of representatives from each of their education-related programs. Members include principals, faith-based partners, parent mentors, GYO candidates, NEIU GYO faculty and staff, and SWOP staff. The group meets every other month to discuss education issues at the individual school level as well as the local, state, and national levels. Immigration, foreclosure, safety, and violence prevention are as intertwined in our discussions as they are in the educational arena.

A "collaborative, multilateral partnership" perspective recognizes, "partnership formation that is open not only to community constituencies—parents and parent organizations, community agencies that work with the same children, and other stakeholders—but also to conjoint collaboration with other institutions and community-based organizations" (Murrell, 2001, p. 30). Adhering to this principle, NEIU participates on the SWOP education team. SWOP holds social, political, and educational events in the community that are attended by the entire constituency noted above. Democratic decision-making processes are used in planning collective actions around key issues. As a result of this work, we have begun to place increasing numbers of non-GYO teacher candidates in the SWOP neighborhood schools. Since a group of NEIU faculty and administrators spent a day with SWOP in January of 2010, this collaborative and multilateral partnership has grown at a rapid pace. We have connected with other SWOP organizers to develop activities for our teacher candidates related to other SWOP work (e.g., afterschool programs, parent mentor training).

A "positionality" perspective ensures that "teachers' work is not simply a matter of acquiring the appropriate skills, techniques, and expertise but also includes being politically reflective and ideologically interpretive"

(Murrell, 2001, p. 31). Our collective work is based on the notion that all teachers, but especially GYO candidates, must be able to learn with and from students and parents in order to be advocates for the community. At NEIU, we believe that you must be politically reflective and ideologically interpretive in context. Building contextual sensibilities requires being deeply embedded in the community in order to understand its strengths, complexities, and possibilities. For example, in the summer of 2009, GYO candidates engaged in a massive rally and phone campaign to regain funding when GYO was drastically cut by the state. Many GYO students participate in the local, state, and national marches for immigration reform. Our candidates are face to face with legislators, fact sheets in hand, on a regular basis. SWOP and NEIU staff discuss these events to ensure that candidates understand the importance of the issues and the implications of their actions for their work in schools and communities.

A "community development agenda" perspective argues for teacher candidates to be grounded in "how to operate within the context of a community development agenda" (Murrell, 2001, p. 31). It is not possible for us at NEIU to be engaged in GYO, which builds a teacher corps for economically distressed communities, without engaging faculty in work that sees community context as part of a larger agenda toward teacher preparation reform. During our January 2010 day in the SWOP neighborhood to launch a community development agenda in the COE, NEIU faculty and staff started the day in a SWOP partner elementary school, where we joined teachers and parents in working on the Parents as Partners component of their 2010–2011 School Improvement Plan. We visited two more schools, one in which SWOP helped to open a comprehensive health-care center. Additionally, we visited the Inner City Muslim Action Network, where we heard about the organization's community projects. Throughout the day, SWOP director Jeff Bartow oriented the faculty and staff to the interconnected issues of foreclosure, immigration reform, and violence and their impact on neighborhood schools. Our GYO candidates contributed their personal perspectives on and experience with each issue.

Through our work with SWOP, we understand that Murrell's typology is limited. Unless we actively involve our teacher candidates and our faculty and staff with issues related to the community, they will never truly learn to work as full partners in the schools. As a result of that day, the faculty and staff attendees have spearheaded a movement to develop a four-pronged plan for our work in the COE that includes: (1) the creation of a GYO fund through the NEIU Foundation supporting scholarships and continued community-based work, (2) a panel presentation by faculty and community participants in the SWOP day with a concomitant critical examination of all COE curricula for the ways in which home-school-community connections are addressed, (3) the development of a set of expertise exchange opportunities, and (4) plans to organize a similar trip to another GYO neighborhood in the fall of 2010.

A community development agenda is not something that can be espoused by the CBO or a few faculty if we are to reform traditional teacher education. It is an agenda that must be embraced as a COE priority. Our visit to the SWOP area was a jump-start to this process.

A "scholar-teacher" perspective includes "visioning and developing a new kind of teacher for effectively meeting the challenges of successful work in urban schools and communities in the 21st century" (Murrell, 2001, p. 32). To ensure that our GYO program reflects a Scholar-Activist-Teacher perspective, SWOP and NEIU overtly share expertise and demonstrate the spirit of collaboration and reflection to our candidates. SWOP shares in, while NEIU takes primary responsibility for, ensuring that all of the candidates meet high academic standards. Likewise, NEIU shares in; while SWOP takes primary responsibility for engaging the candidates in a critical analysis of community issues and activist work around those issues. Examples abound. One SWOP candidate, a secondary mathematics major, accompanied me to Washington, D.C., to testify at a congressional briefing about the power of GYO. Three SWOP candidates addressed NEIU faculty about their route to GYO during our day in their neighborhood. Several men of color excelling academically spoke of the power of GYO to transform not only their lives, but the lives of their families. Because SWOP and COE staffs each operate from a similar philosophical base, the teacher candidates understand that scholar activist is a synonym for teacher.

A "relationships over bureaucracy" perspective describes "a patently antibureaucratic mode of operation among partners that permits flexibility of collaboration and involves all stakeholders in the enterprise of educating and developing children" (Murrell, 2001, p. 32). Relationship-building through communication and shared experiences is a cornerstone of community organizing (Alinsky, 1971). When Jeff Bartow approached me to begin working with SWOP, he visited NEIU to begin the process of understanding each other on a personal, philosophical level. From here, we have engaged our respective staffs in the same type of ongoing communication. The university and the state board of education may always be "patently bureaucratic" places, but we believe strongly in being flexible, collaborative, and humane in our interactions, always quick to remember why we are engaged in the work together. One such example occurred when the Chicago Public Schools mandated that all student teachers apply for positions in the district. A Social Security number was required on the application. This meant that any student teacher who was undocumented may be forbidden to student-teach in CPS or would be too intimidated to apply. I tried to get the policy changed by first using a traditional route, polite discussion. Meeting resistance, I did what my CBO colleagues would have done. I wrote a letter to then CEO Arne Duncan and copied every Latino Illinois legislator. Prior to sending the letter, I shared it with my CBO colleagues to solicit their advice. Jeff came to me privately and said, "Maureen, this is a very good letter and I am behind you 100%, but is there any chance that you could be fired from the university for sending this letter because we will find another way rather than lose you." For Jeff and for SWOP, relationships always trump bureaucracy.

An "expanded roles" perspective requires a "public, community-oriented, and child-focused approach to building partnerships, essential to the project of developing an urban-focused, equity-minded, diversity-responsive, and inquiry-based professional relationship" (Murrell, 2001, p. 33). Our own perspectives in this vein are taking shape, particularly as we work to involve the entire COE. In addition to our four-pronged plan for continued work in the area of home-school-community involvement, we have engaged in parallel activities related to the day-to-day needs of the children and families in the SWOP neighborhoods. Our student Illinois Education Association chapter held a school supply drive for the SWOP schools. At the holidays, the COE faculty provides gifts and food for several families selected by SWOP. We have been witness to the community's devastation as the wish lists changed from items such as toys and gifts for the children to those that many of us take for granted: pot, pans, towels, and toiletries. The seriousness of our work hit home recently when the 18-year-old son of one of our families was shot on the street. Our faculty responded with financial and personal support.

We now place significant numbers of our non-GYO pre-service students in SWOP schools, negotiating with principals to place some of our most promising teacher candidates with their most talented teachers. In these settings, the SWOP GYO teacher candidates are the experts, orienting their peers to the community and its issues. Faculty provide workshops and school and community members are involved in events at NEIU. Thus, our expanded roles continue to evolve and deepen.

A "community as a network of relationships" perspective emphasizes that "what really cements the partnership between school personnel and nonschool personnel is building community through actual physical presence in the schools . . . the measure of our success as agents for change... is our capacity to learn in the company of others" (Murrell, 2001, p. 33). Not only do NEIU GYO leaders sit on the SWOP education team, we also have now engaged in a partnership to extend the collaborative work between the COE faculty and the SWOP network of school and community activists. Faculty members from three different departments connect with

SWOP staff, the parent who leads the parent mentoring program, the school principals, and community leaders. Professors return to the schools, sharing expertise with parents and teachers. Community leaders come to campus to share expertise with faculty and pre-service teachers, and our non-GYO teacher candidates can seek early field experiences in programs sponsored by SWOP.

A "joint responsibility and accountability" perspective requires that "responsibility and accountability be shared by all members of the partnership" (Murrell, 2001, p. 33). All partners, including candidates, attend SWOP Steering Committee meetings. The purpose of these meetings is to organize and share data for the state and to monitor candidate progress. We review the budget and lay out short- and long-term plans. We share perspectives on issues, brainstorm solutions to problems, and update each other on work outside of GYO. We have become each other's biggest advocates and serve as sources of support for our collective practice. For example, when two otherwise outstanding candidates stopped showing up for GYO events, we called them in for a conference. Their rationale was that they were far ahead of their peers, they were busy, and they didn't see the need to help others. After a lengthy discussion, the candidates left, but the GYO partners stayed to discus our need to do a better job of collectively fostering the notion of reaching back while moving forward, a foundational aspect of GYO. Indeed, jointly responsible for all aspects of GYO, we are accountable not only to a state agency, but also, and more importantly, to each other.

These ways in which our work approximates Murrell's (2001) nine characteristics of collaboration only begin the process of building a program that is not only good for GYO teacher candidates, but also good for all prospective teachers. We are a work in progress, but the web of connections that are developing with SWOP provides hope and possibility in justice-oriented, community-based teacher education.

CONCLUSION: BECOMING A FORCE WHEN WE'RE TOGETHER

GYO has committed to provide the state with a specific number of teachers in the coming years. That 4 years of funding have produced only about two dozen graduates underscores the time and commitment required to grow our own teachers. Through building and institutionalizing collaborative structures in GYO, NEIU intends to create a program that will benefit all of our candidates. We want every graduate, teacher, principal, counselor, and reading specialist to leave NEIU having gained the perspectives and commitment of insiders, even if they do not work in GYO communities. Although we know that our GYO candidates will be strong teachers for their communities, we expect our non-GYO candidates to bring the sense of community and the collective responsibility for everyone's children wherever they teach. It was then-Senator Barack Obama who moved the 2004 Democratic Convention crowd with his words, "If there's a child on the South Side of Chicago who can't read, it matters to me, even if it is not my child. . . . It is that fundamental belief that I am my brother's keeper, I am my sister's keeper that makes this country work." This fundamental belief should drive the education of all of our candidates.

Our work with SWOP and the other CBO personnel in GYO programs at NEIU has shown us the promise of the GYO teachers model. As our partnerships grow and deepen, everyone involved is beginning to expand their vision and see the possibilities for a radically different type of community-based COE. Many see the intimate and complex relationship between the school, the community, and the university in a way that is far beyond anything that the organizers of GYO most likely had in mind when they conceptualized the program.

Commitment to the tenets of GYO requires adherence to the principles of effective community organizing and excellent teaching in urban schools. How does GYO ensure that the relationships, structures, and processes are in place to maintain successful and sustainable partnerships in each of the consortia so that the work lives on past any financial or bureaucratic impediments that arise? Barber and Fullan (2005) warn that reformers can easily fall into the trap of investing a lot of money into a project absent the capacity for implementation. Given GYO's reliance on state funds and the challenging economic times, we need to be vigilant about balancing speed and capacity to ensure the lasting success of this promising model.

REFERENCES

Alinsky, S. (1946). *Reveille for radicals*. New York: Random House.

Alinsky, S. (1971). *Rules for radicals*. New York: Random House.

Barber, M., & Fullan, M. (2005). Tri-level development. *Education Week, (24)25*, 32–35.

Boyle-Baise, L. (2005). Preparing community oriented teachers. *Journal of Teacher Education, 56*(5), 446–458.

Corwin, R. (1973). *Reform and organizational survival*. New York: John Wiley & Sons.

Darling-Hammond, L. (2010). *The flat world and education*. New York: Teachers College Press.

Fullan, M. G. (1999). *Change forces*. New York: Routledge.

Gamble, M. (1989). Educating for inner-city schools: Hunter College's field-based training tomorrow's teachers program. In J. DeVitis & P. Sola (Eds.), *Building bridges for educational reform.* Ames, IA: State University Press.

Gold, E., Simon, E., Brown, C., Blanc, S., Pickron-Davis, M., Brown, J., & Navarez-La Torre, A. (2002). *Strong neighborhoods, strong schools.* Chicago: Cross City Campaign for Urban School Reform.

Hill, D., & Gillette, M. (2005). Teachers for tomorrow in urban schools. *Multicultural Perspectives, 7*(3), 42–50.

Illinois Association of Deans of Public Colleges of Education (IADPCE). (2009). *Teacher graduate assessment.* Macomb, IL: Author.

Illinois Board of Higher Education. (2010). *Illinois higher education enrollments and degrees systems.* Retrieved February 10, 2010, from http://www.ibhe.org/EnrollmentsDegrees/

Mediratta, K., Shah, S., & McAlister, S. (2009). *Community organizing for stronger schools.* Cambridge, MA: Harvard University Press.

Murrell, P. (2001). *The community teacher.* New York: Teachers College Press.

Obama, B. Keynote Address, The 2004 Democratic National Convention. Retrieved August 30, 2004, from http://www.pbs.org/newshour/vote2004/demconvention/speeches/obama.html

Payne, C. (2008). *So much reform, so little change.* Cambridge, MA: Harvard Education Press.

Putnam, R. (2000). *Bowling alone.* New York: Simon and Schuster.

Skinner, E. (2005). *Latinas in higher education: Learning from their experiences.* Unpublished doctoral dissertation, University of Illinois at Chicago.

Warren, M. (2005). Communities and schools: A new view of urban education reform. *Harvard Educational Review, 75*(2), 133–173.

13

Developing Powerful
Teaching and Learning

Grow Your Own Teachers Within the
National Educational Reform Context

LINDA DARLING-HAMMOND

I'm delighted to be here, because I love Grow Your Own for all the things you represent and all the things you do. What you do is bring a critical pipeline of great people into teaching, into the schools where they're most needed. What you represent, in addition, is the power of community, the possibilities of transformation for individuals and for organizations, and the potential of creating a new and stronger profession.

This work is both pedagogical work and political work, and it's something I learned when I entered teaching myself. My first student teaching experience was in Camden, New Jersey, before I worked in the Philadelphia area. I learned three things when I began teaching. First of all, I learned that I was underprepared for the challenges of the job that I had to do, as many of us are, because I was teaching high school English, and I didn't know how to teach reading to the students who came to my classroom unable to read. I didn't know how to work with English language learners (ELLs) who were in my classroom. I was unprepared to work with students with special education needs. I could go on.

The work of teaching is so incredibly complex, and the charge of preparing teachers is a sacred trust. To be sure that teachers have all of the tools that they need to be able to do an excellent job from the day they start in the classroom is something that we owe every person in this country who takes on this important work. And, unfortunately, in this country we drop the ball on that charge many, many times over. The U.S. practice is very different from high-achieving nations elsewhere. If you were coming into teaching in Finland or Singapore, you would go into a 3- or 4-year teacher education program completely at government expense with a salary or stipend while you train. And then, you would go into the profession earning as much as an engineer or more. In Singapore, you would earn as much as a beginning doctor in government service. You would then have extensive mentoring on the job, and 15 to 25 hours a week in your teaching day to collaborate, plan, work, and learn with other teachers to polish your craft. I don't even have to tell you the contrasting side of the story in the United States. But the efforts that Grow Your Own is making to really create a strong preparation pipeline are beginning to point in a new direction.

The second thing I learned when I was teaching in big, urban, comprehensive high schools is that such schools are not designed to allow teachers to care effectively for their students or to be accountable for what actually happens to them. I found I could create a little oasis in my classroom, but I could not have any effect on what happened to students when they left my classroom. I didn't plan and organize teaching with other teachers who shared my students. We didn't have the context within which we could be truly accountable.

I learned that lesson when I was working with a student who had failed his classes the year before—I had the students who failed English the year before because who else would you give them to but a beginning teacher?—and I finally got this young man writing. His writing was so tiny, you could barely read it; I had to use a magnifying glass. I think there must be a psychological interpretation of that handwriting. It turned out he was brilliant. He had a lot to say when he finally got working. We were really beginning to make headway, and then he stopped coming to class. When I tried to figure out where he was, I finally found out that he'd been expelled for using drugs, and nobody had even bothered to tell me. The teacher is just a cog in that big wheel of the urban comprehensive high school. I realized then that we had to transform schools so that teachers can care effectively for their students.

The third thing that I learned was that we have great inequalities in access to resources for our schools. At that time, Camden's per-pupil expenditures were about half of what they were in Princeton, South Brunswick, and other New Jersey suburbs. There were very few books in the book room, large classes, underprepared teachers, and all the other suboptimal conditions that we know about in urban schools. That was 1973. It is over 35 years later later, and we are still struggling with these conditions. So this work is both pedagogical, and it is political.

My work over the subsequent years has really been about creating teacher education programs, schools, and school funding systems that get us to a place where we can offer students what they need. And we're not yet making as much progress as we need to make. The two schools that I have co-founded were both community-rooted. One was called the Children's Community School, and it was a parent-teacher collaborative. The other is East Palo Alto Academy High School in a community that had lost its high school during desegregation in 1975. At that time, it was an all-Black community; all the students were bused out, two-thirds of them were not graduating. We put a school back in the community, training teachers there so that we could demonstrate that in collaboration with community, you can create another reality both for individual students and then, gradually, for the community as a whole. So it's very important, this work you're doing that puts communities at the core.

Communities in this country start at schools. When I was in Philadelphia, I saw how busy the Quakers and the other Founding Fathers were in creating schools. There are more schools and colleges than you can shake a stick at in that small area from Center City to Swarthmore. But creating schools to serve the needs of different communities has often involved substantial commitment and struggle on the part of the people. In the South, schools for enslaved people were started by communities of those people in cabins in the woods, where people would come at night, having to risk capture and awful punishment just to get an education. Teachers and communities of people came together. Teachers were of the people and worked with the community to create education. In all of the lawsuits leading up to Brown v. Board of Education, it was teachers working with lawyers and community members who brought the cases, who collected the data, who figured out the strategies to work toward equitable education. So what you are doing here to develop teachers for the community comes from a long line of struggle and a long line of progress.

THE IMPORTANCE OF GOOD TEACHERS

Strong preparation and a strong profession are needed because, as you know, good teaching cannot be teacher-proofed. Teaching is not just opening up children's brains and dumping little facts in, and having them come out on a test. Students have their own ideas. They have their own experiences. There is no one lecture or instructional packet that will ensure that students learn. They come to school with their own ideas and they try to make sense of the information that we give them. They filter through it, and this produces sometimes unpredictable results. What great teachers do is figure out where students are, and they take them where they want them to go.

Great teachers help students learn to very high levels, but it is a torturous process between here and there. Moreover, we know that the challenges of 21st-century teaching are much greater than they were in the 20th century. We have a greater need for education in society. Seventy percent of jobs now are knowledge-work jobs. That proportion was only 5% back in the early 1900s when we invented the schools that we're still trying to operate today. Teachers are being called up to help most students learn the kind of thinking curriculum that used to be rationed to only 5 or 10% of students who were selected into gifted-and-talented programs or honors programs. The rest of the students were just supposed to learn the basics. Now we're trying to teach that kind of curriculum to virtually all of our children. There are now much higher standards for learning, and much more diverse students. We have had waves of immigration in the last couple of decades. Because of the success of public education, students with special education needs are now entitled to more education. We are trying to keep students in school longer, and that diverse set of needs means that teachers cannot just get through the book. They have to figure out how to teach every child. And, of course, we're expecting a great deal more of schools to ensure success.

It used to be that the job of a teacher was just to get through the curriculum. Now the job is actually to produce high levels of learning—a very different mission for schools. Yet we're still struggling to redesign schools to achieve this mission of teaching for understanding and teaching for diversity. This mission means teachers need deeper and more flexible content knowledge. You not only have to know the subject in the way that you've learned it with one way of doing things, but you have to be able, when the students come up with something, to figure out how to relate what they know to the broader content they're trying to learn. All of teaching and learning is embedded in language, so teachers have to know a lot about language and literacy development, both for first- and second-language learners. Teachers need greater capacity to diagnose learning strategies and needs. You have to be able to figure out how are students learning—How does Paolo understand this material? Where is Katie in terms of her readiness for this skill?—and build pedagogies that will allow them to get from where they are to where they need to be. Teaching requires more sophisticated scaffolding of learning and more individualized support. It's a more and more challenging job.

And we know from a lot of research that one of the most important determiners of student learning is teachers' knowledge and skills. Ronald Ferguson (1991) did a study back in 1991 called "New Evidence on How and Why Money Matters" to combat the common argument that money doesn't matter. I always wondered, when that claim is made, if money doesn't matter, why don't rich people want to give it up? Why don't the people who send their students to private schools that spend more than $20,000 per pupil think that they could do just as well on $8,000 per pupil? We really ought to ask that question.

Ferguson found that the most important schooling input is teachers and that money matters, especially when you spend it on highly skilled teachers. As Figure 13.1 shows, about 40% of the explained variation in student learning outcomes in his study was attributed to teacher qualifications—in this case, teacher education, experience, and licensing examination scores. Class size also made a difference, while home and family factors accounted for about half of the variation. Basically, the moral of the study was that the core building blocks of achievement were teachers who know what they're doing in settings where they know the students well. All the other special programs we create to make up for the lack of skilled teaching are like barnacles on the side of a ship. If you don't have teachers who know what they're doing, working in settings where they know the students well, you then need to create all kinds of dropout prevention programs, truancy prevention programs, compensatory education programs, remedial education programs, and summer school programs because the school didn't make the right investments in skilled, personalized teaching in the first place.

Figure 13.1. Variation in Student Learning Outcomes

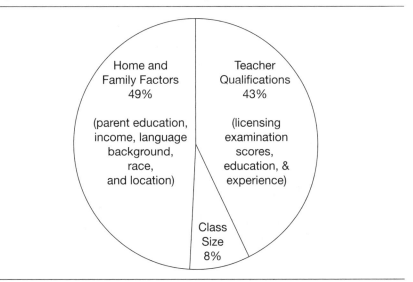

Source: National Commission on Teaching & America's Future (1997).
Note: Developed from data presented in R. F. Ferguson (1991).

THE INEQUITABLE DISTRIBUTION OF TEACHERS

The other thing Ferguson found is that if teachers were equitably distributed to children in Texas, the Black-White achievement score gap would have been almost entirely erased.

However, teachers are one of the most inequitably distributed school resources in state after state. This inequity has been clear in my service as an expert witness in many school finance lawsuits from South Carolina to New York, Massachusetts, and California. As Figure 13.2 shows, in California, at the time of the Williams v. California lawsuit, the probability of students getting teachers who were not fully prepared and credentialed was about five times higher in segregated minority schools and in high-poverty schools than it was in predominantly White, more affluent schools (Shields, Humphrey, Wechsler, Riel, Tiffany-Morales, Woodworth, Young, & Price, 2001).

Among the strategies used to address teacher shortages in such high-need districts has been a range of alternative certification programs, offering varying amounts of preparation for teachers. A study examining these

Figure 13.2. Distribution of Uncertified Teachers by Poverty, Race, and Achievement Levels

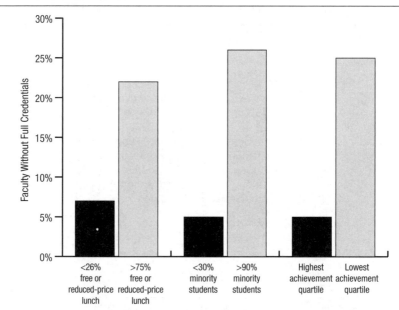

Source: P. Shields et al. (2001).

routes found, as has previous research, that alternative candidates (AC) who were still taking courses while teaching were significantly less effective in both reading and mathematics than their traditional route counterparts (TC) (Constantine, Player, Silva, Hallgren, Grider, & Deke, 2009). Furthermore, the students of teachers from what the study called "low-coursework" alternative programs (AP) actually declined in their reading and math achievement between fall and spring. Students taught by teachers from "high-coursework" programs did better and gained some, and those taught by their traditional route counterparts did better still (see Figure 13.3). Under Race to the Top, policies to expand low-coursework alternative route programs would actually promote more of the least effective entry pathway into teaching.

We need to reconsider the notion that we should address shortages by bringing in people who are underprepared to teach, especially for our highest-need students in our highest-need schools. In the United States, we don't have overall teaching shortages. There are approximately three times as many credentialed teachers in this country as there are jobs. There is, however, a shortage of people who want to work for low salaries under poor working conditions. A lot of people have left teaching because the

Figure 13.3. Fall-to-Spring Test Score Gains/Losses of Students Taught by Alternatively Certified (AC) and Traditionally Certified (TC) Teachers

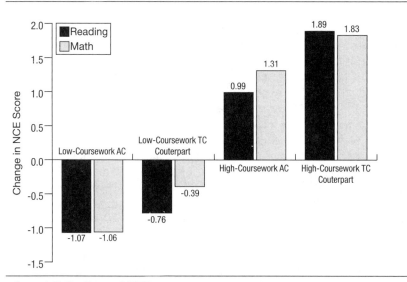

Source: L. Darling-Hammond (2009).

Figure 13.4. U.S. PISA Results, by Subgroup, Compared to OECD Average

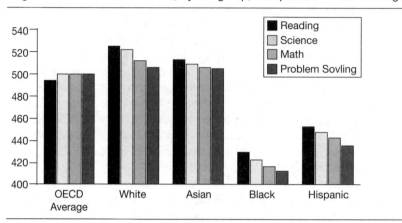

conditions and salaries for teaching are not what they need to be. When you have a situation with unequal funding, unequal salaries, and unequal working conditions, guess what? Underresourced districts have more difficulty attracting and retaining teachers. We know that those who have more experience past the first couple of years are more effective, and that those who have more training are more able to meet the needs of the wide range of students who are right there in that classroom. If we really want to have well-prepared teachers in all schools, then we need to change the incentive structure for teaching and be sure that we're giving people the incentives to come in and stay in a profession.

The consequences of under-education for communities are reflected in the individual and societal costs of high school dropouts. One-third of our students nationally do not graduate from school, and the proportions are over 50% in many low-income communities. Recent dropouts have less than a 50% chance of getting a job; that percentage is less than 20% if the young person is an African American male. And if the young person finds a job, it pays on average less than half of what the same job would have earned 20 years ago, which is not enough to make a living, buy a house, and raise a family. Dropouts cost this country more than $200 billion a year in lost wages, taxes, and social costs. (For a discussion of these issues, see Darling-Hammond, 2010.)

This set of problems is very tightly tied to the school-to-prison pipeline. Eighty percent of inmates are high school dropouts, and most inmates are functionally illiterate. Yet, we are now spending a lot of the money that we should be spending on education in prisons. In fact, corrections costs have increased by 900% while public education costs have increased by 25%. In five states, we are spending more on prisons than on public higher education today. Although the United States is 35th out of 40 top nations in the world in math achievement, and 29th out of 40 in science, we are first in the world in the number of inmates. We have 5% of the world's population and 25% of the world's inmates, and we are creating a bifurcated society primarily because of the way we are inequitably allocating access to good education.

This approach makes no sense in a world in which investing in the education of one's people is the primary route to individual success and to societal success. We cannot sustain a democratic society with our current investment pattern. One of the underrecognized realities is that inequality of investment in education strongly influences those low U.S. rankings. White and Asian students on average are reading, doing science, and achieving in mathematics at levels at or above the OECD country average (see Figure 13.4). However, African American and Hispanic students are doing so much less well that it drives the entire national ranking down. These inequalities in outcomes are associated with the unequal allocation of resources (Darling-Hammond, 2010).

Clearly, we need to equalize resources for schools serving students of color and staff them with well-prepared teachers who plan to stay in the community, like those being developed through the Grow Your Own program.

DEVELOPING EXPERT INSTRUCTION

The key question is how we ultimately improve the quality of teaching, so that all students can experience high-quality instruction. In the 20th century, most people thought of teaching as basically knowing a lot of content and saying it out loud so that students could learn it. Of course, we now know much more from research about what effective teaching really is. A lot of this research is summarized in the National Research Council's book, *How People Learn* (Bransford, Brown, & Cocking, 1999) and in the National Academy of Education's *Preparing Teachers for a Changing World* (Darling-Hammond & Bransford, 2005).

We know that effective teachers organize active learning. Students are actively engaged in applying their knowledge so that they can use it and make sense of it. Effective teachers not only use a wide variety of teaching strategies, but they know when to use what strategies for what purposes and for which students to ensure learning.

One of our perennial problems in the United States is the series of recurring curriculum wars. Fighting these wars takes a lot of time and effort that we don't need to be spending on unproductive squabbles. For example, in the reading wars, there is a fight about whether to emphasize phonics or whole-language teaching. In mathematics, the debate has been over learning math facts or learning mathematics for reasoning and comprehension. Yet, every great teacher knows that one has to do both—that a teacher has to build the capacity for students to decode text and also has to give them a rich literacy environment in which they're reading real books and talking about them, getting excited about them, writing, and so on. A good teacher knows how to manage the classroom so that students who need certain kinds of supports get those things, and so that students meanwhile have an environment in which they are always making meaning of texts and concepts, and using their minds in creative ways.

The curriculum wars stem from the assumption that teachers can't be trusted to make decisions about when and how to use different strategies for students. Policymakers then often decree a single approach: "Everybody is going to do phonics and only phonics." When that is not enough, the pendulum swings back and the next policy mandates: "Stop doing that. Now we're all going to do whole language." And then, when that by itself isn't enough, we zigzag back again. Instead, we should be saying, "Let's understand what great teachers do. They have a toolkit. They know how to use it. They can use expert judgment about how to apply these skills in the classroom." In order to do this, we have to put knowledge in the hands of teachers, not decide that somebody way up at the top of the system is going to make decisions and hand them down to teachers to be implemented as though they were robots.

Effective teachers know how to assess student learning continuously and adapt teaching to student needs. One of the wonderful findings of international research on formative assessment is that when teachers are continually paying attention to how students learn as well as what they know (this means looking at student work and listening to students talk, not just looking at 2-digit scores), when teachers give effective feedback that students can act upon, some of the strongest learning gains of any intervention in education can occur. We need teachers to know not just how to give grades at the end of the unit or the year, but how to assess continuously how students are learning in the context of ambitious tasks: for example, undertaking scientific investigations, writing research papers, developing mathematical models and tools. Students then need the opportunity to get feedback and revise this challenging work.

This is actually one of the most important things to produce equitable outcomes. Every classroom will have students who come to it with different kinds of experience and prior knowledge that they can share with one another. That variability is just a fact of life: The imaginary model classroom where every student is learning in the same way at the same pace at the same time is never going to happen, has never yet happened, and is not going to happen in the future—and teachers need to be able to deal with that. But students can learn at high levels if they have the opportunity to undertake a challenging task with clear guidance and scaffolding, and if they receive feedback from peers with a rubric so that they can see what the standards are, and then attempt it again with the idea that revision is always expected. This is how human beings learn: We learn by trying and revising and trying again.

When we teach in this way, we can get to a higher standard and begin to close the achievement gap. The students who are already doing well will do even better with these opportunities, while the students who started with less experience will improve at an even faster pace, because they've had the chance to figure out this new material with help and the opportunity to try and retry. We need to figure out strategies both for teaching and curriculum that allow for those clear standards, constant feedback, and opportunities for revising work.

Finally, effective teachers know how to create and manage a collaborative classroom in a way that students can learn with each other; they know how to respect and start from student experiences in building instruction; they know how to scaffold instruction and activate multiple intelligences; and they know how to create a psychologically safe, secure environment so students can explore and learn from their mistakes. They help students build both their competence and their confidence; this is why students' opportunities to get feedback and to revise their work are so important. Students need to build the notion that "if I put forth more effort, with guidance I will become more competent." If you think about an Olympic skater or a musician, or anyone engaged in a complex performance, she will try something—that triple axle for instance—and, perhaps, might fall on her behind. Now, is the coach going to say, "That's a D minus. We're moving on to the next thing"? No! He's going to say, "Here's what you need to try to do. Try it again, and try it this way, or that way." What you get is not a failure experience but a learning experience that eventually translates into competence and confidence. We have to figure out how to do that in the classroom as well.

What guides the practices of equitable teachers? It is not just the technical competence of the teacher but also how the teacher relates to the child, the family, and the community. That is one of the things that is so important in the work that you're doing here with Grow Your Own teachers. How do we see the child? Is this our child or some other person's child? Do we see the child as marginal or as a central member of the community? What is our stance toward the child and the family? I don't care where you come from, or where you've been, or where you're going, there will always be students who push your buttons. There will be students who are easy for you to teach because you understand their experience and perspective and communication style. Then there will be students who are more challenging. How do we come to a place where we can see, understand, care for that child enough to teach him or her? How do we find the strengths of that child, working in collaboration with the family, so that we can see a child more holistically? How do we find the place from which we can understand this child?

What tools do we have to learn about children's strengths, experiences, and prior knowledge? We need a two-way pedagogy. Teaching is not just talking at the students. It's also learning from students through journals, conversations, opportunities for them to share their experiences, and check-in moments where we say to students, "Let's take some time to hear what's going on with you." Learning from students also occurs when teachers give multi-modal opportunities for students to show what they know and to demonstrate the expertise they are drawing on, so then it can be used in the classroom. We need a lot of tools for this kind of two-way pedagogy. We also need a large repertoire of practices for teaching a wide range of learners and for scaffolding the curriculum. And we need strategies to reinforce the sense of competence and attachment for students in the classroom, and means to attach children to school.

I want to just add a couple of words about the insights that come from the How People Learn (HPL) framework (Bransford, Brown, & Cocking, 1999), regarding what we know about how people learn and what effective teaching is in that context. The HPL framework offers four key elements: Effective classrooms are learner-centered, knowledge-centered, assessment-centered, and community-centered.

In terms of knowledge-centeredness, effective classrooms provide authentic learning opportunities that emphasize using knowledge through research and writing, problem-solving, and experimentation. A well-planned classroom that has these opportunities carefully managed will actually reduce a lot of "discipline problems" that occur when students are bored by tasks that are not meaningful to them, but you have to have the tools and skills to manage an inquiry classroom. Such classrooms feature modeling and demonstrations illustrating what students are being asked to do—and they need to have the opportunity to exhibit understanding and proficiency.

When we first started the high school that I mentioned to you in East Palo Alto, the students who came to us from a very low-income district with a lot of challenges in the schools they had previously attended weren't used to doing work. Many did not do work in class; most did not know how to do homework. It just wasn't part of what they'd experienced before. Part of what we were trying to figure out was how to get the students actually to engage in the work. Ultimately, we developed a project in which students had to do research in the East Palo Alto community; they had to write about it, create a videotape, and bring it to Stanford to present to students and faculty. Then, all of a sudden, everybody did their work. The exhibition became the tool to engage around the work, and then to revise the work, and then to take pride in the work, and then to push the work forward. Those habits could then continue throughout the rest of the high school experience. Authentic work that is exhibited beyond the teacher is part of the magic that's needed to get students engaged and feeling that the knowledge is for them. It's not just for getting a grade; it's not just for getting points; it's actually for becoming an empowered human being.

Effective classrooms are learner-centered. They offer the two-way pedagogy that builds connections to students' lives, experiences, and prior knowledge. They are diagnostic: When there's a problem, teachers ask, "What can we find out? What can we do?" They are culturally responsive. They are aware of what students and families and parents can bring to the learning process. They access the funds of knowledge that Luis Moll and colleagues (1992) talk about, and then they are able to exhibit in many ways that you belong in this classroom, that we are learning about ourselves and each other, and that this is not "somebody else's" school.

Effective classrooms are assessment-centered. I've already talked about the fact that it really needs to emphasize this formative assessment and what I call a culture of revision and redemption. There is always the opportunity to do better, to improve, to succeed, to redeem. That's what's going to get students hooked on learning.

Finally, effective classrooms are community-centered. They create a sense of common mission and co-membership in the classroom. One of the things teachers need to figure out is, "What do I have in common with each of my students?" Teachers need to spend that first week of school (and significant time thereafter) really coming to know their students. What do they care about? What do they do outside of school? Where can I hook into their experiences and relate the curriculum to them? Great teachers know that this is time well spent because they can draw from that bank of knowledge to draw those connections between and among students and with the students to create that co-membership in that classroom.

Teachers have to know a lot about how to manage peer collaboration, because everybody has had bad experiences with group work at one time or another. Just putting students together and saying "do group work" is not a recipe for success. You need a lot of tools to understand how to set group-worthy tasks, to give students roles and teach them how to play those roles, to elicit their participation in ways that are distributed across the group. Of course, that means teaching skills of discourse and mutual support that enable students to become part of the academic community. Then they can connect to the community beyond the classroom in a variety of ways: making sense of the resources that are theirs, connecting to parents, and so on.

Being in and of the community is so important, and it is so much of what Grow Your Own is about. The community in this framework becomes a resource, not an obstacle. All children are our children. They are not "those" children or "other people's" children. They are our children, and we can work and learn in partnership with families. One of the very important things in both in the teacher's toolkit and in the school's toolkit is to have ways to work effectively with families. In the teacher education program that my colleagues and I started in Stanford, one of the things teachers do in their classroom management class is that they have to make positive phone calls home to parents. They need to learn to pick up the phone and say, "It's so great to have Josue in this classroom. Here is what he's doing. I'd like to learn more about what you're thinking, what your goals for him are, what you want me to know about him as a learner, how we're going to work together." Parents usually are shocked when they get a call from a teacher, especially at the high school level, saying, "I want to tell you about what a great kid you have." We usually ask teachers to start with the students who are the most challenging to teach, and to find a positive basis on which to make that phone call home, and to make sure all parents are contacted in the beginning of the year to create that relationship. Sometimes creating these relationships also depends on home visits and parent meetings and conferences, so that teachers and parents can then figure out how to do the work together. This means that if there are issues that come up later, you've got a relationship to build on. It changes everything. Over and over again, parents and teachers say how much this changes the dynamic. And students will say, "Oh my goodness! My teacher called home and said nice things about me." These things create a transformation in that relationship in the classroom.

We also need times for parents, students, and teachers to come together several times a year and talk about the work. In a high school, that may require an advisory system in which a teacher is responsible for about 15 students. In an elementary school, it may be for all of the students. Parents want to talk about their child, and that's how we're going to engage them in the school. They want to come in and they want to have that conversation, not about what your child didn't do and what grades he or she didn't get, but about what we're building on. Here's the work, where do we need to go, how do we get there together?

Finally, I want to stress the importance of creating classroom and professional community. We need to create common ground and a sense of team, which motivates and enables greater success when we work together, both with students in the classroom and with teachers across the profession.

As the old song says, "We all need somebody to lean on," and we need to do that in the sharing of knowledge. Those of you involved in Grow Your Own are creating communities within and across your universities and school contexts and with community-based organizations. I want to close with this notion of community, while acknowledging that this work that we're doing is very, very challenging. It is three steps forward and two steps back. To get where we need to go, we're going to have to figure out how to join hands and take those steps together.

NOTE

This chapter is an edited transcript (by the author) of a speech from the Grow Your Own Statewide Learning Network, November 19, 2009, Chicago.

REFERENCES

Bransford, J. D., Brown, A., & Cocking, R. (Eds.). (1999). *How people learn.* Washington, DC: National Research Council.

Constantine, J., Player, D., Silva, T., Hallgren, K., Grider, M., & Deke, J. (2009). *An evaluation of teachers trained through different routes to certification.* Washington, DC: Mathematica.

Darling-Hammond, L. (2009). *Educational opportunity and alternative certification: New evidence and new questions.* Stanford, CA: Stanford Center for Opportunity Policy in Education.

Darling-Hammond, L. (2010). *The flat world and education.* New York: Teachers College Press.

Darling-Hammond, L., & Bransford, J. (2005). *Preparing teachers for a changing world.* San Francisco: Jossey-Bass.

Ferguson, R. (1991). Paying for public education: New evidence on how and why money matters. *Harvard Journal on Legislation, 28*(2), 465–498.

Moll, L., Amanti, C., Neff, D., & Gonzalez, N. (1992). Funds of knowledge for teaching. *Theory into Practice, 31*(1), 132–141.

National Commission on Teaching and America's Future. (1997). *Doing what matters most: Investing in quality teaching.* New York: Author.

Shields, P., Humphrey, D., Wechsler, M., Riel, L., Tiffany-Morales, J., Woodworth, K., Young, V., & Price, T. (2001). *The status of the teaching profession 2001.* Santa Cruz, CA: The Center for the Future of Teaching and Learning.

About the Contributors

Joanna Brown is lead education organizer for the Logan Square Neighborhood Association and initiated LSNA's first GYO program in 2000.

Linda Darling-Hammond is Charles E. Ducommun Professor of Education at Stanford University.

Maria Teresa Garretón is professor and chair of Teacher Education at Northeastern Illinois University in Chicago.

Maureen D. Gillette is dean of the College of Education at Northeastern Illinois University in Chicago.

Anne Hallett has been director of Grow Your Own Illinois since 2005. For 30 years, she directed three local and national public school advocacy organizations.

Morgan Halstead works with Northeastern Illinois University and Logan Square Neighborhood Association as a coordinator for Grow Your Own Teachers.

Djanna A. Hill is professor of Secondary Education at William Paterson University of New Jersey and directs a "grow your own" urban teacher preparation program.

Soo Hong is assistant professor at Wellesley College and author of *A Cord of Three Strands: Organizing Parents, Schools and Communities for Collective Empowerment.*

Christina L. Madda is assistant professor in the Department of Reading at Northeastern Illinois University in Chicago.

Kathleen McInerney is associate professor at Saint Xavier University, Chicago, IL, and a professor at the Centers for Interamerican Studies, Cuenca, Ecuador.

Gregory Michie teaches in the Department of Foundations, Social Policy, and Research at Concordia University Chicago

Brian D. Schultz is associate professor in the Department of Educational Inquiry & Curriculum Studies at Northeastern Illinois University in Chicago.

Elizabeth A. Skinner is assistant professor in the Bilingual Education Program, Department of Curriculum and Instruction at Illinois State University.

Mark R. Warren is associate professor at the Graduate School of Education at Harvard University and a fellow of the W.E.B. Du Bois Institute for African and African American Research.

Index

Note: Page numbers followed by "f" or "t" respresent figures and tables, respectively; chapter endnote references are indicated by an "n" and its number, e.g. 46n4